Momentum

MOVING IN THE RIGHT DIRECTION

HEATHER QUINTANA

REVIEW AND HERALD® PUBLISHING ASSOCIATION
Since 1861 | www.reviewandherald.com

Published by Review and Herald® Publishing Association, Hagerstown, MD 21741-1119

Review and Herald® titles may be purchased in bulk for educational, business, fund-raising, or sales promotional use. For information, e-mail SpecialMarkets@reviewandherald. com. The Review and Herald® Publishing Association publishes biblically based materials for spiritual, physical, and mental growth and Christian discipleship.

The author assumes full responsibility for the accuracy of all facts and quotations as cited in this book.

This book was
Edited by Gerald Wheeler
Copyedited by Ida Cavil
Designed by Emily Ford/Review and Herald® Design Center
Illustration Cover by Emily Ford/© Thinkstock.com
Typeset: Minion Pro 10/12

PRINTED IN U.S.A.
16 15 14 13 12   5 4 3 2 1

Library of Congress Cataloging-in-Publication Data
Quintana, Heather, 1975-
   Momentum : moving in the right direction/Heather Quintana.
      p. cm.
1. Christian teenagers—Prayers and devotions. 2. Christian teenagers—Religious life. 3. Christian teenagers—Conduct of life. 4. Devotional calendars—Seventh-Day Adventists. I. Title.
   BV4531.3.Q46 2012
   248.8'3—dc23
                          2012006025

ISBN 979-0-8280-2593-5

Dear Reader,

The Bible doesn't come alive just by reading it—it comes alive by *living* it! So, if you want an out-of-this-world experience with God, you can't just read about following God—you have to get busy following Him.

In this book, you'll be pushed to try new things, form new habits, and get to know God and people on a whole new level. Every day you'll be given a specific challenge to help you put verses and ideas into action. You'll also have the opportunity once a week to document your journey with God. These weekly reviews give you the chance to look back over the past week and make notes about the experiences and ideas that had an impact on you. Now, before you start thinking that sounds a little too much like homework, think again! If you do this every week, I promise you will have an encounter with God that will radically change your life.

So don't keep the ideas in this book trapped on the pages: let them break free and become a part of your life. Let them be the momentum to get you moving in the right direction, closer to God and to the big adventures He has planned just for you.

Heather Quintana

Momentum

MOVING IN THE RIGHT DIRECTION

To order additional copies of *Momentum,* by Heather Quintana,
call 1-800-765-6955.
Visit us at **www.reviewandherald.com** for information on other
Review and Herald® products.

Every Day Is New Year's Day

Therefore, if anyone is in Christ, the new creation has come: The old has gone, the new is here! 2 Corinthians 5:17.

New Year's Day is the ultimate do-over. If you didn't like last year, you get a second chance—a brand-new start. And if you loved last year, well, here's a bright, new year you just might like even more than the last one!

As we turn the page on the calendar, lots of people make New Year's resolutions. Some of the most common resolutions for teens include:

- be a better person
- lose weight/get fit
- get into a good college
- eat healthy
- be happy more often
- do homework on time
- get a job

Those resolutions are great, but they can feel overwhelming and even discouraging if you slip back into old habits. Fortunately, if you want a fresh start, you get more than one chance a year. When you're a Christian, every day is New Year's Day. January 1 isn't the only do-over. God gives us a fresh start every time the sun comes up in the morning. According to Lamentations 3:22, 23, "his compassions never fail. They are new every morning."

The most important resolution you can make today is to share this year with God. Set apart time with Him every day, and all your other resolutions, dreams, and goals will fall into place.

Live it out: Make a New Year's plan with God. Decide a time and place that you will commit to daily devotional time with Him. This will guarantee you get a fresh start—a do-over—every day!

Pray about it: Thank God for a new start. Ask Him to guide you through this new day—and this new year.

JAN 2

A Great Big Bundle of Potentiality

I can do all things through Christ who strengthens me. Philippians 4:13, NKJV.

When I was 6 years old (and my sisters were 3 and 9), my mother came up with the cute idea to have the three sisters sing for church. It would be our musical debut, so we needed just the right song.

After some consideration, we decided on the cheery children's song "I am a Promise." With that catchy tune and lyrics, how could we go wrong? Off we went to the pianist's home for a practice session to ready ourselves for the big performance. There we stood, singing our little hearts out: "I am a promise/I am a possibility/I am a promise with a capital P/I am a great big bundle of potentiality . . ./I can go anywhere that He wants me to go/I can be anything that He wants me to be/I can climb the high mountains/I can cross the wide sea/I'm a great big promise, you see!"

As we belted out those lyrics about how we can do absolutely anything, the pianist interrupted the song and pulled my mother aside for a private chat. I later learned that she had told my mother that one of my sisters couldn't quite carry a tune. Perhaps they should make the song a duet, she suggested, instead of a trio.

I was only 6, but even I knew something just wasn't adding up. If we were all little bundles of potentiality, then why was my sister getting cut from the performance? If we can climb high mountains and cross wide seas, can't we sing a little kiddy song? Apparently not, according to the pianist. The song ended up being a duet, but our hearts just weren't in it after the cutthroat elimination of our sister.

Throughout life, people will say that you can't do things. Some people have grown bitter and disappointed through the years, and they have lost their hope and vision. They don't feel like a bundle of potentiality, so they don't want anyone else to feel like one either! Do not listen to them. Listen to God. If He has called you to climb a mountain, cross a sea, build a church, preach a sermon, sing a song, teach a class, make a speech—then you can do it. Make this your mantra: "I can do all things through Christ who strengthens me" (Philippians 4:13, NKJV).

Live it out: Do something that you feel God is calling you to do. He will give you the strength.
Pray about it: Thank God for seeing and developing your potential.

Festival of Sleep Day

Yes, my soul, find rest in God; my hope comes from him. Psalm 62:5.

Now that all the exciting holidays have passed, are you feeling a little postholi-day letdown? With Thanksgiving, Christmas, New Year's Eve, and New Year's Day all behind us, it seems as if there's not much happening again until spring. But before you start to think this is going to be a plain old ho-hum day, you should know that January 3 is itself a holiday. Today is officially (wait for it . . .) Festival of Sleep Day. Yes, all you sleepyheads, you heard me right. Today honors the joys of taking a nice long snooze.

OK, fine, sleep may not seem exciting enough to earn its own holiday, but according to the Bible, rest is a pretty big deal.

For example, Jesus Himself pointed out to His disciples the importance of resting after busy times. When His disciples had been busy teaching and helping people, Jesus told them: "Come with me by yourselves to a quiet place and get some rest" (Mark 6:31).

Another kind of rest mentioned in the Bible is Sabbath rest. It's so important that it made God's Top Ten List (the Ten Commandments, that is). The fourth commandment says that even God the Creator rested on the seventh day: "For in six days the Lord made the heavens and the earth, the sea, and all that is in them, but he rested on the seventh day. Therefore the Lord blessed the Sabbath day and made it holy" (Exodus 20:11). If God rested and He doesn't even get tired, how much more important is it for us to get Sabbath rest and be reenergized?

Now, before you think rest is just about naps (bor-ing!), keep in mind the bigger picture of rest. Sabbath rest is about taking a guilt-free break from homework and chores. (Now we're talking, right?) It also gives us time to spend with friends, family, and God. And that's something to celebrate. I think rest deserves a holiday of its own, after all.

Live it out: Instead of dreading Sabbath, think of ways you can make it special this week. What kind of activity could you plan that would invigorate you and make you feel closer to God?

Pray about it: Thank God for making room in your life for both activity and rest.

Every Day Counts

This is the day the Lord has made. We will rejoice and be glad in it. Psalm 118:24, NLT.

Last year I decided to try a little something I'll call Project 365. The goal was to take a picture a day for one entire year. Through the years some of my favorite photographs had been candid shots taken on ordinary days, rather than posed shots of special occasions. So why not collect a year's worth of day-to-day memories with a photo a day?

January started with a bang. I was enjoying snapping creative shots-of-the-day. I took pictures at home, at work, even at the grocery store. My friends were getting into it too and were spotting good photo ideas for me. February wasn't so bad either. There were still lots of great ideas.

With each passing month, however, it got harder to find fresh ways to document my life. A few stretches of time were overloaded with long work days (and no vacations or special events), and the days started to blur together. *Did I even take a picture today?* I would ask myself at the end of a drudge of a day. *Oh, well, even if I didn't, tomorrow will look just like today, so I'll take two tomorrow.*

After a few monotonous weeks during which every day seemed like the one before, I realized it was time to snap out of the dull sameness. I needed to stop taking pictures of my stacks of work and computer screen (yes, I did that) and start finding something unique and special about each day. I put the psalmist David's words into action: "This is the day the Lord has made. We will rejoice and be glad in it" (Psalm 118:24, NLT). Searching for beauty and delight all around, I started looking for moments in the day that were worth a photo—and worth rejoicing, as the psalm says. When driving to work, I pulled off the road and got out of my car to take a picture of a cow by a blossoming tree. I snapped a photo of my friends laughing at a joke and of my feet sticking out of the top of a warm bubble bath. I was discovering little moments to delight in and be glad in.

Don't miss out on the small joys of day-to-day living. Soak in every moment, and celebrate another day of life.

Live it out: Pay attention to the little things that make today special—and enjoy every minute.

Pray about it: Thank God for the happiness He sneaks into your daily life.

JAN 5

Live It Out!

For the word of God is alive and active. Hebrews 4:12.

The Bible doesn't come alive just by reading it—it comes alive by *living* it! So don't just read about following God—actually follow Him.

Each week you'll have the opportunity to document your journey with God. Look back over the week's lessons and make notes about the experiences, verses, and ideas that had an impact on you. This isn't just a glorified version of schoolwork. No, it's lifework! Your encounters with God will change your life.

An idea that stood out to me from this week's devotional readings:

_____

_____

_____

A verse from this week's devotions that was powerful to me:

_____

_____

_____

A "Live it out" challenge I tried this week:

_____

_____

_____

Something that happened this week that was a blessing:

_____

_____

_____

My prayer today (thanks, requests, praises):

_____

_____

_____

JAN 6

Turn in Your Bible to Confusions 8:14

I have hidden your word in my heart. Psalm 119:11.

After NFL legend Mike Ditka was fired as the Chicago Bears' coach, he spoke about the situation at a press conference. The team had won only five games all season, and Ditka was obviously disappointed. Choked up, he said, "Scripture tells you that all things shall pass. This, too, shall pass."

When reporters went back to their desks to write up the story, they searched and searched for the Bible verse that Ditka had mentioned. But no one was able to find it. That's because "All things shall pass" isn't in the Bible.

People mistakenly assume quite a few common sayings come from the Bible. Just look at some of these other examples often mistaken as biblical: "God works in mysterious ways." "God helps those who help themselves." "Moderation in all things." "To thine own self be true." "Cleanliness is next to godliness." No, even though there might be similar concepts in the Good Book, none of those quotations are in the Bible.

When asked what their favorite book is, many Christians answer "the Bible." However, many people who claim that they love the Bible haven't even read it. Sure, they've skimmed a verse or two here and there, but they haven't read most of it. As a result, a lot of people aren't sure what the Bible does or doesn't say. Like Mike Ditka, they don't really know whether or not the Bible states that "all things shall pass" or that "God helps those who help themselves" . . . or any other catchy phrase.

Rabbi Rami Shapiro, a Bible teacher at Middle Tennessee State University, notes that his students often get confused about what is in the Bible. In fact, one time Shapiro had a heated debate with a student who was adamant that the saying "This dog won't hunt" is in the book of Proverbs. (No, it's not.)

OK, so the goal isn't to memorize the whole Bible. But it's a great idea to get into the Word more. The more you read it, the more you'll learn and the more you'll see God's love.

Live it out: Read more of the Bible! Choose a book of the Bible you've never read, find a translation of the Bible that is easy to understand, and start reading.
Pray about it: Ask God to help you understand and remember what you read in the Bible.

R U Busy? Txt Me!

I waited patiently for the Lord; he turned to me and heard my cry. Psalm 40:1.

Some people are texting, well, pretty much constantly. (Oh, go ahead and admit it—you know who you are.) In fact, 87 percent of teen texters admit they sleep with or near their phones in case they receive a must-read text during the night.

According to research, one in three teens with phones text at least 100 times a day. That might not seem like a lot to you, but to the adults who still can't figure out how it's possible to type anything at all on those tiny little keys, that sounds huge.

These numbers simply add up to prove that most teens would rather text than talk on the phone, e-mail, send messages on social networks, or even speak face-to-face. They prefer texting for a lot of reasons: it's easy, private, and doesn't cause the crazy nervousness that face-to-face conversations can produce. But perhaps the best thing about it is that it is instant. When you text someone, you expect an immediate response, right? If a few minutes have gone by without an answer, you start to wonder why: *Maybe they are in the shower. Maybe they're mad at me. Maybe their phone fell into the toilet.* We've gotten so used to quick responses that we can't think of many reasons why someone *wouldn't* respond immediately.

It's a funny thing how God communicates. He isn't as rushed as we are. If He had a phone and we texted Him, we'd probably wonder, *Why hasn't He responded? Is He mad at me?* He's not angry. Nor is He disinterested. He just works at a different pace. God's never frantic, never rushed, never early, and never late. Throughout the Bible, people would often have to wait to hear from Him. Even now, His response may not be as immediate as you expect, but it will come. If you allow some quiet time to creep into your life, you will eventually hear Him. The psalmist understood how it felt when he said, "In the morning, Lord, you hear my voice; in the morning I lay my requests before you and wait expectantly" (Psalm 5:3).

Live it out: What can you do to make space in your life to hear God's voice?
Pray about it: Ask God to help you to be sensitive to when He is speaking to you.

Holy Boldness

And who knows but that you have come to your royal position for such a time as this? Esther 4:14.

Drama, power, mystery, conspiracy, and romance. It sounds like the makings for a blockbuster film, but it's actually the setting for one of the greatest Bible stories.

The book of Esther begins with King Xerxes getting wasted at a party. Completely drunk from wine, he commands Queen Vashti to parade herself in front of his guests to show off her beauty. Then things *really* get ugly. The gutsy queen refuses her husband's orders, and the snubbed king calls her bluff. Since she won't do what he thought a queen should do, he says he will get himself a new queen. And that is exactly what he sets out to do.

Try to follow the rapid-fire action that ensues. The king calls for the most beautiful young women in the empire. Esther gets chosen. Her cousin Mordecai, a government official, foils an assassination plot. (I'm telling you, this could be an action movie!) Haman, the arrogant second in command, hates Mordecai because he won't bow down to him. As a result, he tricks the king into agreeing to kill Mordecai, Esther, and essentially the entire Jewish nation. Esther uses her womanly wiles, beautiful banquets, a lot of faith, and some serious holy boldness to ask the king to save her and her people. And that's where I want to press "pause" on this story.

Think of all the events and risks and parties and lies that wove together to set this moment in place. A moment when the future of the Jewish nature depended on one beautiful woman. In a stirring call to action, Mordecai told Esther, "For if you remain silent at this time, relief and deliverance for the Jews will arise from another place, but you and your father's family will perish. And who knows but that you have come to your royal position for such a time as this?" (Esther 4:14).

Although your life may not be filled with intrigue and conspiracy, there will come a God-ordained moment when you, like Esther, will be called to do something risky. When that moment arrives, stand tall, have faith, and live out your God-given role with holy boldness!

Live it out: Read the book of Esther, and find lessons for your life in her story.
Pray about it: Ask God to give you the courage to be ready for "such a time as this"!

What a Funny Accent You Have!

Therefore, if anyone is in Christ, the new creation has come: The old has gone, the new is here! 2 Corinthians 5:17.

In 2011 it was reported that Karen Butler, a woman from Oregon, had emerged from oral surgery with an Irish accent.

In 2010 an African man awoke with an Italian accent after a headache that lasted for weeks.

In 2008 Julie Frazier, from Fort Wayne, Indiana, suffered several months of migraine attacks, resulting in an accent that sounded British or Russian, depending on how tired she was.

In 2010 Sarah Colwill, from the United Kingdom, experienced a headache so extreme she had to call for an ambulance. Later, when she woke up in the hospital, she had a Chinese accent.

OK, I know, you think I'm making this up. But these, and other similar cases, really happened. It's called foreign accent syndrome, and it's a rare medical condition that usually occurs as a side effect of severe brain injury or head trauma. Those suffering from the condition end up pronouncing their native language in a way that sounds foreign to their listeners.

Chances are none of us are ever going to take on a new accent. But the Bible says that when we come to Christ, we become an entirely new person. "Therefore, if anyone is in Christ, the new creation has come: The old has gone, the new is here!" (2 Corinthians 5:17) And when we become new creations, we end up talking differently. We'll speak with more kindness and patience. The more we get to know Christ, the more we will sound like Him.

So, no, you're not likely to end up with a foreign accent anytime soon, but when you become a new creation in Christ, you will gradually start sounding more like Christ. And, in the end, that's even more exciting than developing a Russian accent overnight.

Live it out: Share your beliefs. When opportunities arise, don't be ashamed to speak up about God or to say a nice thing to someone else.

Pray about it: Ask God to help you speak the kind of words that will build people up and represent Him well.

Tears in the Biscuits and Gravy

He changes times and seasons; he deposes kings and raises up others. Daniel 2:21.

I remember the day my classmates made Ms. Miller cry. She was just trying to do her job and teach a bunch of rowdy high schoolers to make biscuits and gravy. As you might imagine, the football players weren't really interested in learning how to make a down-home Southern breakfast from scratch. So before we even had time to preheat the ovens, the guys were making fun of Ms. Miller's voice, her hair, her jacket. Right in front of us she broke down and started crying. When she finally gained her composure, she assigned the rowdies a week in detention—which would give them plenty of time to wish they'd made biscuits instead of jokes.

If a week in detention sounds bad, check out the punishment the young people who made fun of Elisha got. Second Kings 2 tells the story of the kindhearted (and, we should mention, bald) prophet Elisha: "As he was walking along the road, some boys came out of the town and jeered at him. 'Get out of here, baldy!' they said. 'Get out of here, baldy!' He turned around, looked at them and called down a curse on them in the name of the Lord. Then two bears came out of the woods and mauled forty-two of the boys" (2 Kings 2:23, 24).

That's severe. Those boys made fun of an authority figure—and they got mauled by bears! (Fortunately no bears lurked nearby when my classmates and I were making biscuits.) That kind of extreme punishment is rare, but there's a lesson to be learned. God doesn't take it lightly when we make fun of people who are in positions of authority: teachers, pastors, parents, leaders, bosses. Even if they don't seem to deserve respect, God asks us to treat them with it anyway. The Bible says that God chooses leaders: "He deposes kings and raises up others" (Daniel 2:21). God has them—and you—there for a reason. Trust Him to work things out. In the meantime, show respect to those in authority. It will make them better leaders, and it will honor God.

Live it out: When tempted to be disrespectful to a teacher or authority figure, stop yourself. Choose to treat them as God would want you to.

Pray about it: Pray specifically for leaders whom you have a hard time respecting. Ask God to bless them and give them wisdom.

When Love Awakens

I charge you by the gazelles and by the does of the field: Do not arouse or awaken love until it so desires. Song of Solomon 2:7.

I know the cutest little boy who at the age of 5 is already quite the heartbreaker. Full of personality and confidence, he is always talking about his latest "girlfriend." Of course, the closest thing he and his girl have had to a date is a *play date,* in which their parents supervised them at the local park as they raced between the swings and monkey bars. Not to mention, the closest they've come to physical contact is the time he pulled her ponytail, and she whipped around to try to slap him.

Adults often tease young children (and even teens!) about whether or not they have a boyfriend or girlfriend. It's all done in fun, but it actually could have risky results. The point of dating and courtship is to find your life partner—and we all know that a 5-year-old, or even a 13-year-old, isn't ready for marriage. So the constant talk and pressure about getting a girlfriend or boyfriend just starts stirring up this idea long before its time.

Song of Solomon is a book that celebrates not only God's love for us, but the beauty of pure, romantic love between a man and woman. But even in something that honors committed romance, we find a warning. Three times it cautions: "Daughters of Jerusalem, I charge you: Do not arouse or awaken love until it so desires" (Song of Solomon 8:4). The warning applies to guys as well. Don't start stirring up feelings and longings too soon. The earlier you start thinking that you *have* to have a boyfriend or girlfriend, the harder it is to wait for the amazing plan God has for you. If you start rushing relationships, you'll only awaken lust and longings not intended for this time. There's nothing wrong with being 16 years old or 20 years old and not having a boyfriend or girlfriend. Absolutely nothing. God has an amazing ability to match you up with just the right person, and chasing after love before "it so desires" will only make a mess of things. His plan will definitely be worth waiting for just a little bit longer.

Live it out: Are you awakening love before its time with what you watch, listen to, wear, or by how you treat the opposite gender? What can you do to slow down and follow God's timing?

Pray about it: Ask God to be in charge of your love life. He will create something amazing.

19

Live It Out!

Trust in the Lord with all your heart and lean not on your own understanding; in all your ways submit to him, and he will make your paths straight. Proverbs 3:5, 6.

An idea that stood out to me from this week's devotional readings:

_____

_____

_____

A verse from this week's devotions that was powerful to me:

_____

_____

_____

A "Live it out" challenge I tried this week:

_____

_____

_____

Something that happened this week that was a blessing:

_____

_____

_____

My prayer today (thanks, requests, praises):

_____

_____

_____

Silly Little Sheep

You are my sheep, the sheep of my pasture, and I am your God, declares the Sovereign Lord. Ezekiel 34:31.

The Bible consistently describes us as sheep and depicts God as our shepherd. Since God says that we are like sheep, it'd be good for us to know what sheep are all about. Take a look at some of their characteristics:

- **Sheep are stupid.** They would definitely be low scorers on an animal IQ test, and they don't have much common sense, either. All in all, they definitely lack both book and street smarts.
- **Sheep are demanding.** If someone doesn't give them food—and fast—they start bleating (that's sheep language for "whining"). They want their grass or feed, and they want it now!
- **Sheep are stubborn.** Trying to move an obstinate old sheep is like attempting to nudge a hippo. They'll move when they're good and ready.
- **Sheep get lost easily.** Sheep need a navigation system attached to their necks. They wander off course and roam around where they shouldn't.
- **Sheep are needy.** Some animals can do just fine without supervision or help. Sheep, however, are dependent and require the assistance of a shepherd.

All in all, I have to admit that I am like a sheep. Fortunately, God knows we have those characteristics, and He makes up for our weaknesses. Isaiah 53:6 says, "We all, like sheep, have gone astray, each of us has turned to our own way; and the Lord has laid on him the iniquity of us all."

As David admits, "I have strayed like a lost sheep" (Psalm 119:176). And in another psalm, he says, "We are his people, the sheep of his pasture" (Psalm 100:3). As David did, we just need to admit that we are like silly little sheep who must have a Shepherd.

Live it out: Write down areas in your life in which you need help or guidance. Pray over the list, asking God to be your shepherd.

Pray about it: Read Psalm 23. Between each verse, stop and pray about what that passage brings to mind.

Something to Brag About

In God we make our boast all day long, and we will praise your name forever.
Psalm 44:8.

Check out these crazy things people have done to break a world record:

- Xie Qiuping, of China, has been growing her hair for nearly 40 years in order to have the longest in the world. It drags the ground and is more than 18 feet in length!
- In a life-or-death feat, John Evans, of the United Kingdom, balanced a Mini Cooper on his head to break the world record for the heaviest car balanced on a head.
- Zafar Gill, of Pakistan, used a clamp to attach and lift a 136-pound weight with his right ear, thus breaking the world record for the heaviest weight lifted with an ear.
- Professional stuntman Ted Batchelor, of the United States, endured fire burning his body for more than two and a half minutes in order to break the world record for the longest full-body burn without oxygen.

Who even knew there were world records for such things? Nonetheless, all sorts of wild records exist, because people want to have bragging rights to something extraordinary. I'm not sure how many world records the apostle Paul would have been able to break, but I do know he had a lot to brag about. He had a great education and an impressive résumé, but he said none of that mattered. To him, the only thing worth bragging about was Jesus' sacrifice on the cross. The apostle wrote, "May I never boast except in the cross of our Lord Jesus Christ, through which the world has been crucified to me, and I to the world" (Galatians 6:14).

Paul actually wrote a lot about bragging and boasting (Do a word search for "boast" in the Bible, and you'll see just how much he did!). But he always came back to one simple principle: nothing we do or say is worth bragging about. Referring to the words of the prophet Jeremiah, Paul summed it up this way: "But, 'Let the one who boasts boast in the Lord'" (2 Corinthians 10:17).

Live it out: Are you ever tempted to brag? What can you learn from Paul's thoughts about bragging?

Pray about it: Thank God for Jesus' death on the cross. Ask Him to help you to see what things in life are really worth boasting about.

What's in a Name?

You shall not misuse the name of the Lord your God, for the Lord will not hold anyone guiltless who misuses His name. Exodus 20:7.

In the Bible, God's name was serious business. His followers spoke it with great reverence and respect. Such a simple thing—the way they said His name—revealed how they felt about Him. You know the way a girl pronounces the name of the guy she is madly crushing on, all affectionate and excited ("I just got a call from Jooohhhnn!"). Her feelings show in the way she talks about him. Well, in a similar (but less mushy) manner, people reveal their feelings about God in the way they employ His name.

If you do a word search in the Bible for "name" and "God," you'll find stories from cover to cover in which people did things to honor the name of the Lord. Whether they were fighting a battle or building a Temple, they wanted the end result to magnify His name. His name was important, because it carried His personal identity.

It's so common now to hear the names of God and Jesus used lightly. Who hasn't seen a text or message in which a friend wrote something like "OMG! I can't believe it!" If you called someone out on it, they'd likely just say they didn't mean anything by it. And that's exactly the point. When we say God's name, it *should* mean something. We can't see God face to face right now, but we have the privilege to be able to speak to Him and about Him. When we realize how magnificent He is, we'll use His name with a sense of awe and wonder, rather than as a curse or in jest.

When you are tempted to say God's name lightly—or when you hear someone else speak it carelessly—pause and think about how awesome it is that you are friends with God. When we use His name respectfully, we acknowledge His great love and kindness to us.

Live it out: Memorize Psalm 86:12: "I will praise you, Lord my God, with all my heart; I will glorify your name forever."

Pray about it: Talk to God about how humbling and wonderful it is to be loved by Him. Worshipfully speak His name in prayer.

The Big Boss, the Little Person, and Burrito Head

And forgive us our debts, as we also have forgiven our debtors. Matthew 6:12.

There once was an important businessman (we'll call him the Big Boss). He had lots of people working for him (we'll label them the Little People). One day the Big Boss wanted to settle up some business. He went to one of the Little People who owed him $10 billion. When the Big Boss asked for the money, the Little Person began to panic, because the only money he had was his lunch money for the day.

The Big Boss said, "No money, no problem. I'll just sell your wife and kids to pay your debt." Now, the Little Person could live without nice things. He could survive without billions of dollars. But since he couldn't live without his family, he started crying and begging for mercy. In fact, he looked so pathetic that the Big Boss decided to cancel the debt entirely. He didn't demand the $10 billion—and He didn't even take the Little Person's lunch money.

The Little Person was so relieved that he headed over to Taco Bell to relax and eat lunch. There he ran into a friend (we'll call him Burrito Head). Just the week before, the Little Person had bought Burrito Head two bean burritos at Taco Bell. "Hey, man," said the Little Person, "You owe me $2.50! You should pay me back or at least buy my lunch."

Burrito Head explained that he had just spent his last dollars buying his own burritos. "I promise to pay you back next week," he said. The Little Person started screaming to the Taco Bell manager that Burrito Head had robbed him. As a result, Burrito Head ended up in prison.

As luck would have it, the Big Boss owned that Taco Bell franchise. When he heard what had happened, he told the Little Person that he had some nerve not forgiving Burrito Head over $2.50. After all, the Big Boss had forgiven the Little Person $10 billion! The Big Boss thought that was ridiculous, so he immediately sent the Little Person to prison.

Just like the Big Boss, God has forgiven us for tons of huge things. As a result, we have no right to refuse to forgive others for little things. If we forgive others, He will forgive us.

Live it out: To learn more about this story, read Matthew 18:21-35. If there is someone you need to forgive, don't wait any longer. Do it today.

Pray about it: Thank God for forgiving you. Ask for help forgiving others.

A Lesson for Lazybones

Take a lesson from the ants, you lazybones. Learn from their ways and become wise! Proverbs 6:6, NLT.

Ants are so strong that they can carry objects 50 times their own body weight. To put that into perspective, it would be like you carrying around a Volkswagen Jetta.

They aren't just strong, though—they're also smart and hardworking. (If you were a boss looking to hire someone, you would definitely want people who are like ants.) For example, those teeny, tiny little things are able to create supercolonies, massive ant communities that can stretch for miles. Each of the communities has a distinctive chemical profile that enables members to recognize each other and spot intruders.

Considering the smarts, strength, and work ethic of ants, it's really no wonder the Bible says we should look to them for inspiration. Proverbs 6:6-11 puts it this way:

"Take a lesson from the ants, you lazybones.
Learn from their ways and become wise!
Though they have no prince or governor or ruler to make them work,
they labor hard all summer,
gathering food for the winter.
But you, lazybones, how long will you sleep?
When will you wake up?
A little extra sleep, a little more slumber,
a little folding of the hands to rest—
then poverty will pound on you like a bandit;
Scarcity will attack you like an armed robber" (NLT).

Live it out: Don't be a lazybones! Get off the sofa, and live to the fullest! If ants can accomplish great things, so can you.

Pray about it: Ask God for the wisdom and strength to achieve His plan for your life.

JAN 18

Driving God's Car

Share with the Lord's people who are in need. Romans 12:13.

I was driving to church one evening when my car started sputtering and gasping for breath. I could tell it didn't have plans for taking me much farther. Luckily, the old thing managed to roll sluggishly into the church parking lot before completely dying. As if it were a casket, my husband and I stood over the lifeless car wondering what to do with it next. While we discussed calling a tow truck, a fellow church member whipped into the parking lot and pulled up beside us. "What's up?" she asked as she gave us hugs. Manufacturing a cheerful tone, I explained that my car had just broken down, but no problem, we'd get it fixed.

Knowing that my husband and I worked in different towns, she instantly recognized that we would have trouble navigating the next few days with only one operable car. Without hesitation she said, "Why don't you just drive my car until you get yours back from the mechanic?"

Glancing over at her beautiful Lexus, I graciously thanked her, but insisted that we'd be fine. Again she offered, and my husband echoed my gratitude for the offer, but said she should just keep her car, that we'd manage somehow.

"It's God's car. Please, use it," she repeatedly insisted, each time calling the Lexus "God's car." She was completely unselfish. Since she considered it on loan to her from God, she didn't hesitate to lend it to us. Finally we accepted her generous offer.

As I drove "God's car" the next couple weeks, I realized several things: first, that He has great taste, because that was a nice ride! Second, in all seriousness, I recognized how God wants us to treat our possessions—as gifts from Him to be shared without hesitation.

In the book of Acts God's followers gladly shared everything they owned: "All the believers were together and had everything in common. They sold property and possessions to give to anyone who had need" (Acts 2:44, 45). When we realize that everything is God's, it radically changes our relationship with stuff.

Live it out: Treat your possessions as God's possessions. Look for a way to share what you have with others who have needs.
Pray about it: Thank God for what He has given you. Ask for a generous spirit.

Live It Out!

The name of the Lord is a strong tower; the righteous run to it and are protected.
Proverbs 18:10, HCSB.

An idea that stood out to me from this week's devotional readings:

_____

_____

_____

A verse from this week's devotions that was powerful to me:

_____

_____

_____

A "Live it out" challenge I tried this week:

_____

_____

_____

Something that happened this week that was a blessing:

_____

_____

_____

My prayer today (thanks, requests, praises):

_____

_____

_____

A Chunk of Fish Vomit

They knew he was running away from the Lord, because he had already told them so. Jonah 1:10.

Just try running from God, and see how that works out for you. If it goes anything like it did for Jonah, you'll end up as a chunk of fish vomit on the shoreline. (Hey, if that grosses you out, take it up with God. I'm just reporting the facts from the Bible.)

It all started when God asked Jonah to go to the great, powerful city of Nineveh and preach against it, because it was so wicked. "But Jonah ran away from the Lord" (Jonah 1:3). He fled in the opposite direction. Actually he sailed in the opposite direction, jumping on the first boat to Tarshish.

During his runaway ship ride, a violent storm arose, frightening even the most experienced of the sailors. When they cast lots to figure out who was responsible for the calamity, the lot fell on Jonah. They grilled him with questions, trying to figure out what he had done and what god he served. He explained that He worshiped the God who made the sea. "This terrified them and they asked, 'What have you done?' (They knew he was running away from the Lord, because he had already told them so)" (verse 10).

Apparently, fleeing from God was a much more serious business than Jonah first realized. In an attempt to save themselves, the sailors threw him overboard, and the sea grew calm. Even though the prophet was on the run, God was still gracious to him. Instead of letting him drown, "the Lord provided a huge fish to swallow Jonah" (verse 17). The fugitive preacher had three days and nights in the stinky, hot, wet digestive system of a fish to think about what he had done. Finally he made peace with God. "And the Lord commanded the fish, and it vomited Jonah onto dry land" (Jonah 2:10).

Jonah learned the gross, hard way that running from God never pays. If you go where God directs you, you'll be happier. You'll also greatly decrease your chances of ending up as fish vomit.

Live it out: When God asks you to do or say something, don't run from the responsibility. Trust His leading, and be courageous.

Pray about it: Ask God to direct you, so that you will end up exactly where He wants you to be.

Seaweed Wrapped Around His Head

I will offer sacrifices to you with songs of praise ... For my salvation comes from the Lord alone. Jonah 2:9, NLT.

Jonah had three reeking, putrid days inside a fish belly to think about the consequences of running away from God. He could have gotten angry with the Lord or even with himself. Instead, he actually ended up saying a prayer of thanks! When he wasn't holding his nose or throwing up his breakfast from the day before, he was thanking God for saving him. Read just a part of his prayer:

"I cried out to the Lord in my great trouble,
    and he answered me.
I called to you from the land of the dead,
    and Lord, you heard me!
You threw me into the ocean depths,
    and I sank down to the heart of the sea.
The mighty waters engulfed me;
    I was buried beneath your wild and stormy waves. . . .
I sank beneath the waves,
    and the waters closed over me.
Seaweed wrapped itself around my head. . . .
    But you, O Lord my God,
snatched me from the jaws of death!
    As my life was slipping away,
I remembered the Lord" (Jonah 2:2-7, NLT).

And when Jonah thanked God for sending a fish to save him, a funny thing happened: "Then the Lord ordered the fish to spit Jonah out onto the beach" (verse 10). Jonah's gratitude led to his salvation.

Live it out: When you are in a horrible, stinky situation, do you get bitter or grateful? Take a hint from Jonah, and try to find something for which to be thankful.
Pray about it: Like Jonah, thank God for saving you and giving you a second chance.

Rotten With Envy

A heart at peace gives life to the body, but envy rots the bones. Proverbs 14:30.

Imagine this: two new kids, a brother and a sister, transfer to your school. They seem to have everything going for them. You name it, they've got it: great looks, star athletic ability, good grades, stylish clothes, charming personalities, a loving family, new cars (one for each of them, of course). To top it off, all your classmates are tripping over themselves to become friends—or get a date—with one of them.

How would you feel about the new kids? You might think they're great. Then again, you might consider them conceited and acting "better than" you. Either way, if you're like a lot of teens, you might feel a little jealous. And if you do, your jealousy can make you feel resentful or negative toward them.

In the Bible, teenage Joseph seemed to have everything going for him. Genesis 37:11 records that "his brothers were jealous of him." Remember what their jealousy caused them to do? They took it out on Joseph.

Just like Joseph's brothers, we may think our jealousy is between us and the person who has made us envious. But when we are jealous of someone, our problem really isn't with that person: it is with God. Deep down, we believe that He was unfair and ripped us off. He could have made *us* gorgeous, wealthy, popular, athletic, or super-smart—He could have, but He didn't. It makes us feel as if we got cheated.

However, we have a limited perspective and cannot fully understand what God is doing. According to Scripture, He brings good things and bad things into the lives of the righteous and unrighteous (see Matthew 5:45). Even though we cannot comprehend His master plan, we *can* trust that God will give us what we need. As long as we think He owes us something, we will continue to be jealous of other people who have what we want. The best way to block rotten feelings of jealousy is to focus on being thankful for what we already have.

Live it out: Are there people to whom you are unkind because you are jealous of them? Start today to treat them better.

Pray about it: Thank God for the blessings He has given you. Tell Him you trust Him to bring just what you need into your life.

Who, Me, Jealous?

Anger is cruel and fury overwhelming, but who can stand before jealousy?
Proverbs 27:4.

As happened in the story of Joseph and his brothers, jealousy can cause people to do some pretty mean things. And often when people are jealous, they don't even realize the root of their meanness is actually envy. Consider if there's anyone in your life toward whom you feel a trace of jealousy. As long as that envy remains—even if it seems buried beneath kind words and smiles—your relationship with that person cannot be what God intended it to be.

Fortunately, there's no reason to allow jealousy to have power over you. Declare a war on those envious feelings. Free yourself to have the healthy, happy relationships that God wants for you.

Here are a few things you can try this week to help you overcome jealousy:

- **Celebrate the lives of the people you envy.** If you are envious of someone's sense of humor and energy, tell her how much fun she is to be around. Congratulate the person who got the highest grade in the class. With each compliment and praise you will be retraining your mind to be happy for others. This is not insincere or dishonest—you are telling them what you truly believe ("You always look so put together"; "What an amazing car!"; "Your family is so much fun"). Saying such honest compliments will begin to break the silent stronghold that envy has on your heart.
- **Don't compare yourself with others.** It will make you feel either ripped off or arrogant. Everyone's life is different, and God gives blessings to everyone, so don't try to estimate who is "better."
- **Trust that God will give you what is best for you.** He is working on a long-term plan, so He doesn't get caught up worrying about earthly possessions. His goal is to save us, so He shapes our life circumstances in a way to try to bring us closer to Him.

Live it out: Choose a person you can "celebrate" today by giving them a compliment.

Pray about it: Start your day with this prayer, "Heavenly Father, I trust You will bring into my life what I need. Help me to celebrate the lives of others and not to compare myself to them. Please forgive me for the times I have been unappreciative and envious."

Dumpster Diving for Jesus

Do not conform to the pattern of this world. Romans 12:2.

Don't look now, but somebody might be eating out of your trash can. Let me explain. Freegans are a group of people who boycott money-driven society by choosing not to buy all the stuff the rest of us purchase every day. They are often highly educated people with good jobs that pay good money. Even though they could afford to buy new clothes and cars and food, they don't. Rather, they believe that our society buys way too much stuff, and our excessive shopping causes us to throw things away and replace them too quickly. This creates an amount of waste so enormous that many people can be fed and supported simply off our society's trash. And that's what freegans do. Living off your trash, they dumpster dive. (Although they call it "urban foraging," that doesn't make it stink any less.) Among other more sophisticated practices, they regularly rummage through the garbage of homes, stores, and restaurants to get useful items, including the food they eat.

Freegans summarize their beliefs by saying they embrace community and generosity and oppose materialism, conformity, greed, and moral apathy. That sounds a little like what Christians believe . . . but I haven't seen anybody from my church dumpster-diving for Jesus.

OK, I'm not saying that God is calling us to eat out of dumpsters (and I'm really glad about that, because I'm a little obsessive-compulsive about food expiration dates and germs). But maybe we can learn something here, even from people who eat trash. They believe something passionately, so their actions match up with their beliefs. While they have money and could drop serious money on themselves, they don't.

Jesus said, "Do not store up for yourselves treasures on earth, where moths and vermin destroy, and where thieves break in and steal. But store up for yourselves treasures in heaven . . . For where your treasure is, there your heart will be also" (Matthew 6:19-21). Where we put our money is a good indicator of what matters to us. With every purchase, we can make a statement and align ourselves with the God's values—or with the world's.

Live it out: Before purchasing something, stop and pray about it. Does how you spend your money line up with what the Bible teaches or what the world teaches?
Pray about it: Ask God to help you know the best use for your cash.

Dead Plants, Mullets, and Good Looks

The Lord does not look at the things people look at. People look at the outward appearance, but the Lord looks at the heart. I Samuel 16:7.

Have you ever made a quick judgment about a person or place based on their appearance? I recently did that when I went to an appointment with a new doctor. Within just a few minutes I was ready to leave! Let me set the scene. First, the plants in the office were all dead. (*If he can't keep plants alive, is he going to be able to help me stay alive?*) Second, he was wearing a faded Hawaiian shirt instead of a doctor's coat, and he had a long, greased-back, balding mullet. (*That look doesn't really help me take him seriously.*) Third, the doc had left his half-eaten lunch (*was that yesterday's lunch?*) on a shelf by the skeleton spinal cord and medical supplies. (*I know it's not a restaurant, but aren't there some health codes we need to follow here?*) Fourth, when I was sitting on the exam table, if I moved my head just the right way, I could see a huge storage box stowed on a ledge. The label on the box said "Deceased" in what appeared to be size-96 font. (*What deceased things are in there? Deceased plants? Deceased people?*)

Turns out, though, you really can't judge by appearances. The doc ended up being one of the best physicians I've ever met. He had excellent bedside manner; made eye contact and joked; and was attentive, optimistic, and thorough. Once I calmed down, I even realized the storage box probably only had files of *papers* about deceased people—and that didn't seem so scary after all.

Is there someone you've judged harshly because you thought they looked nerdy, snobby, or out of touch? Chances are, if you'd get to know them, you'd discover things you really like about them. You'd notice how good they are in geometry, or how funny they are, or how they like the same foods and TV shows as you do. Once you start focusing on their great characteristics, you won't be so worried about whether their shirt is stained or they don't have the latest haircut. Like me in the doctor's office, you'll begin to see others as God does. "People look at the outward appearance, but the Lord looks at the heart" (1 Samuel 16:7).

Live it out: Is there someone you didn't give a fair chance because you judged them on appearance only? Do something today to give them a second chance.
Pray about it: Ask God to help you see people as He sees them.

JAN 26

Live It Out!

God is our refuge and strength, an ever-present help in trouble.
Therefore we will not fear, though the earth give way and the mountains
fall into the heart of the sea, though its waters roar and foam and the mountains
quake with their surging. Psalm 46:1-3.

An idea that stood out to me from this week's devotional readings:

_____

_____

_____

A verse from this week's devotions that was powerful to me:

_____

_____

_____

A "Live it out" challenge I tried this week:

_____

_____

_____

Something that happened this week that was a blessing:

_____

_____

_____

My prayer today (thanks, requests, praises):

_____

_____

_____

Lowercase Gods

You shall have no other gods before me. Exodus 20:3.

On God's list of top 10 ways to live a God-honoring, joyful life, number one is "You shall have no other gods before me." Of the Ten Commandments, this might seem like one of the easier ones. It's not as if you're going to worship pagan gods, right? Well, there are a lot of other things that fall under the category of gods with a lowercase "g."

Today, do a spiritual checkup to see if you have any lowercase gods in your life. Timothy Keller, the author of *Counterfeit Gods,* says the best way to identify them is to examine these areas of your life:

- **Your daydreams.** When you don't have to think about something, such as when you are waiting for the bus, what do you daydream about? If you are obsessive about something, that might be a god.
- **Your money.** Where do you spend your money most effortlessly? That might be a god.
- **Your areas of persistent guilt.** Is there an area in your life in which you have thought, "I know God forgives me for this, but I can't forgive myself"? If so, there is something in your life that is more important to you than God—and that is a god.
- **Your greatest fears.** What is your most terrifying nightmare? Is there something that could happen that would make you feel as if you have no reason to live? That's a god.

When you look at it that way, you realize the commandment not to have other gods isn't just about pagan deities after all. If you recognize gods in your life, it's time to do everything you can to allow Jesus Christ to capture your affection. Instead of being obsessed with other things or people, the goal is to be madly in love with Him. It doesn't happen overnight, but the more you pray, learn about His love, and recognize His blessings, the more the lowercase gods will lose their grip on you.

Live it out: Go through the list above and identify any gods in your life.
Pray about it: Every day, ask God to help you recognize and to release the gods in your life. Pray for strength and desire to give God first place in everything.

JAN 28

That's a Law? You've Got to Be Kidding Me

The law of the Lord is perfect, refreshing the soul. The statutes of the Lord are trustworthy, making wise the simple. Psalm 19:7.

Consider yourself warned! Here are some laws that are actually still on the books in cities and states across the United States:

- If you park your pet elephant at a meter in Orlando, Florida, you'll need to deposit the same amount of money in the parking meter as you would for a motor vehicle.
- If you happen to be in Normal, Oklahoma, don't even think of teasing your dog by making an ugly face at it. That's the law . . . and, people of Normal, that kind of law is definitely *not* normal.
- In Farmington, Connecticut, even though cows don't have drivers' licenses, they do have the same rights as motorists on the road. So be sure not to pass them on a double yellow line!
- Married women of Michigan, if you have an appointment at a hair salon, you might have to cancel it. A law there states that you can't change your hairstyle without your husband's permission.

Such laws are so outdated that they are laughable. Nevertheless, they are technically still valid, because they have never been repealed.

Not all old laws are ridiculous, however. The Ten Commandments, for example, are ancient laws that have stood the test of time. On that list, God only included guidelines that would still make sense a day later, a decade later, or even a millennium later. He is way too wise to have included any rules about elephants and parking meters.

Live it out: Using Exodus 20:1-17 as a guide, write out the Ten Commandments in modern terms that speak to you.

Pray about it: After reading through the Ten Commandments, ask God if there are particular areas He wants you to focus on right now.

Weakness Isn't for the Faint of Heart

My grace is sufficient for you, for my power is made perfect in weakness.
2 Corinthians 12:9.

I'm a fainter. The slightest thing can make me faint. I have fainted at the dentist, the dermatologist, the family doctor. I have fainted when I visited a sick friend. And I have fainted skiing on the top of a mountain in Colorado. (The uber-friendly ski patrolman who came to my rescue was quick to assure me it happens all the time. "Don't sweat it," he said. "This happens every day to people like you who are visiting and aren't used to the altitude." Maybe because I was half-conscious or maybe because I was embarrassed, I didn't tell him that I *lived* in Colorado and was at high altitude every day.) I've also fainted while driving on a busy road. After the tow truck hauled away my totaled car and the ambulance raced me to a five-day hospital stay, the doctors gave me an anticlimactic diagnosis: "You're a fainter."

Fortunately, God does His very best work when we are weak. That's good news for all sinful humans, but especially for faint people like me who are, shall we say, a little delicate. Your weakness probably isn't fainting. Maybe it is a habit that you can't break, anger you can't manage, or fears you can't tame. Whatever your weakness, God promises He will be strong enough for both of you. In fact, He thinks your weakness is the perfect backdrop for His awesomeness. He told Paul, "My grace is sufficient for you, for my power is made perfect in weakness" (2 Corinthians 12:9).

Isaiah 40:28-31 records God's promise to anyone who feels weak: "Do you not know? Have you not heard? The Lord is the everlasting God, the Creator of the ends of the earth. He will not grow tired or weary, and his understanding no one can fathom. He gives strength to the weary and increase the power of the weak. Even youths grow tired and weary, and young men stumble and fall; but those who hope in the Lord will renew their strength. They will soar on wings like eagles; they will run and not grow weary, they will walk and not be faint."

Live it out: Memorize Isaiah 40:28-31, and repeat it whenever you feel tired, weak, or discouraged.
Pray about it: Talk openly to God about your weaknesses. Ask Him to be strong on your behalf.

JAN 30

A Sleepover With the Big Cats

He rescues and he saves; he performs signs and wonders in the heavens and on the earth. He has rescued Daniel from the power of the lions. Daniel 6:27.

If you think being bitten by a vicious dog is bad, what if it were a lion! Take it a step further, and imagine being thrown into a pit of starving, vicious lions. At that point, being *bitten* by a lion would be the absolute best case scenario. Being *torn to shreds* would be the more likely outcome.

The story of Daniel in the lions' den sounds like a fable, but it is actual history. The prophet's enemies tricked King Darius into making a decree that anyone who prayed to any god or person other than the king for 30 days would end up in the lions' den. So it was that any renegade prayer warrior would face a bloody, painful death.

The threatening decree didn't stop Daniel, though. He continued his long-standing tradition of praying to God three times a day in front of his window. When his nemeses tattled to the king, the king found himself trapped. He had to enforce the decree, even though he admired and respected Daniel. In despair, the king threw him to the circling felines, with a heartfelt cry: "May your God, whom you serve continually, rescue you!" (Daniel 6:16).

And God did deliver him. When the king arrived the next morning to see what had happened, Daniel called out, "May the king live forever! My God sent his angel, and he shut the mouths of the lions. They have not hurt me, because I was found innocent in his sight" (verses 21, 22).

It was an absolute miracle. Daniel had spent the night with hungry beasts, and they hadn't even nipped at his ankles! "The king was overjoyed and gave orders to lift Daniel out of the den. And when Daniel was lifted from the den, no wound was found on him, because he had trusted in his God" (verse 23).

Next time you find yourself in a situation that seems hopeless, remember Daniel. When you feel as if lions are circling and there's no way of escape, remember Daniel. If you start to lose hope and feel that God has left you to suffer all alone, remember Daniel. What God did for Daniel, He can do for you too! Trust Him, even when you feel as if you're in a lion's lair.

Live it out: Think of a time in your life that God has protected or helped you. Thank Him again.
Pray about it: Thank God for protecting you in the overwhelming situations that you face.

Prayers, Lions, and a Changed Kingdom

I issue a decree that in every part of my kingdom people must fear and reverence the God of Daniel. Daniel 6:26.

When you trust God during difficult circumstances, people notice. Your faith helps build *their* faith.

The morning after Daniel got thrown into the lions' den, King Darius raced to the pit to find out what had happened. He could have sent a servant, but he wanted to see for himself. When the Hebrew prophet shouted up from the pit that he was safe, Darius was amazed and delighted at God's protection. Just a few weeks before, he had made a decree that everyone in the kingdom had to pray to him. But after he saw what happened in the lions' den, he issued a new decree. He ordered that everyone in the kingdom now had to fear and reverence Daniel's God instead!

King Darius declared:

"For he is the living God
    and he endures forever;
his kingdom will not be destroyed,
    his dominion will never end.
He rescues and he saves;
    he performs signs and wonders
in the heavens and on the earth.
    He has rescued Daniel
from the power of the lions" (Daniel 6:26, 27).

That is a serious change of heart! Many people came to have reverence and respect for the true God because Daniel stood up for his beliefs. He kept praying, despite the risk of death.

When you hold on to your faith even when things seem hopeless, it will change not only you, but also others. Like Daniel, you might even influence a kingdom full of people.

Live it out: Is there a situation in your life in which you feel called to stand up for God? Trust Him and remain firm for what's right!

Pray about it: Ask God to help you be like Daniel—daring and courageous in your faith.

Learn to Laugh

A joyful heart makes a cheerful face, but when the heart is sad, the spirit is broken.
Proverbs 15:13, NASB.

One of my friends likes to stir things up and is always cracking jokes. Another friend is so shy that she rarely says a thing if people are nearby. Yet another friend is a sports fanatic who constantly talks about his favorite team and can easily be spotted in a crowd because he is always wearing his team's colors. Still another friend is pleasantly proper, hates sports, and prefers to talk about God and church.

Even though my friends are all very different, they all have one thing in common. (No, silly, not that they are all friends with me. Although that is *another* thing they all have in common.) It is a trait that all my friends since kindergarten have had: they like to laugh. I love people who laugh. I love people who make jokes. I love people who laugh at my jokes (even when they aren't really funny). I love people who laugh at themselves. (By the way, once you are comfortable laughing at your own mistakes, you'll have lots of material for jokes. We all mess up sometimes, so it's better to learn to be happy and laugh through it instead of being miserable and upset at yourself.)

The Bible agrees with me that it is a fantastic thing to be cheerful and light-hearted. You don't have to be a standup comedian to enjoy life—you just have to learn to look on the bright side. Proverbs 15:15 says, "All the days of the afflicted are bad, but a cheerful heart has a continual feast" (NASB). In other words, if you're always looking at the negative, every day is miserable. But if you learn to smile and laugh and be cheerful, life is like a constant celebration!

Live it out: First things first: turn that frown upside down! Smile! Laugh! You don't need to be phony, but make an effort to be happy.
Pray about it: Thank God specifically for 10 people or things that have brought happiness and cheer into your life. Repeat as needed when you start to feel down.

Live It Out!

I consider that our present sufferings are not worth comparing with the glory that will be revealed in us. Romans 8:18.

An idea that stood out to me from this week's devotional readings:

_____

_____

_____

A verse from this week's devotions that was powerful to me:

_____

_____

_____

A "Live it out" challenge I tried this week:

_____

_____

_____

Something that happened this week that was a blessing:

_____

_____

_____

My prayer today (thanks, requests, praises):

_____

_____

_____

FEB 3

A Road Trip in a Limo, the Super Bowl, and Keeping Your Integrity

Am I now trying to win the approval of human beings, or of God? Galatians 1:10.

What would you do for two tickets to the Super Bowl? My football-loving friend Erin found out just what she would—and wouldn't—do for those tickets.

A few years ago Erin was one of seven lucky finalists in the "Super 7 Misfits to the Super Bowl Contest." She competed against six other women for two tickets to the hottest sporting event of the year. In the final round, she and her opponents faced a series of crazy challenges held during a road trip from Dallas to San Diego. So the seven women piled into a Ford Excursion stretch limo with a driver named Doc, a DJ named Big Al Mac, and one change of clothes each.

Along the way, the contestants had to perform stunts. The winners advanced to the next city, and the losers went home in a Greyhound bus. They did all sorts of feats: they built downhill slides with $20 worth of supplies; they spent the night in a pizza parlor; they asked NFL players for interviews.

With each task, Erin had to decide how badly she wanted to win the tickets. She decided it was more important to keep her integrity than to win, so she never compromised her beliefs. For example, one challenge involved lying, but she chose not to lie. Another challenge involved gambling, but she wasn't a gambler. Plus, throughout the road trip, the other contestants drank alcohol, leaving them hung over and shaky for each day's challenge. While her competitors threw back drink after drink, Erin stayed sober.

Sticking to her morals paid off: Erin won the competition. She and her husband got two tickets to the Super Bowl. If you ever meet Erin, have her tell you about that wild road trip in a limo with strangers. She still laughs about it, and she still insists that she won because she kept her integrity.

Live it out: Don't give in to the pressure! It's not cool to lose your integrity. Next time you're faced with a compromising situation, stick with what you believe.
Pray about it: Ask God for the courage to live what you believe.

Hey, Big Talker

For it is the one who is least among you all who is the greatest. Luke 9:48.

If you think bullies are tough guys, then they have gotten in your head and made you believe their lies. The truth is that even in Bible times, the *real* tough guys— the heroes!—were usually the people being *picked on* by bullies.

Take David, for example. He was the little guy, the underdog, fresh meat for a bully. For 40 days Goliath had shown up to pick a fight with the Israelites. When David came to meet the challenge, Goliath roared and cursed the little shrimp of a kid: "Am I a dog, that you come at me with sticks? . . . Come here, . . . and I'll give your flesh to the birds and the wild animals!" (1 Samuel 17:43).

And then there's Joseph. His brothers bullied him so much that they even sold him to strangers. (And you thought *your* big brother was bad.)

Even Jesus Himself was bullied while on earth.

The best part of all of these stories is that each of them stayed true to God's plan for their lives. They were real heroes! Just check out what happened later for each of those bullied individuals.

David, the little guy no one believed could hold his own against Goliath, became king, of course, and ironically, "all the people of Israel and Judah loved David because he led them well in battle" (1 Samuel 18:16, NCV).

What about Joseph? Years later he became one of the most powerful people in the land. He confidently told his tormenters: "You intended to harm me, but God intended it for good to accomplish what is now being done, the saving of many lives" (Genesis 50:20).

And, of course, Jesus' death became our salvation. There's no greater ending to a bully story than that! Isaiah 53:5 records, "The punishment, which made us well, was given to him, and we are healed because of his wounds" (NCV).

The hero in the story is never the bully. It is the person who is on God's side.

Live it out: Make a commitment never to bully anyone and to stand up for those being bullied.

Pray about it: Thank the Lord for standing up to the bully Satan for you.

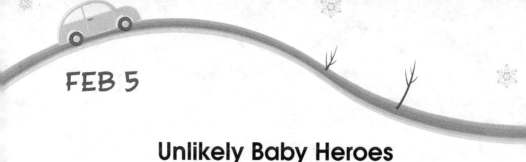

Unlikely Baby Heroes

You are barren and childless, but you are going to become pregnant and give birth to a son. . . . He will take the lead in delivering Israel from the hands of the Philistines. Judges 13:3-5.

God enjoys doing the unlikely. One of His favorite accomplishments in the Bible, for example, was arranging for women who couldn't possibly get pregnant to have babies. When God needed special heroes, he often arranged for them to be born as miracle babies to entirely improbable mothers. Sarah became pregnant with Isaac when she was in her 90s. Elizabeth had John the Baptist when she was an old woman. Mary gave birth to Jesus Christ when she was a virgin teenager.

Samson, the strongest man who ever lived, was also a miracle baby. An angel appeared to his mother and said, "You are barren and childless, but you are going to become pregnant and give birth to a son. . . . He will take the lead in delivering Israel from the hands of the Philistines" (Judges 13:3-5).

Unfortunately, Samson didn't always act like a hero. He made some big mistakes in his life. But in the end, he recognized his dependence on God. Even though he messed up, Hebrews 11 lists him as one of the heroes of faith.

If you feel as if God could never turn you into someone strong and mighty, remember what He has done in the past. He has created heroes of faith from tiny babies whose birth was technically impossible. Constantly He has brought up heroes from the most unlikely situations. You are never too weak or messed up for Him to transform you into a hero of faith. If He can turn an unlikely baby into a hero, he can do the same for you.

Live it out: Ask your mom about when you were born. Was she excited or scared when she found out she was pregnant? What were her dreams and hope for you?

Pray about it: Thank God for giving you life. Pray that He will help you become a hero of faith.

When a Man Loves a Woman

He fell in love with a woman ... whose name was Delilah. Judges 16:4.

When people get attracted to someone, it makes them do crazy things. Take Samson, for instance. Judges 16:4 says, "He fell in love with a woman in the Valley of Sorek whose name was Delilah." She just sounds like trouble, doesn't she? *Delilah.*

There's nothing wrong with falling in love. But to do so with the wrong person, well, that's another story. Delilah was definitely the wrong one. Samson's enemies, the Philistine rulers, asked her to lure him into telling the secret of his power. (Samson was, after all, the strongest man they had ever met. If they could figure out his power source and cut it off, they would be able to defeat him.) The leaders offered to pay Delilah in shiny silver shekels if she came up with any information that would lead to Samson's defeat.

Delilah could be bought. She began Operation Power Source. The first time she tried to get him to admit where his strength came from, he gave her the fake out. He told her he would lose it if tied with seven new bowstrings. So the devious woman arranged for Samson to be bound with bowstrings. When he easily ripped his way free, she asked him again. Once more he lied to her, this time claiming that new ropes would restrain him. As before, he effortlessly broke free.

A third time gorgeous Delilah batted her eyes at the man who was in love with her. She kept pestering him about the source of his strength. A third time he lied, and a third time she fell for it. Knowing that she still had power over the starry-eyed man, she told him to stop making a fool of her.

Crazy in love, Samson revealed his most important secret to a woman he had a crush on. As soon as Delilah learned that Samson would lose his power if his hair was cut, she sold him out. She lured Samson to sleep, and she allowed his enemies to give him a buzz cut—stealing his amazing hair and his amazing strength.

Live it out: When you think you're in love, don't lose your mind and do crazy things! Keep a level head, stay in prayer, and listen to godly advice. Don't let your heart overrule your mind.

Pray about it: Ask God to help you to make good decisions in your relationships, so that you don't end up doing stupid things when you fall in love.

On the Job With
Ethel K. Finkelsteinenbakker

Serve one another humbly in love. Galatians 5:13.

Imagine that you have just graduated from high school and need a job. Pronto. Your parents say that unless you go to college you're going to have to get your own place—and you know rent is going to cost a lot more than the $18 you've got wadded up in your pocket. In desperation, you've accepted the only job offer you've gotten: to be the personal assistant for a wealthy, elderly woman. That wouldn't be so bad, except your new employer, Ethel K. Finkelsteinenbakker, is notorious for being a pinch-fisted Scrooge who pays her employees in nickels and dimes, despite the piles of money she has in the bank. You definitely won't earn much, and Ethel K. Finkelsteinenbakker is a demanding old thing, so being her "personal assistant" essentially means you'll be her *servant*.

By 10:00 a.m. on your first day as Ethel K. Finkelsteinenbakker's servant you start thinking there *has* to be a better way to get money in this world. At the end of your first day (the longest eight hours of your life) you drive immediately to the local college and pick up an application. There's no way you're going to be a servant for the rest of your life.

No one wants to spend their entire life as a servant. That's why it doesn't sound like much fun when Jesus says that if we follow Him, we're going to end up as a "servant of all" (Mark 9:35). Amazingly, however, God promises that we will actually find joy and reward if we are servants on His behalf.

But how can you stay happy and loving if you're serving the likes of Ethel K. Finkelsteinenbakker? There's a little trick buried in Ephesians 6:7 that will help you serve absolutely anyone: "Serve wholeheartedly, as if you were serving the Lord, not people." That's the trick: remember your true Master is God, not Ethel K. Finkelsteinenbakker—or anyone else, for that matter. Considering how much He has done for you, what would you be willing to do for Him? Now, with that in mind, do those same things for the people whom He loves (which is everyone). That's how we can serve anyone anytime anywhere.

Live it out: Today, do an act of service that takes you out of your comfort zone.
Pray about it: Pray, "Lord, help me to be willing to serve. Remind me that my service is for You, not to impress people or to look good."

I Can't, but God Can!

I am the Lord, the God of all mankind. Is anything too hard for me?
Jeremiah 32:27.

Your palms are sweaty, your heart is pounding, and you're getting a little light-headed . . . When you're facing a scary situation, nervousness can sweep over you and convince you that you just can't handle it. Some situations can definitely feel intimidating, whether it is speaking in front of a crowd, trying to get to know a new person, or approaching an adult to have a difficult discussion.

I've often heard that the best way to overcome nervousness is to build your self-confidence, but I actually know an even better trick. Rather than worrying about self-confidence, it's time to get some God-confidence! Here's the problem with self-confidence without God: while part of your mind tries to convince you, "I can do this!" the other part is saying, "No, I can't! I *can't* do this!" In contrast, when you have God-confidence, you can tell yourself, "I feel as if I can't do this on my own, but with God I can. With God all things are possible!"

God-confidence comes with a guarantee and a proven track record. The Bible actually promises that with Him all things truly are possible. If you want to build your God-confidence, here are some verses to memorize and repeat to yourself during nerve-wracking situations:

- "With man this is impossible, but with God all things are possible" (Matthew 19:26).
- "I am the Lord, the God of all mankind. Is anything too hard for me?" (Jeremiah 32:27).
- "Everything is possible for one who believes." (Mark 9:23).

Live it out: Build your God-confidence by reading biblical stories of what God has done. From cover to cover, the Bible shows how He used regular, nervous people to do amazing things.

Pray about it: When facing scary situations or dreadful days, assert your faith by praying, "God, I know You are powerful. With You all things are possible."

FEB 9

Live It Out!

But those who hope in the Lord will renew their strength. They will soar on wings like eagles; they will run and not grow weary, they will walk and not be faint. Isaiah 40:31.

An idea that stood out to me from this week's devotional readings:

_____

_____

_____

A verse from this week's devotions that was powerful to me:

_____

_____

_____

A "Live it out" challenge I tried this week:

_____

_____

_____

Something that happened this week that was a blessing:

_____

_____

_____

My prayer today (thanks, requests, praises):

_____

_____

_____

Three Genius Pounds

I praise you because I am fearfully and wonderfully made; your works are wonderful, I know that full well. Psalm 139:14.

Three pounds of anything doesn't seem like much. A bag of flour or a sack of potatoes weighs more than three pounds. So do most people's backpacks or purses. And frankly, if you gained or lost three pounds, it wouldn't be enough to be noticeable to most people.

Yet, it is a mere three pounds of wrinkly matter that forms your brain, the very headquarters of your body—the command center for every single thing you do and say. The three pounds of the brain are arguably one of the most complex, marvelous things in our universe. Just check out some facts about the human brain:

- **Your brain is faster and more powerful than a supercomputer.** Say, for example, that your baby sister starts toddling over to play with a vicious dog. Your brain quickly calculates when, where, and at what speed you'll need to dive to grab her before she reaches the dog. Then it sends orders to your muscles in time for you to save little sis from disaster.
- **The neurons in your brain create and send more messages than all the phones in the entire world combined.** Tiny chemical and electrical signals constantly race along the neuron highways of your brain. And when I say racing, I mean exactly that. Motor neurons can relay information at more than 200 miles per hour.

Now, if you think the human brain is amazing, just consider how mind-blowing God's mind is compared to ours. The Bible records just how much more advanced He is than we are: "'For my thoughts are not your thoughts, neither are your ways my ways,' declares the Lord. 'As the heavens are higher than the earth, so are my ways higher than your ways and my thoughts than your thoughts'" (Isaiah 55:8, 9). God is unquestionably brilliant enough to handle anything that you bring to Him!

Live it out: Strengthen your God-given brain by reading Scripture and inspirational books.

Pray about it: Pray the words of David in Psalm 139:14: "I praise you because I am fearfully and wonderfully made."

An Explosion of *Stuff*

Do not store up for yourselves treasures on earth.... But store up for yourselves treasures in heaven, where moths and vermin do not destroy, and where thieves do not break in and steal. Matthew 6:19, 20.

Ever since I was a teenager my closet has been an absolute explosion of clothes. I have way more clothing than closet space, and piles of it cascade down like waterfalls of color and pattern. Truth be known, at any given time I've probably had enough clothing for 10 girls.

Alas, after our wedding my husband realized he had just agreed to take on a wife—and the equivalent of a small department store of clothing and accessories. During the early years of our marriage I somehow convinced him that it's normal for girls to thieve all the closet space. Just when he seemed to have made peace with the fact that he could not have both a wife and a closet of his own, we visited our friend Katelyn.

She is a teenager who is bubbly, cute, and stylish. As Katelyn gave us a tour of her family's home, she showed us all the bedrooms and even the closets. Each closet neatly held only a few clothing items, leaving the majority of each closet empty. Remembering how stylish Katelyn's dresses were, my husband looked at her minimal closet and asked, "Where are all your clothes?"

"This *is* all my clothes," she answered. "I can only wear one thing at a time, so I don't need a lot. Every month I go through my closet and give everything I don't need to charity."

Seeing Katelyn's closet inspired me to clean out my own. I filled trash bags full of all the extra things I owned. Some I gave to girls I knew who needed it, and the rest I donated to charity.

Here's a message for the guys who stuck through this entire devotional about clothes: you may not have a closet full of clothes, but you might have a lot of other stuff. Whether you're a guy or a girl, take a look around your room. Do you have more CDs, games, sports equipment, clothes, books, or decorations than you really need? If so, why not share it with someone who could use it? After all, it feels so much better to share it than to try to cram it all into the closet.

Live it out: Simplify and share. Go through your room and pull out things you don't need or use regularly. Give items to charity or to people that you know could use them.
Pray about it: Ask God to bless the people who end up with the things you give away.

I  Love

Do everything in love. I Corinthians 16:14.

Love, love, love. We (especially girls!) love to love stuff. We love ice cream. We love football. We love weekends. We love summer break. We love that good-looking new student.

Because we say it so much, you would think that we *love* everything. There has even been a grassroots campaign on Facebook demanding the addition of a "love" button, because the "like" option just isn't a strong enough word to describe some photos and statuses.

People use the word "love" to describe a number of feelings: liking, lust, enjoyment. But love is actually not a feeling at all. It is a series of choices. First Corinthians 13:4-8 gives one of the most instructive and enlightening descriptions of what love really is: "Love is patient, love is kind. It does not envy, it does not boast, it is not proud. It does not dishonor others, it is not self-seeking, it is not easily angered, it keeps no record of wrongs. Love does not delight in evil but rejoices with the truth. It always protects, always trusts, always hopes, always perseveres. Love never fails."

Based on that definition, I guess we don't really *love* ice cream and football after all. We just like them. Love truly is an action. It is the choice to be kind and selfless, trustworthy and forgiving—even when we don't feel like it.

Say, for example, you get mad at your dad for not letting you go out with your friends. You definitely don't *feel* loving toward him. In fact, you're starting to feel as if you hate him. The only way to spark a sense of love again is to *choose* to act loving again. If you're not sure what that kind of love looks like, refer back to 1 Corinthians 13:4-8. It shows us exactly how love chooses to act.

Live it out: Is there someone in your life you don't feel very loving toward? Put 1 Corinthians 13:4-8 to the test. How can you show them love today, even if you don't *feel* loving?

Pray about it: Thank God for His extravagant, never-ending love for you. Ask Him to help you have the patience and endurance to become more loving.

Loving Out Loud

God is love. 1 John 4:16.

If you're looking for a perfect example of love lived out loud, search no further. According to 1 John 4:16, it's this simple: "God is love." Well, it sounds simple, but it's really profound. Love is at the very heart of Christianity. We can be saved, because God is love. The most famous Bible verse in the world explains the role that love played in salvation: "For God so loved the world that he gave his one and only Son, that whoever believes in him shall not perish but have eternal life" (John 3:16).

As a reminder of what love is, look again at 1 Corinthians 13:4-8: "Love is patient, love is kind. It does not envy, it does not boast, it is not proud. It does not dishonor others, it is not self-seeking, it is not easily angered, it keeps no record of wrongs. Love does not delight in evil but rejoices with the truth. It always protects, always trusts, always hopes, always perseveres. Love never fails."

Now, keep in mind that God is love, and love is God. In that case, if you want to know what God is like, you can replace the word "God" for "love" in those same verses. Check out how it works: "[God] is patient, [God] is kind. [He] does not envy, [He] does not boast, [He] is not proud. [He] does not dishonor others, [He] is not self-seeking, [He] is not easily angered, [He] keeps no record of wrongs. [God] does not delight in evil but rejoices with the truth. [He] always protects, always trusts, always hopes, always perseveres. [God] never fails."

Satan will try to make you feel that God doesn't love you. Don't fall for that lie. The Bible promises that God loves you. Yes, you.

Live it out: Do your beliefs about God match what the Bible says about Him? When you picture what He is like, do you imagine Him as endlessly loving? If not, memorize 1 Corinthians 13:4-8 with the word "love" replaced with "God." Let the words soak into your heart.

Pray about it: Praise God for sending Jesus to die—all in the name of love!

FEB 14

Love Enough for Everybody

A new command I give you: Love one another. As I have loved you, so you must love one another. John 13:34.

Valentine's Day is one of my favorite holidays. A day filled with flowers, choco-late, cards, balloons, hugs, and love—what's not to like about that? According to my husband, a lot. He's certain that money-hungry executives have hijacked the holiday to create heart-shaped junk just so they can make a quick buck off all of us romantics. My husband does make a good point, but I'm still willing to play along and let those execs earn a buck off me.

Even though it might seem like it, Valentine's Day isn't just for people who are dating or married. It's a great day to express love to anyone special in your life. One of my most memorable Valentine's Days was when I was single and away at college. I didn't expect any gift or card that day, but to my surprise, I received gifts from a couple of my girlfriends, candy from my roommate, flowers from a classmate, and a couple care packages from family members. I felt so loved!

Don't let the romantics (or money-hungry executives) keep Valentine's Day all to themselves. Express love to someone today. Guys, give your mom a flower, or hug her and kiss her on the cheek. Tell her you love her. She'll melt right there in front of you. (And don't be surprised if she even gets a little teary-eyed.) Girls, call your grandparents and tell them you love them. Or send messages to your closest friends letting them know that you're glad they're in your life.

Never miss an opportunity to show someone you care about them. You don't even have to spend a penny or buy a heart-shaped box of candy. Love can be ex-pressed in thousands of ways. Find a creative way to do so today.

Live it out: Express love to at least one person today. Make a card, send a mes-sage, give a hug—let them know you think they are special.
Pray about it: Thank God for His bigger-than-life love. Ask for the confidence and assurance to show love to others.

Do a Grouch a Favor Day

Be kind and compassionate to one another. Ephesians 4:32.

Once again, my not-so-sophisticated research for this book has revealed yet another not-so-important fact. Buried in the shadow of Valentine's Day is a not-so-popular holiday: Do a Grouch a Favor Day. (How did we all go so long without knowing this?) The special holiday promotes just what it says: finding a grouchy person and doing something nice for them. Just because.

Today, look around for someone who is in a grouchy mood. Or perhaps you know someone who is *always* in a grouchy state. If so, that perpetual grouch would definitely be a nice candidate to receive your attention today. After taking in their situation, think of a small kindness you could do for them. Now, remember, you can't tell them why you are doing it, because even a grouch would be insulted to know they were targeted for Do a Grouch a Favor Day.

If you're thinking this silly holiday doesn't deserve your attention, you should keep in mind that the Bible says pretty much *every* day should be Do a Grouch a Favor Day. Just look at these verses in defense of doing a grouch a favor:

- "I tell you, do not resist an evil person. If anyone slaps you on the right cheek, turn to them the other cheek also. And if anyone wants to sue you and take your shirt, hand over your coat as well. If anyone forces you to go one mile, go with them two miles. Give to the one who asks you, and do not turn away from the one who wants to borrow from you" (Matthew 5:38-42).
- "If your enemy is hungry, feed him; if he is thirsty, give him something to drink. In doing this, you will heap burning coals on his head" (Romans 12:20).
- "Bless those who persecute you; bless and do not curse" (Romans 12:14).

Live it out: Get out there and find a grouch! Then do a favor for them.

Pray about it: Ask God for forgiveness for the times you've been a bit of a grouch yourself.

Live It Out!

For the Spirit God gave us does not make us timid, but gives us power, love and self-discipline. 2 Timothy 1:7.

An idea that stood out to me from this week's devotional readings:

_____

_____

_____

A verse from this week's devotions that was powerful to me:

_____

_____

_____

A "Live it out" challenge I tried this week:

_____

_____

_____

Something that happened this week that was a blessing:

_____

_____

_____

My prayer today (thanks, requests, praises):

_____

_____

_____

FEB 17

From the Land Down Under to the Land Under Snow

For whoever wants to save their life will lose it, but whoever loses their life for me will save it. Luke 9:24.

Wayne Scullino was born and raised in Australia. He was Aussie through and through. His job, house, friends, and family were all in Australia. But at the age of 30 Wayne quit his job, sold his house, and convinced his wife to leave the land down under to move to the chilly, snowy state of Wisconsin.

It didn't make sense to his friends, but Wayne had one reason that compelled him. It wasn't a job or friends or a sense of adventure, but so that he could cheer for his favorite team, the Green Bay Packers. No joke. The man left everything behind and moved halfway across the planet so that he could be near his favorite football team. He wanted to be able to attend their games and be in the middle of the action. "At some point," Wayne said, "you've got to start living the life you want to."

Wayne gave up everything to have the life he wanted—and a lot of people thought he was crazy for doing it. In a way, God asks us to do something even crazier with our lives. He asks us to give up everything without even knowing for sure what we'll get instead. In fact, Jesus said that if we try to hold on to our life instead of surrendering it to God, that we'll lose our life. It almost sounds like a riddle: "For whoever wants to save their life will lose it, but whoever loses their life for me will save it" (Luke 9:24). In other words, God is asking you to be sold out, all-in for Him. If you live for yourself, you'll end up with nothing.

During His famous sermon on the mount, Jesus presented this same idea of losing your life in order to gain it. He explained that if you live for yourself, you'll end up with nothing—but if you live for God, you'll have everything: "But seek first his kingdom and his righteousness, and all these things will be given to you as well" (Matthew 6:33).

Live it out: Are you living for yourself or for God? What is holding you back from surrendering your life to Him?

Pray about it: Pray a prayer of surrender, offering your life to God.

56

The Day Mama Fettuccine Died

Whoever has been forgiven little loves little. Luke 7:47.

In the town of Spaghettiville, you don't mess with Frankie Fettuccine Napolitano. No one does. Frankie is a rich and powerful man who owns everything in Spaghettiville—the bank, the park, the roads, the houses. Everything.

So it's no surprise that everyone owes him money. Lenny Linguine Botticelli, for example, owed him $500 for back rent on a tiny, dingy apartment. Frankie held a mortgage totaling $500,000 for a new, gorgeous house bought by Tony Tortellini Calibrese.

It just so happened that the very month that both Lenny and Tony were due to pay up, Frankie Fettuccine Napolitano suffered a terrible loss. His mother, affectionately known around town as Mama Fettuccine, died suddenly. Heartbroken, in his grief Frankie decided to honor his mother by canceling the debts of everyone who owed him money that month. So it was that Lenny didn't have to pay back that $500, and Tony could forget the $500,000.

Now, Mama Fettuccine died many years ago, but Tony still tells this tale today. He'll never forget the man who forgave his debt of a half million dollars. On the other hand, the story of the canceled $500 slipped out of Lenny's mind a long time ago.

Jesus told a parable very much like this story: "Two people owed money to a certain moneylender. One owed him five hundred denarii, and the other fifty. Neither of them had the money to pay him back, so he forgave the debts of both. Now which of them will love him more?" (Luke 7:41, 42).

Simon replied that the one who had been forgiven the bigger debt probably loved the moneylender more. Jesus replied, "You have judged correctly" (verse 43).

Christ's story illustrates that the most appreciative people are those who realize how much debt God has forgiven them.

Live it out: Consider how your life and future would be if you were not forgiven. How can you express your appreciation to God for His forgiveness?

Pray about it: Sincerely thank God for canceling your debt—for forgiving you and loving you.

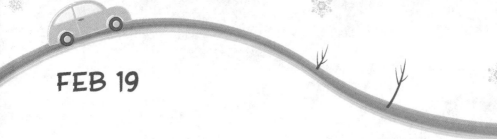

FEB 19

Well, Would You Look at That

But we all, with unveiled face, beholding as in a mirror the glory of the Lord, are being transformed into the same image from glory to glory. 2 Corinthians 3:18, NKJV.

What are your favorite TV shows? your favorite movies? your favorite music videos?

Now think about the saying "By beholding you become changed" (*Christ's Object Lessons,* p. 355). In other words, you will become like what you look at, or behold. If you often watch ("behold") violence, you're destined to be more violent. Guys, if you focus on men in sports and entertainment who prioritize fame, money, and sex, that value system will influence your own attitudes. Girls, if you constantly view shows or videos in which women are shallow, flirtatious, and interested in plastic surgery and landing a rich man—it will impact your values.

I know, you're probably thinking, *That's not true. I just watch this stuff for fun. It's only entertainment.* However, each time an idea is reinforced in your mind, it becomes a stronger part of you. Fortunately, if you spend time with—and "behold"—people who pray often, the value of prayer will shape you. If you frequently watch films or hear stories about real people who have done great things for God or humanity, it will inspire you. And if you behold Jesus by studying His life, you will slowly become more like Him and embrace His values.

Before you decide on a show, movie, or video, ask yourself, *If I watch this, will I be beholding—and changing into—what God wants me to be?* If not, come up with an alternative activity. Call a friend. Read a good book. Select an inspiring video on YouTube or an uplifting DVD. That one question will really narrow down your options, because most things in pop culture won't make it through that filter. Fortunately, there are positive alternatives. As you select what you behold, remember Romans 12:2: "Do not conform to the pattern of this world, but be transformed by the renewing of your mind. Then you will be able to test and approve what God's will is—his good, pleasing and perfect will."

Live it out: Filter your media choices with the question *If I watch this, will I be beholding—and changing into—what God wants me to be?* If the answer is no, pass on it.

Pray about it: Ask God to help you behold the things that will make you more like Him.

Memorizing the Bible
for Less Than Minimum Wage

I have hidden your word in my heart that I might not sin against you. Psalm 119:11.

When I was 10, my pastor and Bible teacher offered $30 to anyone in our class who would memorize the Sermon on the Mount. Everyone's ears perked up at the idea of earning 30 bucks, but almost everyone's interest dropped when they realized the Sermon on the Mount really was as long as a sermon. It is, after all, three entire chapters of the Bible—Matthew 5-7.

I, however, would not be deterred. Having set in my mind that I would memorize it, I would let nothing stop me. Maybe it was childhood innocence, the call of ambition or cash, or because I thought that that pastor was the coolest thing to hit the ministry scene since the actual Sermon on the Mount. Whatever it was, I was motivated. (If I had stopped to think about it, I would have realized that gig did not pay well at all. If you average out how much I made an hour to memorize that passage, it was well below minimum wage. Who are we kidding? It was well below *sweatshop* wages. But in my defense, I was a little kid, so 18 cents an hour probably felt as if I were making serious bank.)

The big day came when we memorizers would recite the passage during a church service. Of all the kids in the school, only two of us took the challenge. (I should go ahead and admit that the other girl who did it was a first grader, which really impressed all the adults and showed me up. I mean, she didn't even know how to write in cursive or do long division, but here she was reciting three chapters of the Bible!) Both of us made it through, earning a few amens, a round of applause, and some cold, hard cash.

No joke—to this day, I still remember the Sermon on the Mount. I know it better than any other passage in Scripture. I have memorized other verses since, but none of them have come so easily or quickly, or stuck with me so deeply, as the Sermon on the Mount. Something almost supernatural happens when you memorize parts of the Bible. God honors your efforts, and He will bring those passages back to your mind for the rest of your life. The verses you learn right now really will guide and comfort you for years to come.

Live it out: Pick a passage in the Bible, and start today to memorize it. Better yet, memorize a verse every week. You'll never regret it.

Pray about it: Make Psalm 119:11 your prayer. Ask God to help you love His Word.

FEB 21

If Looks Could Kill

You shall not murder. Exodus 20:13.

When it comes to the Ten Commandments, the sixth, "You shall not murder," seems a little, well, *obvious*. Most of us are fairly confident we'll be able to make it through life without murdering anyone. The stories of killings in the Bible might even be so unsettling that you've wondered how they made it into the Holy Book at all.

But like everything in Scripture, there is more to this verse than what you catch with a quick reading. The book *Patriarchs and Prophets* (p. 308) offers an eye-opening look at this commandment. It says that the following acts—to a greater or lesser degree—are ways we commit "murder" and break this commandment:

- strong negative feelings that lead us to wish someone harm or to injure them
- acts of injustice that shorten life
- an attitude of hatred and revenge
- selfish neglect of suffering or needy people
- self-indulgence or behaviors that damage our health

This list is a powerful reminder of the sacredness of life. We can "murder" by speaking harsh words, feeling hatred, ignoring others' needs, or neglecting our health. It's not just the act of murder that kills: our thoughts and daily actions can chip away at life too. First John 3:15 reinforces this idea: "Anyone who hates a brother or sister is a murderer."

Fortunately, there is also a positive side to consider. Just as our harsh words or acts can cause death, so right words and actions can promote life. When you make healthy decisions, offer someone help, or show love, you are doing just what God said: you are causing life to flourish.

Live it out: Do something kind this week that will cause life to flourish.
Pray about it: Ask forgiveness for ways that you have promoted death, and ask God to help you find ways to foster life.

Jesus Is on the Guest List

"The Son of Man came eating and drinking, and you say, 'Here is a glutton and a drunkard, a friend of tax collectors and sinners.'" Luke 7:34.

It seems to me from reading the Gospels that Jesus liked a good dinner party as much as the next guy. In fact, He ate so frequently with people labeled as "sinners" that He got the reputation of being a "friend of sinners" (Luke 7:34). If you ask me, that is one seriously awesome reputation for God to have. He could have stayed in beautiful, perfect heaven with angels singing His praises, but instead He came down to our messed-up planet to save sinners. He healed sinners. He told stories to sinners. He laughed with sinners and cried with sinners. He looked sinners in the eye and listened to their problems. And He went to parties with sinners and ate dinner with sinners.

One day when He was eating at Matthew's house, the Pharisees asked His disciples, "Why does he eat with tax collectors and sinners?" (Mark 2:16). Jesus overheard the question and answered: "It is not the healthy who need a doctor, but the sick. I have not come to call the righteous, but sinners" (verse 17).

Obviously, the idea of Jesus hanging out with the riffraff made the religious leaders of His day very uncomfortable. But, honestly, aren't we all sinners? It's a beautiful part of the gospel that Jesus is willing to listen to us, talk with us, spend time with us.

If you ever feel messed up or desperate, cheer up! You are exactly the kind of person Jesus would like to hang out with. If you had been around while He was on Earth, and you had asked Him to dinner, He would have lit up at the invitation. "What time should I be there?" He would have asked excitedly. After all, that's why He came to earth—to give all of us sinners a future and a hope.

Live it out: Do you see potential in people the way that Jesus did? How can you show others the kind of love He displayed?

Pray about it: Thank God for the beautiful plan of salvation that allowed Jesus to come to earth and be our friend.

FEB 23

Live It Out!

Peace I leave with you; my peace I give you. I do not give to you as the world gives. Do not let your hearts be troubled and do not be afraid. John 14:27.

An idea that stood out to me from this week's devotional readings:

_____

_____

_____

A verse from this week's devotions that was powerful to me:

_____

_____

_____

A "Live it out" challenge I tried this week:

_____

_____

_____

Something that happened this week that was a blessing:

_____

_____

_____

My prayer today (thanks, requests, praises):

_____

_____

_____

A Life-changing Experiment

This is the day that the Lord has made. Let us rejoice and be glad today!
Psalm 118:24, NCV.

Here's an experiment I challenge you to try. (If you do it, I'm warning you, it will change your life!) This is the mission, if you choose to accept it: "Do something every day to improve, beautify, and ennoble the life that Christ has purchased with His own blood" (*The Ministry of Healing*, p. 491). In other words, every day do something—anything—that will make life better, beautiful, and noble. Jesus died so that you could have a life, so don't make it a boring, mediocre one. Do everything you can to make it count for something. Take risks: do kind things, do noble things, do beautiful things!

I've taken this challenge for the past year, and it has helped me be braver, more thoughtful, and more tuned in to God. Once you try it, you'll see that every day He will bring opportunities into your life to help you meet the challenge. Here are some ideas to get you started:

- Listen to Christian music instead of the latest secular hits.
- Tell someone thank you for what they've done for you.
- Choose a healthy meal instead of junk food.
- Listen compassionately to someone who seems down or discouraged.
- Take a walk outside, breathe deeply, and notice the beauty in nature.
- Smile at people.
- Paint, sing, write—use whatever talents God has given you.

Remember, when you take this challenge, it won't just make your life better. It will honor God and improve life for the people around you too.

Live it out: Keep a copy of this challenge somewhere you will see it every day, and always be on the lookout for ways to live it out.
Pray about it: Ask God to help you be aware of opportunities to make life better, beautiful, and noble.

FEB 25

Standing Tall Like a Tree

That person is like a tree planted by streams of water, which yields its fruit in season and whose leaf does not wither—whatever they do prospers. Psalm 1:3.

The Redwood National and State Parks in California are home to the tallest trees in the world. And when I say tall, I mean *tall*. The highest known redwood tree is 379 feet. To put that into perspective, it would be as high as if you had a friend stand on your shoulders . . . and then had 65 more of your friends perched on top of that.

Redwood trees aren't just tall. They're also resilient and strong. They even get better with age, producing more and better wood as they age. Not to mention, they can live to the ripe old age of 2,000 years old (and you thought your parents were ancient!). They also can hold their own against the elements: large ones are even resistant to fire.

Every houseplant that has ever entered my home has died. Usually it's a slow, cruel death, either from neglect or overwatering. I don't mean to do it. I really don't. I want them to live, but for some reason they wilt under my care. The contrast is quite sad, actually: my miniscule, struggling houseplant gasping for life in comparison to a majestic, thriving, robust 300-foot-tall redwood.

The Bible says that people who trust in God will be like redwoods, not my houseplants. Jeremiah 17:7-9 records, "But blessed is the one who trusts in the Lord, whose confidence is in him. They will be like a tree planted by the water that sends out its roots by the stream. It does not fear when heat comes; its leaves are always green. It has no worries in a year of drought and never fails to bear fruit."

If you ever feel like a wilting plant, put your trust in God. He promises to give you strong roots, protect you from harm, and make you flourish and grow. Just like a massive, majestic tree.

Live it out: Think of a person you know who is like a strong tree because they trust in God. Talk to them, and ask how they came to love and trust the Lord.
Pray about it: Say a prayer of surrender. Tell God you trust Him to grow you in a way that will make you stronger and better each year.

A Boatload of Problems

He got up, rebuked the wind and said to the waves, "Quiet! Be still!" Then the wind died down and it was completely calm. Mark 4:39.

Jesus was exhausted. It was evening, and He had just finished a long day of teaching and healing. His ministry was so important—and the people had so many needs—that it was difficult for Him even to take a break to rest or eat. At last, weary and starving, He said to His disciples, "Let's get in the boat and cross over to the other side of the lake" (see Mark 4:35).

Once they were in the boat, it didn't take long for Jesus to fall asleep. While He snoozed, darkness settled in, and a violent storm spread across the Sea of Galilee. Now, this was no small rainstorm. It was a *fierce* storm. (Even today the Sea of Galilee gets wild storms, sometimes with waves 20 feet high.) It's no wonder the disciples thought they were going to die!

Remember, of course, that some of the disciples were master fishermen. So when the storm first struck, they immediately went to work battling it. It was part of their job, after all, to work with the sea. However, by the time the waves were breaking over the boat and the water was pouring faster than they could bail it out, all they could do was scream, "Teacher, don't you care if we drown?" (verse 38).

Jesus slept through the wind. He slept through the rain. He slept through the waves drenching His hair and His robe and His friends. But He did not sleep when His followers called out to Him. When they pleaded for help, He woke up and calmly told the winds and the waves to be still. Mark 4:39 records, "Then the wind died down and it was completely calm."

Like the disciples, sometimes we try to confront storms alone. We feel panic sweep over us as the wind roars and the waves crash. As we start frantically bailing buckets of water out of our sinking boat, we forget that everything—wind and waves and all of life's problems—respond to Jesus' command to be still. Next time a storm blows into your life, remember that He will hear and help anytime you, like the disciples, say, "Jesus, there's a storm! I need Your help!"

Live it out: Are there any storms in your life that you need Jesus to calm? Ask for His help.

Pray about it: Talk to Jesus about any areas in life in which you feel you are drowning.

The God Who Can Do Anything

I will remember the deeds of the Lord; yes, I will remember your miracles of long ago. Psalm 77:11.

Let's just take a moment to think about a few of the amazing things that God has done.

In the Old Testament He sent food from heaven (little manna snowflakes) and parted humongous bodies of water so that people could walk across dry land. He made a donkey speak, water flow from a rock, and frogs, flies, and locusts appear at His command. After the Exodus He put into the sky a cloud during the day and a ball of fire during the night, so that His followers would know where to go. Later He made oil multiply for a widow. Besides stopping hungry lions from eating one of His followers, He protected three of his followers who were thrown into an inferno, so that they walked out of the flames not even smelling like smoke. Through the centuries He raised up cities and destroyed His followers' enemies.

In the New Testament Jesus continued to reveal the magnitude and power of God. Miracles and wonders filled His few short years of ministry on earth. He fed thousands of people with a handful of food and told the wind and waves what to do—and they did it. Christ healed lepers and cast out demons. Bringing sight to the blind, sound to the deaf, and the ability to run to those who were crippled, He also offered unrestrained amounts of health, hope, and forgiveness to messed up people. And, according to John, what we read in the Gospels only *begins* to tell the story: "Jesus did many other things as well. If every one of them were written down, I suppose that even the whole world would not have room for the books that would be written" (John 21:25).

Now, let's take a moment to think about the things that upset and worry you. Are your problems any bigger than those in the Bible? Is what you're facing today any more difficult for God to solve than what He handled in Scripture? Definitely not. God is as powerful and loving and ready to help as ever. As A. W. Tozer wrote: "Anything God has ever done, He can do now. Anything God has ever done anywhere, He can do here. Anything God has ever done for anyone, He can do for you."

Live it out: When tempted to worry, remind yourself of God's power.
Pray about it: Praise God for the power and help and compassion He offers to people on earth.

Life Is a Highway

And God said, "I will be with you." Exodus 3:12.

A couple years ago my friend Bill took a long road trip alone. After hours of endless highway, poor radio reception, and spotty cell phone reception, all that quietness and aloneness began to wear on him. Certain the time would fly by if he just had someone to talk to. Suddenly he saw a clean-cut hitchhiker on the side of the road and he swerved off the highway to invite the stranger to be his travel companion. He knew this could be dangerous (and he definitely doesn't recommend it), but he said a little prayer and let the hitchhiker into his car.

Bill enthusiastically greeted the stranger as he imagined the hours and miles passing by as they exchange riveting conversation. However, Bill's plan was foiled when the hitchhiker used hand motions to thank Bill for the ride—and to explain that he was deaf and mute. Definitely an unexpected turn of events for Bill! Wondering what the odds were of picking up a deaf hitchhiker, he calmly pulled back onto the highway—and settled in for many more quiet hours on the road.

Like Bill, as we head through life's journey, we want companionship. We want to be able to talk and listen to someone and share the experience. It especially would be nice to hear from God on the journey. How great it would be if He would just call or text or e-mail us—or better yet, be with us in person along the way. Unfortunately, sometimes it feels as if God is like that hitchhiker, neither able to hear us or talk to us. But, the Bible promises that God always hears and is always trying to send us messages through the Bible, the Holy Spirit, nature, and godly people.

On life's journey, when you feel as if God can't hear you, claim this promise: "Listen! The Lord's arm is not too weak to save you, nor his ear too deaf to hear you call" (Isaiah 59:1, NLT). And when you want to hear from Him, remember this verse: "Whether you turn to the right or to the left, your ears will hear a voice behind you, saying, 'This is the way; walk in it'" (Isaiah 30:21).

Live it out: Set a time every day to talk—and listen—to God.
Pray about it: Pray about whatever is on your heart. Then be quiet and listen to what God has to say to you.

MAR 1

Useful, No-nonsense Advice

Do not forget my teaching, but keep my commands in your heart, for they will prolong your life many years and bring you prosperity. Proverbs 3:1, 2.

Adults are just full of advice, aren't they? What you should wear; what you should do; what time you should go to bed; whom you should definitely never, ever date ("Young man, you'll date her over my dead body!"). Well, some of those examples aren't advice—they're orders (but that's OK, because God has asked us to respect the wisdom of authority).

Nevertheless, the advice we get at home or church doesn't always match what we hear from our friends. With so many differing ideas floating around, how do you know the very best thing to do when facing a tricky situation?

One way to get wisdom is to study the book of Proverbs. It has incredible, can't-fail advice that couldn't be any more practical. Fortunately, God is all wisdom, and He wants us to be wise too. That's why He preserved this collection of insights. Proverbs covers a wide range of topics, including youth, friends, money, family, temptation, marriage, and self-control. (Once you read the book for yourself, you'll probably even see where the Christian adults in your life are coming up with some of their advice!)

Here's an easy, fun way to read this book of wisdom. Proverbs has 31 chapters: that's one for every day of the month. At a set time during the day (morning is a good time), read the chapter of Proverbs that corresponds with the date of the month. On March 1 read Proverbs 1, Proverbs 2 on March 2, and so forth. Then in April, start all over again. I know, you're thinking it's going to get boring reading the same book again and again, but it is so interesting that you'll find something new every single time you go through it. The more often you read it, the more its wisdom will sink into your heart. It will prepare you to live well now and in the years to come.

Live it out: Each day this month, read the chapter of Proverbs that corresponds with the day's date.
Pray about it: Ask God to use the wisdom of Proverbs to teach you exactly what He wants you to know.

Live It Out!

In this world you will have trouble. But take heart! I have overcome the world.
John 16:33.

An idea that stood out to me from this week's devotional readings:

_____

_____

_____

A verse from this week's devotions that was powerful to me:

_____

_____

_____

A "Live it out" challenge I tried this week:

_____

_____

_____

Something that happened this week that was a blessing:

_____

_____

_____

My prayer today (thanks, requests, praises):

_____

_____

_____

MAR 3

If Pets Had Thumbs Day

So God created mankind in his own image, in the image of God he created them. Genesis 1:27.

Mark your calendars, folks. Today is If Pets Had Thumbs Day. As you may have picked up in science class, our opposable thumbs truly set us apart from most everything else in nature. It's a little thing (literally), but the thumb allows us to build and create things that a dolphin or kitten just never could.

Since it is If Pets Had Thumbs Day, go ahead and imagine what it would be like if they did indeed have thumbs. Right now your dog Buster would probably be twisting open that jar of dog treats you store in the kitchen. And if Buster only had a little more brains to go with his newly acquired thumbs, he might even pick up your phone and text that cute little dog down the street.

We know, of course, that our thumbs aren't the only things that differentiate us from our pets. The Bible says that we are actually made in the image of God. (Just let that sink in, and you will be amazed.) Genesis 1:26, 27 declares: "Then God said, 'Let us make mankind in our image, in our likeness, so that they may rule over the fish in the sea and the birds in the sky, over the livestock and all the wild animals, and over all the creatures that move along the ground. So God created mankind in his own image, in the image of God he created them; male and female he created them.'"

All the animals are special to God (even the tiny little birds), but no creatures are more important to Him than us, the ones made in His very image. Jesus said, "Are not five sparrows sold for two pennies? Yet not one of them is forgotten by God. Indeed, the very hairs of your head are all numbered. Don't be afraid; you are worth more than many sparrows" (Luke 12:6, 7).

You are set apart and special to God (and not just because of those thumbs of yours). He has particular plans for you and wants to have a friendship with you. When you stop to think about it, that's more amazing than if your pet had thumbs.

Live it out: Think about or journal ways in which you are made in God's image. What characteristics do you have that are like Him?
Pray about it: Praise God for making you in His image. What a privilege!

Why Do You Have to Be So Mean?

Therefore encourage one another and build each other up, just as in fact you are doing. I Thessalonians 5:11.

There is a simple rule about human beings that will forever change your social life. Once you know it, you will see situations in a whole new light. Take it in, because it will help you understand people for the rest of your life. The rule? *A person is most comfortable when they feel as if they are equals with the person(s) around them.*

I'll explain with an example. Let's take Shawn, for instance. When Shawn feels inferior around others, he is going to do whatever he can to regard himself as an equal. That way he will feel comfortable again, right? In a desperate attempt to feel equal to others, he has two choices to level the playing ground: (1) he can cut down the other person to try to bring him or her down, or (2) he can brag about himself in an attempt to try to raise himself up.

When someone cuts you down or brags, remember this rule. They are seeking to feel like an equal. They desperately want to feel comfortable, accepted, and valuable. It's hard to take the high road in such situations as this, but when someone boasts or attacks you, don't get mad. Instead, be kind to them. Build them up with kindness and acceptance. Remind yourself that they must be struggling to assure themselves that they are adequate.

Fortunately, once people learn to get their sense of worth and acceptance from Christ, they won't have to react this way anymore. Nevertheless, in the meantime, you'll meet people who are still tearing others down or bragging about themselves. When you come across this situation, keep your cool and do what Paul suggested: "Encourage one another and build each other up" (1 Thessalonians 5:11). Don't roll your eyes or take it personally. Instead be like Christ to them, and love and accept them. It will help them realize that there are better rules to live by.

Live it out: Pay attention to how you interact with people. Do you boast or belittle others? If so, pray about it and ask God to help you realize the worth He has placed on you and everyone else.

Pray about it: Thank God for accepting and loving you. Ask Him to fill you with love and acceptance for yourself and others.

Less Talk, More Action

Go back and report to John what you have seen and heard. Luke 7:22.

John the Baptist was so devoted to announcing the arrival of the Messiah that he completely opted out of mainstream life. Instead of getting a steady job, a wife, a house, and kids like the other guys in the neighborhood, he went out into the wilderness shouting, "Repent, repent!" He was probably a bit of a quirky fellow, because the Bible says this wilderness preacher wore clothes made of camel's hair, and his diet consisted of locusts and wild honey.

It seems that he was also an acquired taste—the type of person you either love or hate. John spoke so openly and freely about sin and God that people found themselves either drawn to him or appalled.

But even someone who is completely on fire for God can have their doubts from time to time. After Herod threw John the Baptist into prison, John had a lot of long dark hours to think. Doubts began to slither into his mind: *If Jesus is really the Savior, why hasn't He become the reigning king?* John was a straight shooter, after all, so when doubts troubled him, he confronted Jesus as best he could from prison. He sent a messenger to ask Him, "Are you the one who is to come, or should we expect someone else?" (Luke 7:19) In other words, "Are you really the Savior, or are you just some poser running a con on us all?"

Scripture gives no indication that Jesus took offense at the inquiry. Instead, He sent this message back: "Go back and report to John what you have seen and heard: The blind receive sight, the lame walk, those who have leprosy are cleansed, the deaf hear, the dead are raised, and the good news is proclaimed to the poor" (verse 22). Jesus didn't go into some debate to prove Himself to John—rather, He let His actions speak for themselves. He wanted John to know that amazing things were happening, so of course He was the Promised One!

If you, like John, ever have dark times when you wonder if God is for real, do what Jesus told John to do: focus on the amazing things that God is doing and has done. Look around and see how He is at work in people's lives. It will remind you that He is the real deal!

Live it out: Think of 10 things you have seen or heard that demonstrate God is truly the God of the universe.

Pray about it: Thank God for the miracles and great things He has done all around you.

Never Too Young
to Make a Difference

Don't let anyone look down on you because you are young, but set an example for the believers in speech, in conduct, in love, in faith and in purity. I Timothy 4:12.

You can't get your driver's license until you're 16. Nor can you get married without your parents' permission until you are 18. And don't even think about running for president of the United States until you are 35.

A lot of things in life have minimum age requirements, but there is no age limit on when you can start making a difference in the world around you. Some of the most astonishing accomplishments in history resulted from young people who believed anything is possible. They hadn't outgrown the wonder of childlike faith. As a result, they saw mind-blowing happenings from God.

Just think, Mary, the mother of Jesus, was pregnant with the Savior of the world when she was still a teenager. By the age of 12 Jesus was in the Temple courts with the teachers, asking probing questions and sharing insights. Not to mention the brilliant and resourceful Old Testament hero, Joseph, who was sold into slavery as a teenager. David, of course, was another teen hero, when he fearlessly defeated the giant Goliath. Samuel wasn't even a teen yet when he heard God's call and responded, "Speak, for your servant is listening" (1 Samuel 3:10). And because of a confident young servant girl who was willing to share her faith, Naaman was healed of leprosy.

As Paul told the young Timothy, "Don't let anyone look down on you because you are young, but set an example for the believers in speech, in conduct, in love, in faith and in purity" (1 Timothy 4:12). You're never too young to be a disciple and do big things for God.

Live it out: Think of one way you can make a difference in your school, home, church, or community. Now, without making any excuses, set to work doing it. If necessary, involve a teacher, pastor, parent, or friend. No task is too small or large if God is calling you to do it.

Pray about it: Thank God for using teenagers to make a huge difference in the world. Ask for a God-given mission for your life and for the courage to follow it!

MAR 7

Working Hard or Hardly Working?

And in praying use not vain repetitions. Matthew 6:7, ASV.

I experienced a little culture shock when I graduated from college and went into the workforce. In college, students rolled out of bed and headed to class in pajama bottoms, a T-shirt, and flip-flops. Taking a shower or brushing your hair before an early-morning class was considered optional. And if you were awake at midnight, you could easily find company, because someone would always be nearby cramming for a test or eating Taco Bell take-out.

In the workplace, however, I was surrounded by people who operated by a completely different code. The office setting demanded that I retire all hoodie sweatshirts and build a professional wardrobe (at the age of 22, I wasn't even sure where to buy business clothes). Showing up even two minutes late wasn't fashionable—or even acceptable. And from the sounds of it, all my coworkers headed to bed in the 9:00 hour so that they and their children could squeeze in enough zzz's to make it through the next day.

The first months of my new job involved dozens—make that hundreds—of new experiences. Every day was different and held lots of surprises. Only one factor remained constant: Pete. Every day my colleague Pete would come into the office and say the exact same thing, "Are you working hard or hardly working?" For the first few days I tried to have clever responses. Mix it up, you know. Show a little wit. But by the twentieth time, I was fresh out of cleverness and just gave a forced, fake little chuckle.

For the duration of my time in that job, Pete asked me that. Every single day. His question had seemed charming at first, but after I had heard it a few hundred times, it was just meaningless marshmallow words—full of air and not much else.

Apparently God doesn't want us to say the same thing again and again to Him, either. Jesus taught that when we talk to God, we need to mix it up a little: "And in your prayer do not make use of the same words again and again, as the Gentiles do" (Matthew 6:7, BBE). Jesus wants a fresh, growing relationship with us. That requires that we talk honestly about all sorts of things, instead of repeating the same old phrases.

Live it out: Make a list of the phrases you commonly pray. Find new, sincere ways to say them.
Pray about it: Today talk to God about things you've never prayed about before. Keep it fresh.

74

That Piece of Junk
Is Worth *How Much?*

Indeed, the very hairs of your head are all numbered. Don't be afraid; you are worth more than many sparrows. Luke 12:7.

Ever wondered what your grandparents watch on TV when you're not around? Besides the local news, a favorite with the 60-plus set is *Antiques Roadshow*. It's a program in which antiques appraisers travel to various regions of the country to look at people's antiques and determine their value. In other words, regular people drag old junk out of their attics and basements and schlep it over to a large auditorium where men and women in suits tell them whether their junk is worthless . . . or priceless.

In one episode a woman took in a simple, striped Navajo blanket for evaluation. She wasn't sure how old it was or if it was even an original. There was, after all, a factory in Oregon that made exact replicas of that blanket, and tourists can buy them for a mere $3. As the suits evaluated the blanket, though, they became quieter and more fascinated with it. They began to handle the blanket very carefully. After a little research they told the owner of the blanket that it was definitely worth more than $3. It was, in fact, worth $500,000. A plain, boring blanket from her attic was worth a half million dollars!

Who doesn't love a story like that? (Be honest, it makes you want to go look for valuables in your attic, doesn't it?) Everyone likes to hear that something we thought had no value actually has incredible worth.

That's exactly how God sees us. You may feel as if you don't have value. Maybe the people around you don't seem to think you have any worth either. But God sees you as priceless—worth far more than a half million dollars. In fact, Jesus thinks your value is immeasurable: you are worth dying for. You are a priceless treasure.

Live it out: Try to see the value in people. Even if they seem quirky or odd, treat them as a priceless one-of-a-kind creation.
Pray about it: Ask God to help you view people as He does.

Live It Out!

Give your burdens to the Lord, and he will take care of you. Psalm 55:22, NLT.

An idea that stood out to me from this week's devotional readings:

_____

_____

_____

A verse from this week's devotions that was powerful to me:

_____

_____

_____

A "Live it out" challenge I tried this week:

_____

_____

_____

Something that happened this week that was a blessing:

_____

_____

_____

My prayer today (thanks, requests, praises):

_____

_____

_____

The Secrets We Keep

"Who can hide in secret places so that I cannot see them?" declares the Lord. "Do not I fill heaven and earth?" declares the Lord. Jeremiah 23:24.

When it comes to secrets, there are two kinds of *people:* those who can keep a secret and those who can't. As soon as something hits some people's ears, it leaks out of their mouths. It is a rare, wonderful thing to find a friend who will carefully guard your hush-hush information.

And when it comes to secrets, there are two kinds of *information:* someone else's and your own. It seems it's always easier to tell another's confidences than your own. We might repeat a clandestine story about someone else without remorse, but when it comes to our own stealth behaviors and thoughts, we remain tight-lipped.

The other day someone said to me, "I have no secrets. I'm an open book." While they seemed relieved not to have any skeletons in the closet, most of us don't have that same certainty. Just like adults, many teens walk around with top-secret information—facts about themselves that they do not want anyone to know. Maybe it is a habit or a feeling they are ashamed of. Or perhaps it is something they did or something that happened to them. They would be embarrassed and humiliated if anyone ever found out.

Psalm 44:21 says that God knows what you hide in your heart, but don't let that scare you. It should actually bring you relief. Although He knows your deepest, darkest matters, He loves you anyway. He knows those secrets, and He died on the cross so that you wouldn't have to be a slave to them. He doesn't want your secrets or shame to hold you captive anymore.

If something is holding you captive and making you feel ashamed, trust that God's grace is greater than your sin. Claim Romans 5:20 as a promise from God to you: "Where sin increased, grace increased all the more."

Live it out: Break the silence. If you have a secret problem that is eating away at you, don't let it have power over you anymore. Talk to a trustworthy adult, and ask for help.

Pray about it: If you feel shame about a secret in your life, take it to God in prayer. Confide in Him—and don't be afraid to cry, scream, or ask Him what He wants you to do next.

The Fanciest and Most Fabulous Sweet 16 Party Ever!

Blessed is the one who will eat at the feast in the kingdom of God. Luke 14:15.

Fancy Felicia Fabulousness was indeed both fancy and fabulous (Yes, of course, Fancy Felicia Fabulousness is a made-up character, but go with me on this anyway.) For her sixteenth birthday she wanted to have the fanciest and most fabulous sweet 16 party anyone had ever seen. Her parents were loaded, not to mention equally obsessed with creating the fanciest and most fabulous party, so they offered Fancy Felicia Fabulousness $5 million for her party budget.

Their daughter got right to work planning every last detail. She arranged for all the winners of *Top Chef* to prepare her favorite foods. Also she had all the winners from *American Idol* come to perform live. Finally, she added the final touches: a three-ring circus, a pool where guests could swim with dolphins, helicopter rides, hot-air balloons, new iPads as party favors, and limo pickup service for all the guests.

Obviously Fancy Felicia Fabulousness planned on inviting only the cool kids, since they would be the only ones who would truly appreciate how great the party was. She was sure they would all drop their plans to be at what was obviously the It party of the year. However, to her shock, people started making excuses. One after another, all the cool kids blew her off.

On the day of the party, there sat Fancy Felicia Fabulousness, surrounded by dolphins and hot-air balloons, with no one coming to her stupendous party. Her father, enraged that there wasn't a single guest at this extravagant party, sent the butlers and maids out to invite bums off the street and homeless people from the local shelters. There would still be a party, but the guests would just be a different sort than originally invited.

In Luke 14:15-23 Jesus told a similar story to describe God's kingdom. Christ explained that people are privileged to get an invitation to the kingdom. If they turn it down, they will miss out on an amazing opportunity. But even if people don't accept the invitation, others will still be a part of the fancy, fabulous celebration. Why not accept the invitation and join the celebration!

Live it out: Do you feel God asking you to give your heart to Him? Don't make any more excuses. Just accept the invitation—and celebrate!

Pray about it: Ask God to make you a part of His kingdom celebration.

Love, Peace, and an End to War

I have set my rainbow in the clouds, and it will be the sign of the covenant between me and the earth. Genesis 9:13.

The account of the Flood doesn't begin with Noah building the ark. We have to back up and see what was happening before that. The soggy story actually started when God looked around Planet Earth and recognized a problem: "The Lord saw how great the wickedness of the human race had become on the earth, and that every inclination of the thoughts of the human heart was only evil all the time. The Lord regretted that he had made human beings on the earth, and his heart was deeply troubled" (Genesis 6:5, 6).

God made a tough decision: "I will wipe from the face of the earth the human race I have created—and with them the animals, the birds and the creatures that move along the ground—for I regret that I have made them" (verse 7).

Things on the planet were so bad that He had to wipe the slate clean and start over. When the Flood began, it must have felt as if God and earth were at war. The disaster swept people, animals, homes, and all earthly possessions away and buried them in a watery grave. However, the sad, wet story doesn't have an entirely sad ending. God saved some righteous people and a troupe of animals so that the earth could have a fresh start.

God promised that He would never flood the earth a second time, and made a covenant with humanity, one that involved a rainbow, to show that He would not be at war with them again. "I have set my rainbow in the clouds, and it will be the sign of the covenant between me and the earth. Whenever I bring clouds over the earth and the rainbow appears in the clouds, I will remember my covenant between me and you and all living creatures of every kind" (Genesis 9:13-15).

When you see a rainbow in the sky, remember that God is not at war with you. He wants to save you, not destroy you. He is fighting *for* you, not against you.

Live it out: When you see a rainbow, thank God for being at peace with you.
Pray about it: Thank God for fighting to save you and flooding you with love.

Never Too Good to Be True

No good thing does he withhold from those whose walk is blameless. Psalm 84:11.

My friend Rachel had the mind of a businesswoman—even when she was young. Once when she and her stepsister were home alone, they decided to have a yard sale to earn a little spending money. Having seen the neighbors do it before, they pulled out some things from their house and set them in the yard. It would have been a fair and honest way to earn a little money, except for two small details. One, they took things that were actually in use in the house, such as lamps from the end tables and decorations hanging on the wall. Two, their parents didn't know about their yard sale bargain blowout.

When neighbors saw what nice stuff was being sold, they quickly became interested. Even more important, they were shocked and delighted at how low the prices were. "Just $1 for this gorgeous vase your mom got on vacation last year? I can't believe it! This seems too good to be true!"

The sale was a discount-lover's dream. Everything sold at rock-bottom prices. The neighbors were delighted, and Rachel and her stepsister walked away with cash in their pockets. Everyone was happy, that is, everyone except Rachel's parents. When they returned to a home stripped of all its valuables, they were outraged. They immediately made the girls go from neighbor to neighbor collecting the items—and returning the profits.

Rachel's neighbors had been skeptical. They thought those prices and yard sale items were too good to be true—and they were right. Whenever we see something that seems absolutely wonderful, we start wondering if it is for real. The cool thing about God is that He is always doing amazing things. He makes big promises—and He keeps them. And He gives good gifts and offers us salvation, peace, and joy. As Ephesians 3:20 says, He "is able to do exceedingly abundantly above all that we ask or think" (ASV). In other words, He repeatedly does things that seem too good to be true—but everything about them is absolutely, positively real indeed. Everything He gives you or offers you is yours for the asking. No gimmicks, no empty promises, no asking for it back.

Live it out: Make a list of at least 10 good things that God has done for you.
Pray about it: Thank God for being so good that He almost seems too good to be true!

Anger Alert:
Hothead Approaching!

Whoever is slow to anger has great understanding. Proverbs 14:29, ESV.

You may have an anger problem if you've done any of these things lately: slammed a door, punched a wall (or a person), ignored someone, screamed at someone, felt as if you were going to explode emotionally, cursed someone, or given someone the cold shoulder. Anger can express itself in many ways. Even God Himself got angry in the Bible. Thankfully, He handles it better than we do. He is slow to get angry: "But you, Lord, are a compassionate and gracious God, slow to anger, abounding in love and faithfulness" (Psalm 86:15).

We humans can do a few things to be slow to anger like God. Check out these ways to keep yourself from exploding in anger:

- **Don't make such a big deal out of everything.** Sometimes the best way to respond to something that offends you is to overlook it. Otherwise, you'll end up angry every single day of your life. "Good sense makes one slow to anger, and it is his glory to overlook an offense" (Proverbs 19:11, ESV).
- **Let it go before you go to bed.** Try to make peace about what has you upset before the day ends. If you take today's anger into tomorrow, and the next day's anger into the day after that—you'll have such a heavy load of anger, it will be like dragging around a huge bag of rocks! "Do not let the sun go down while you are still angry, and do not give the devil a foothold" (Ephesians 4:26, 27).
- **Don't hang out with hotheads.** If you spend time with people easily upset, you will become just like them. Instead, associate with people who seem calm, cool, and collected, and observe how they handle life. "Do not make friends with a hot-tempered person, do not associate with one easily angered, or you may learn their ways and get yourself ensnared" (Proverbs 22:24, 25).

Live it out: If you struggle with anger, choose one of the techniques above and begin to put it into practice this week.

Pray about it: When you feel anger boiling up inside, take a deep breath and ask God to help you be slow to anger, as He is.

Zip Your Lips, Tame Your Tongue

Whoever would love life and see good days must keep their tongue from evil and their lips from deceitful speech. 1 Peter 3:10.

It's often the little things that get us into big trouble. According to James 3, the tongue is one of those little troublemakers. Sometimes we just mouth off and say something with that tongue of ours, and it causes big problems. It's little, but it's hard to tame: "All kinds of animals, birds, reptiles, and sea creatures are being tamed and have been tamed by mankind, but no human being can tame the tongue. It is a restless evil, full of deadly poison" (James 3:7, 8).

James cleverly explains the impact of the words that slip off our tongues:

"When we put bits into the mouths of horses to make them obey us, we can turn the whole animal. Or take ships as an example. Although they are so large and are driven by strong winds, they are steered by a very small rudder wherever the pilot wants to go. Likewise, the tongue is a small part of the body, but it makes great boasts. Consider what a great forest is set on fire by a small spark. The tongue also is a fire, a world of evil among the parts of the body. It corrupts the whole body, sets the whole course of one's life on fire, and is itself set on fire by hell" (verses 3-6).

If you're ready to take on the big job of taming the little tongue, here's the first step: think before you speak. Train yourself to pause before words escape your mouth. When you feel the urge to lash out angrily at someone, zip your lips and count to 10. Breathe deeply, and calm down before you say a word. If you're trying to break the habit of cursing, set yourself a penalty (such as making yourself give a dollar to charity every time you use a swearword). If you are just dying to send a nasty e-mail or text, wait! Wait for hours—or better yet, wait until tomorrow. Allow your fiery tongue to cool down before you let the words fly.

Taming your tongue isn't just a suggestion. It's a central part of leading a spiritual life: "Those who consider themselves religious and yet do no keep a tight rein on their tongues deceive themselves, and their religion is worthless" (James 1:26).

Live it out: Slow down, breathe deeply, and think before you speak today.
Pray about it: Ask for help and forgiveness as you tame your tongue.

MAR 16

Live It Out!

And my God will meet all your needs according to the riches of his glory in Christ Jesus. Philippians 4:19.

An idea that stood out to me from this week's devotional readings:

_____

_____

_____

A verse from this week's devotions that was powerful to me:

_____

_____

_____

A "Live it out" challenge I tried this week:

_____

_____

_____

Something that happened this week that was a blessing:

_____

_____

_____

My prayer today (thanks, requests, praises):

_____

_____

_____

Jesus and Desperate People

Praise the Lord, my soul, and forget not all his benefits—who forgives all your sins and heals all your diseases. Psalm 103:2, 3.

Have you ever felt a little under the weather and stayed home sick from school? Sometimes days like that don't turn out so badly. If you've got, say, just a cough (and you aren't throwing up your breakfast), then the day might even be restful and relaxing, because you can lounge around on the sofa and your mom won't even make you take out the trash.

But have you ever been ill for a week? Now, *that* is an entirely different situation. After a few days you start to feel as if you're missing out on the world beyond pajamas and thermometers. Now imagine what it would feel like to be that way for a month . . . or a year? Then consider what it would be like to be sick for 12 years nonstop.

That's how long the woman in Luke 8 had been suffering. Doctors said there was no hope for her—they just turned her away. She had no idea what else to do except ask Jesus for help. She was *desperate.*

Thankfully, Jesus specialized in helping desperate people. The woman pushed through the crowd to touch His robe. She believed that it would make her well—and it did indeed. Her desperation did not turn Jesus off. He loved that she put all her hope and every little ounce of faith she could muster into Him. After she was healed, Jesus said to her, "Daughter, your faith has healed you. Go in peace" (Luke 8:48).

If you feel desperate about something, take it to God. He will have compassion on you. Tell Him you really need Him, and He will help you. Gather up all the faith you have—even if it is just a tiny amount—and put it all into Him. Act as if He is your only hope, because, honestly, He really is.

Live it out: Read the story of this woman in Luke 8:43-48. Close your eyes and think about an area of your life that seems out of control or hopeless. Imagine yourself pushing through the crowd so that you can take that problem to Jesus. Picture in your mind what it would feel like to have Him look at you and say you are healed.

Pray about it: Pray about the areas in your life that seem most desperate. Put your faith wholeheartedly into God.

When Donkeys Talk

Then the Lord opened the donkey's mouth. Numbers 22:28.

Toward the end of their 40-year stretch in the desert, the Israelites were finally learning how to trust God. Their faith and obedience increased, and things started to turn around for them. They still faced problems, though, including all the kings and others trying to keep them out of their land. But each time someone picked a fight, the Israelites won. One battle at a time, they were becoming mighty conquerors.

When King Balak and his people, the Moabites, heard about this, they began running scared. They dreaded what the Israelites might do to them. In their own words, the Israelites were "going to lick up everything around us" (Numbers 22:4).

Balak needed a plan—and fast. His best idea was to ask a sorcerer, Balaam, to curse the Israelites. I know, that's kind of like sticking needles into a voodoo doll of Moses and hoping it would hold back the Israelites. No surprise, God told Balaam not to curse them. Balak wouldn't take no for an answer, though. He wouldn't let up until Balaam agreed to go to Moab.

Now, this is where the story gets straight-up wacky. On the way to Moab, Balaam's donkey acted strangely three times: he ran off the trail into a field, he crushed Balaam's foot against a wall, and he lay down in the middle of the road. Each time Balaam was embarrassed and angry, and each time he beat the donkey. After the third beating, the creature spoke (yes, like a human): "What have I done to you to make you beat me these three times?" (verse 28).

If you've been looking for a wild and crazy story in the Bible, you just found it, folks. That donkey opened its mouth and talked. Balaam soon realized the animal had been behaving oddly because it was trying to dodge an angel blocking the path. The angel was seeking to keep Balaam from doing something stupid. The moral of this wacky story? If God tells you not to do something, just don't do it. If you have a plan and God has a different one, just go with His.

Live it out: Has God convicted you not to do something, but you keep doing it? Listen to Him. If you need help, talk with an adult you trust.
Pray about it: Ask God to interrupt your plans if you, like Balaam, are on the wrong path.

Turning Curses Into Blessings

The blessing of the Lord be on you. Psalm 129:8.

Dolphins communicate with each other, as do dogs and even bees. While this greatly impresses me, you've got to remember that they are, after all, speaking in dolphin, dog, and bee languages. How much *more* impressive would it be if they learned to communicate in human language? You know, a dolphin at Sea World makes his own announcements over the loudspeaker: "*Ladies and Gentlemen,* allow me to introduce to you the one, the only, Shamu!" Or a dog gets a column in the Washington *Post* and tells us all his opinions about war and politics and pop culture.

Balaam's donkey is the only animal I've heard of who started a conversation with a human. When He saw an angel trying to stop Balaam—and Balaam couldn't see it himself—that donkey just opened his mouth and talked to the foolish guy.

Balaam, you'll remember, was on his way to Moab at the request of King Balak, who wanted him to curse the Israelites. Once the donkey and the angel tag-teamed to persuade Balaam out of it, Balaam finally offered to return home and forget the whole thing.

Surprisingly, though, the angel told Balaam to go to Moab. But there was one catch: Balaam was to speak only what God told him to say.

When King Balak saw Balaam roll into town, he was thrilled and certain he would get a curse for the Israelites out of him. The king took Balaam to a mountain peak overlooking the camp of Israel and told him to curse the Israelites. But when Balaam opened his mouth, a blessing came out instead. He couldn't help himself—those were the words God put in his mind! The king tried two more times to get a curse out of Balaam, but every time blessings for the Israelites poured out instead of curses!

Like King Balak, Satan wants to curse you. But God wants to bless you. Thankfully, God can turn all of Satan's attempts to curse you into blessings. He can make good things come from bad. His blessings always win out!

Live it out: Think of a bad experience in your life that God has turned into something good.

Pray about it: If you are going through a difficult time, ask Him to turn the curses into blessings for His glory.

Mean People

Hatred stirs up conflict, but love covers over all wrongs. Proverbs 10:12.

Sometimes people deliberately say or do things they know will hurt someone. Which leaves us asking the question: "Why are they so *mean?*" There's no simple answer, but here is a simple truth that will help you understand it a little better: hurt people often strike out at others. In other words, people who have been wounded themselves will often injure others.

For example, 16-year-old Josh's father and older brothers constantly tease him. They call him a sissy, laugh at him, and say he'll never be smart enough to graduate from high school. It's no surprise, then, that Josh recently got in trouble at school for picking on younger, weaker boys. Hurt people hurt people.

When someone is cruel to you, remember they are causing pain because they are themselves in pain. It doesn't make what they are doing right, but it will help you have compassion on them despite their cruelty.

Proverbs 10:12 says, "Hatred stirs up conflict, but love covers over all wrongs." When people have experienced hatred toward them (or when they hate themselves), they pass on the hostility to others. In contrast, when people feel loved, they share the love. The more you soak in God's love for you, the more natural it will be for you to display love to others.

The greatest way to respond to hatred and meanness is by returning love: "If your enemy is hungry, give him food to eat; if he is thirsty, give him water to drink. In doing this, you will heap burning coals on his head, and the Lord will reward you" (Proverbs 25:21, 22). After all, those who really need kindness and love are those injured individuals who go around hurting people.

Live it out: Think of those who are often mean to others. Find a way this week to show kindness to them.

Pray about it: Follow the advice of Matthew 5:44, and "pray for those who persecute you."

Painful Love

They spit on him, and took the staff and struck him on the head again and again.
Matthew 27:30.

Hundreds of years before it happened, Isaiah wrote that the Savior would suffer. When Jesus lived as a man on earth, He read those very scriptures predicting what He would go through. He knew without a doubt that it would be painful to save us.

Isaiah described not only the pain Jesus would endure, but also the quiet strength with which Christ would respond:

"He was oppressed and afflicted,
      yet he did not open his mouth;
  he was led like a lamb to the slaughter,
      and as a sheep before its shearers is silent,
  so he did not open his mouth" (Isaiah 53:7).

The stories recorded in Matthew, Mark, Luke, and John confirm that Isaiah's prophecy was indeed true. Read here just one small portion of Mark's description of Jesus' experience: "The soldiers led Jesus away into the palace (that is, the Praetorium) and called together the whole company of soldiers. They put a purple robe on him, then twisted together a crown of thorns and set it on him. And they began to call out to him, 'Hail, king of the Jews!' Again and again they struck him on the head with a staff and spit on him. Falling on their knees, they paid homage to him. And when they had mocked him, they took off the purple robe and put his own clothes on him. Then they led him out to crucify him" (Mark 15:16-20).

Jesus has such extravagant love for us that He endured humiliating torture. He took on undeserved pain to give us undeserved love.

Live it out: Read Isaiah 53. As the words create a mental image of Jesus' suffering, focus on your appreciation for His great sacrifice.
Pray about it: Say a prayer of thanks for Jesus' life, suffering, death, and resurrection.

You Can't Un-see Something

I keep my eyes always on the Lord. Psalm 16:8.

The first time your parents leave you alone at home feels like a small rite of passage. There you are, on your own, practically an adult . . . At least it feels that way until you start hearing noises *(Is there someone trying to break in?)*, or you have a small catastrophe (broken glass or burned food).

My first time on my own was a couple short hours one Saturday night. As my parents pulled out of the driveway, I felt the world was mine for the exploring—one big adventure. I could do anything—absolutely anything! I settled for watching television. OK, that's boring, but there was still adventure to be had, because I could watch anything—absolutely anything!

As I flipped through the channels, I landed on a horror film. I had never seen one before, so this was part of the adventure, right? I watched only one scene, and it is still seared into my brain. It left me unsettled and scared. I won't even describe it lest it disturb you too. For years the image haunted me, especially when I was at home alone.

Here's the thing: you can't un-see something. Once you put it in your mind, it's there to stay. That's one of the reasons it is important to select and filter what you see. Whether it is a gory movie, a pornographic image, or a violent video game, once that image is in your brain, it has become a part of you. It can influence what you think, feel, and do.

Thankfully, God is in the business of making us new. As we focus on Him, those ugly images will gradually fade. If your mind is cluttered with lots of junk, it's time for a Trash Pickup Day in your brain. Start by praying this prayer: "Turn my eyes away from worthless things" (Psalm 119:37). Then turn your eyes toward God: "And let us run with perseverance the race marked out for us, fixing our eyes on Jesus" (Hebrews 12:1, 2).

Live it out: Eliminate all the images that are keeping you from feeling close to God. Get rid of movies and video games, throw away magazines, delete images or videos from your computer and phone. Ask God to help you fix your eyes on Him, and don't be ashamed to ask for an adult's help too.

Pray about it: Kneel down and pray Psalm 119:37: "Turn my eyes away from worthless things."

MAR 23

Live It Out!

So do not fear, for I am with you; do not be dismayed, for I am your God. I will strengthen you and help you; I will uphold you with my righteous right hand. Isaiah 41:10.

An idea that stood out to me from this week's devotional readings:

_____

_____

_____

A verse from this week's devotions that was powerful to me:

_____

_____

_____

A "Live it out" challenge I tried this week:

_____

_____

_____

Something that happened this week that was a blessing:

_____

_____

_____

My prayer today (thanks, requests, praises):

_____

_____

_____

Saddle Up Anyway

Be strong and courageous. Deuteronomy 31:6.

My husband is brave and a quick learner—a killer combination. For example, he tried archery, and—bam—he was good at it. When he started skiing—bam—he soared at that. You see the pattern. The only problem is he seems to think *I* should be as brave and as quick a learner as he is. (Have I mentioned that I'm a little clumsy, and a tad bit slow at acquiring new skills?)

I've landed in some pretty risky situations because of his optimistic faith that I'll bravely, quickly be able to pick up on any ability. For example, after only a short snow skiing lesson (I'm talking minutes here, people, not hours), my husband declared I was ready to move past that lame little bunny slope. So he escorted (by *escorted*, I mean *dragged*) me over to a chairlift to tackle a real Colorado mountain. The ride up seemed to last 15 hours—we just kept going higher and higher and higher. All I could think was *How in the world am I going to get back down?* My anxiety only worsened when the person beside me on the lift started talking about how this run was far superior to the ones she had crushed the week before in the Swiss Alps.

And then there was the time we went mountain biking on terrain far beyond my beginner's skill level. When we finished, my husband admitted an experienced cyclist had recently suffered serious injuries on that trail after biffing it, flipping his bike, and hitting a tree.

While these and other similar instances were happening, I didn't feel brave. I was scared to death. But when it was all over (and I lived to tell about it), I felt totally brave! I was proud of myself.

John Wayne, the actor who became famous for playing rugged-cowboy roles, once said, "Courage is being scared to death but saddling up anyway." God told Joshua a similar message when he was facing a scary situation: "Be strong and very courageous" (Joshua 1:7). God knew things would all turn out fine in the end. And He understands that we all encounter scary situations too, and He commands us to meet them with courage. When it's all said and done, we'll look back and feel stronger and braver. Our faith will grow when we saddle up anyway while facing frightening situations.

Live it out: Think of trying something that frightens you, then saddle up anyway!

Pray about it: Ask God for the courage to do what He wants you to do.

MAR 25

Today Is the Day

The Lord has done it this very day; let us rejoice today and be glad. Psalm 118:24.

God is all about doing as much as possible *today*. Throughout Scripture, He encourages us to live to the absolute fullest right now. You've probably heard the old motto "Don't put off until tomorrow what you can do today." If God were a regular ol' person down here on earth, He would have that motto plastered everywhere: on a mug, a T-shirt, a poster, a screensaver! Just look at the things He says that we should always do today instead of tomorrow:

- **Do nice things today.** If you feel God prompting you to do something nice for someone, don't let another day go by. Do it now. "Do not withhold good from those to whom it is due, when it is in your power to act. Do not say to your neighbor, 'Come back tomorrow and I'll give it to you'—when you already have it with you" (Proverbs 3:27, 28).
- **Say nice things today.** If there is any kind thing you could tell someone, say it to them now. Don't wait until later, because you may never do it. "But encourage one another daily, as long as it is called 'Today'" (Hebrews 3:13).
- **Respond to God today.** If the Holy Spirit is speaking to you, don't wait another day to respond. "So, as the Holy Spirit says: '*Today*, if you hear his voice, do not harden your hearts'" (verses 7, 8).

Make the most of today. There are no do-overs, so take every opportunity to make today the very best day possible.

Live it out: Think of something you have been putting off, and do it today. Call a friend, pay back a loan, give a present, buy lunch for someone. Whatever you've felt impressed to do but haven't done yet, do that thing today.

Pray about it: Surrender your life to God today. Don't let today slip away without teaming up with God.

Jesus' Farewell Dinner

I am going away and I am coming back to you. John 14:28.

Jesus knew His time on earth was almost over. He had been dropping hints and trying to get the disciples to understand that He would die but rise again. It was all too much for them to comprehend, though, so they still had no idea what the next few days would hold.

Jesus didn't want to face His crucifixion without one more special dinner with His 12 followers. He included a lot of important elements into the dinner: He humbled Himself and washed His followers' feet, He warned them that one of them would betray Him, and finally He gave them a lot of encouraging words.

Read some of those hope-filled words Jesus spoke at His farewell, and let them encourage you too:

- "Do not let your hearts be troubled. You believe in God; believe also in me. My father's house has many rooms; if that were not so, would I have told you that I am going there to prepare a place for you? And if I go and prepare a place for you, I will come back and take you to be with me that you also may be where I am" (John 14:1-3).
- "I will not leave you as orphans; I will come to you" (verse 18).
- "If you remain in me and my words remain in you, ask whatever you wish, and it will be done for you" (John 15:7).
- "I no longer call you servants, because a servant does not know his master's business. Instead, I have called you friends" (verse 15).
- "In this world you will have trouble. But take heart! I have overcome the world" (John 16:33).

Live it out: Read all about Jesus' farewell dinner, including all the things He told His disciples in John 13-17. As you read it, imagine what Jesus was feeling and the disciples were thinking.

Pray about it: Jesus was thoughtful and sensitive enough to leave His followers with encouraging words. Thank Him for preserving them in Scripture so that you can be encouraged by them too.

Before the Rooster Crows

Again Peter denied it, and at that moment a rooster began to crow.
John 18:27.

Assertive and outspoken, Peter would just say or do whatever came to mind. During the Last Supper, for example, he eagerly promised Jesus, "I will lay down my life for you" (John 13:37). But Jesus knew better. "Then Jesus answered, 'Will you really lay down your life for me? Very truly I tell you, before the rooster crows, you will disown me three times!'" (verse 38) Jesus knew that before the night was over, impulsive Peter would forget his promise and betray Him three times.

Later that night Jesus was arrested. As the Temple police bound and took Jesus away, Peter followed. When they arrived at the high priest's courtyard, Jesus went in, but Peter remained outside the door. The girl on duty there asked if Peter was one of Jesus' disciples. Frightened, he responded, "I am not" (John 18:17). *Strike one.*

As he continued to wait, the disciple joined a group of servants and officials warming themselves around a fire. There someone asked him, "You aren't one of his disciples too, are you?" (verse 25) Again, his response: "I am not" (verse 25). *Strike two.*

One of the high priest's servants then challenged Peter, saying he was almost certain he had seen Peter with Jesus earlier that night. "Again Peter denied it, and at that moment a rooster began to crow" (verse 27). *Strike three.*

Like Peter, we think we would never renounce Jesus—but then we end up in a sticky situation and our confidence waivers. Our denials may look different than Peter's, but they are denials all the same. When we compromise our beliefs at a party or a sporting event, or are cruel or pick on others, we deny our relationship with Jesus. We reject Him in thousands of ways.

Thankfully, Jesus forgave Peter for his denial. In fact, Peter went on to become a bold, brave spokesperson for Jesus! And thankfully for us, Jesus forgives our denials and allows us to have a fresh start too. Every morning a rooster crows welcoming the sunrise, and we all wake up to a fresh start, another chance to stand up for Jesus.

Live it out: Are there ways you have denied Jesus? If so, ask for a fresh start, and move forward.

Pray about it: Pray for forgiveness for the times you have renounced or abandoned Jesus.

How a Real Man Handles a Fight

There is a time for everything . . . a time to be silent and a time to speak.
Ecclesiastes 3:1-7.

You don't have to attend every argument you're invited to.

If someone says something upsetting or tries to pick a fight, you don't have to get into it. Keeping calm and quiet isn't a sign of weakness: sometimes it is the ultimate sign of *strength*. Jesus was the perfect example of calm composure when unfairly tried and condemned to death.

Just look how He responded when He was invited to "attend an argument": "When he was accused by the chief priests and the elders, he gave no answer. Then Pilate asked him, 'Don't you hear the testimony they are bringing against you?' But Jesus made no reply, not even to a single charge—to the great amazement of the governor" (Matthew 27:12-14).

He remained so calm, cool, and collected that it *amazed* the governor. How could someone do that?

Jesus knew the truth, having spoken it openly to crowds of people during the previous few years. But He knew this wasn't the right time to try to prove something. Instead, He surrendered Himself to the will of the heavenly Father and quietly and calmly trusted God. This wasn't cowardly—it was courageous!

Live it out: If someone tries to start something with you, don't react without thinking. Take a few breaths, say a silent prayer, and think about how you should respond. Remember: you don't have to attend every argument you're invited to.

Pray about it: Ask God to help you develop the inner strength that Jesus displayed in times of crisis.

MAR 29

Raised From the Dead

But when they looked up, they saw that the stone, which was very large, had been rolled away. Mark 16:4.

Take time today to reflect on the story of Jesus' resurrection, imagining what that day must have been like for His followers—and for His critics. Here is just part of the story, in the words of Matthew the disciple:

"After the Sabbath, at dawn on the first day of the week, Mary Magdalene and the other Mary went to look at the tomb.

"There was a violent earthquake, for an angel of the Lord came down from heaven and, going to the tomb, rolled back the stone and sat on it. His appearance was like lightning, and his clothes were white as snow. The guards were so afraid of him that they shook and became like dead men.

"The angel said to the women, 'Do not be afraid, for I know that you are looking for Jesus, who was crucified. He is not here; he has risen, just as he said. Come and see the place where he lay. Then go quickly and tell his disciples: "He has risen from the dead and is going ahead of you into Galilee. There you will see him." Now I have told you.'

"So the women hurried away from the tomb, afraid yet filled with joy, and ran to tell his disciples. Suddenly Jesus met them. 'Greetings,' he said. They came to him, clasped his feet and worshiped him. Then Jesus said to them, 'Do not be afraid. Go and tell my brothers to go to Galilee; there they will see me'" (Matthew 28:1-10).

Live it out: Find a way to express your gratitude for Jesus' resurrection, such as praying with someone or talking about Jesus with a friend.

Pray about it: Praise God for the Resurrection! Give thanks that Jesus is alive!

Live It Out!

Cast all your anxiety on him because he cares for you. I Peter 5:7.

An idea that stood out to me from this week's devotional readings:

_____

_____

_____

A verse from this week's devotions that was powerful to me:

_____

_____

_____

A "Live it out" challenge I tried this week:

_____

_____

_____

Something that happened this week that was a blessing:

_____

_____

_____

My prayer today (thanks, requests, praises):

_____

_____

_____

Keep It Simple

This is all that I have learned: God made us plain and simple, but we have made ourselves very complicated. Ecclesiastes 7:29, TEV.

Keep It Simple is a principle that reminds us not to make things too complicated.

Teachers often use Keep It Simple as a guideline for how to write a paper or give a speech. However, the principle applies to lots of other areas of life too. Sometimes we make all kinds of things more complicated than they need to be. As Solomon, the wisest man who ever lived, wrote in Ecclesiastes 7:29: "This is all that I have learned: God made us plain and simple, but we have made ourselves very complicated" (TEV).

When it comes to the important things in life, if you want to Keep It Simple, here are a few things you can do:

- **Speak simply.** Say what you mean clearly, kindly, and honestly. Don't make promises you don't plan on keeping, and don't swear on the Bible or your mother's grave. According to Jesus, "All you need to say is simply 'Yes' or 'No'" (Matthew 5:37). Sometimes we go on and on when a short and simple answer would have done the job.
- **Shop simply.** Buy things for their usefulness, not their status. When you are choosing what to purchase, select the thing you need, not what you think will impress people. That's easier said than done in a society that is all about status. But, remember, in God's society, status isn't what matters.
- **See things simply.** Don't turn everything into a big deal. If someone didn't invite you to a party, don't raise a fuss about it. Maybe their parents limited the number of people they could invite. Or if someone doesn't return your call, maybe they were working and couldn't make personal calls. When we make something bigger than it really is, it just leads to fights and hurt feelings.

Live it out: Think of one way to Keep It Simple today. For example, instead of giving a long excuse when asked a question, give a clear, direct answer.

Pray about it: Ask God to help you keep things simple.

All That Glitters Is Not Gold

There is a way that appears to be right, but in the end it leads to death.
Proverbs 14:12.

Looks can be deceiving. The young, hip chef Craig Thornton proves it all the time. Craig loves to surprise people by giving them food that looks like one thing but tastes like another. For example, he makes a "dessert" that appears just like a yogurt parfait topped with blackberries. In reality, though, it's not a dessert at all. It's actually a golden beet salad with onions and radishes whipped up until it resembles vanilla yogurt. Those "blackberries" aren't even really blackberries. They have the exact shape and color of berries, but they are really beet juice poured and frozen in blackberry-shaped molds.

When people take a bite of Craig's masterpieces, they're baffled. One man tasting a fake blackberry said, "It's so confusing! It looks like a blackberry, so my mind wants to think it is a blackberry—but it tastes like a beet!"

One of Satan's specialties is making things appear as something they aren't. He can make something look glamorous, but underneath the appearance it will really be a disaster. Premarital sex, drugs, and alcohol can all seem thrilling and cool on TV, the Internet, and music videos. But looks can be deceiving. Premature sexual activity can lead to broken hearts, devastated self-image, and feelings of isolation and bitterness. While advertising and music make drugs and alcohol seem sexy and hip, substance abuse can result in depression, lost friendships, poor health, problems in school, and the inability to get a job—to name just a few of the problems.

Don't make decisions based on appearances. It's too easy to be tricked, because looks really are deceiving. To ensure that you don't get fooled by Satan, base your choices on what the Bible says. Otherwise, you might end up eating whipped beet salad when you thought you were getting a blackberry parfait.

Live it out: When making choices, trust what the Bible says instead of appearances. Don't be fooled by glitz and glamour.
Pray about it: Ask for wisdom to not be fooled by looks.

Laughing at God

Then the Lord said to Abraham, "Why did Sarah laugh and say, 'Will I really have a child, now that I am old?' Is anything too hard for the Lord?" Genesis 18:13, 14.

Sometimes God does the impossible, and sometimes He does the outright laughable. The things that fall into that latter category are acts so unlikely that humans actually burst out laughing at the Lord.

One of those laughable miracles happened for Sarah and Abraham. When Abraham was 75 and his wife Sarah was 65, God promised that Abraham would have as many offspring as stars in the sky. Only problem, the patriarch didn't have even *one* child yet, and the clock was ticking. It would have been crazy enough if God had presented them with a child then, at that advanced age. That would have seemed impossible. God, however, waited 25 more years before he gave them a child, just to make the miracle outright laughable.

And laugh, Sarah did. When God told Abraham that within a year they would have a son, Sarah actually laughed at the thought. "Then the Lord said to Abraham, 'Why did Sarah laugh and say, "Will I really have a child, now that I am old?" Is anything too hard for the Lord?'" (Genesis 18:13, 14). Well, technically, she laughed because she was 90 and her husband was 100, which makes them old enough to be your great-great-grandparents. And who wouldn't find the idea of a great-great-grandma having a baby hard to believe?

God didn't hold Sarah's laughter against her, though. Genesis 21:1, 2 says, "Now the Lord was gracious to Sarah as he has said, and the Lord did for Sarah what he had promised. Sarah became pregnant and bore a son to Abraham in his old age, at the very time God had promised him." Apparently Sarah had a great sense of humor, because the couple named that sweet little baby Isaac, which means, "He laughs." She even said, "God has brought me laughter, and everyone who hears about this will laugh with me" (verse 6).

God definitely got the last laugh, though, because He came through with an outright laughable miracle. When you are tempted to think something is impossible, remember what God told chuckling Sarah and Abraham: "Is anything too hard for the Lord?"

Live it out: When faced with an obstacle, remind yourself that nothing is too hard for the Lord.

Pray about it: Praise God for being all-powerful and able to do the impossible.

All for One, One for All

Defend the weak and the fatherless; uphold the cause of the poor and the oppressed. Psalm 82:3.

Every year a group from my church takes a mission trip to an orphanage in Central America. We pack our work clothes and go prepared to help in any way we can. And when we're not working, we have the chance to spend time with the orphans and the staff.

Each of the orphans has a story, but one of the young boys is especially memorable. Tony is always respectful and kind to us, but because of his very troubled past, he has another side.

Last year at school Tony was frequently in trouble. Time and again his bad behavior landed him in the principal's office. Finally the principal had taken all he could. Frustrated, he called the orphanage director and said the boy had been expelled and would not be welcome back at the school.

The orphanage director hadn't given up on Tony, though. He knew the boy had lots of potential to learn and grow. Since Tony didn't have a father, the director had become a father figure to him, just as he had for the other 80 orphans. He would stand up for Tony and wouldn't let him get kicked out without a fight.

"If Tony goes," the orphanage director said to the principal, "then we all go." The school principal was shocked: the school wouldn't be able to operate if all the children from the orphanage stopped attending. The orphanage director would not back down. He wanted Tony to have another chance to get a good education.

The principal saw a father's love and protection in the orphanage director, and he agreed to allow the boy to stay. And when Tony saw that someone was on his side, it motivated him to behave better. He wanted to show respect for the orphanage director by doing his very best.

When Satan comes to condemn you and tell you that you've run out of chances, don't lose hope. God will step in and defend you. Making it clear that He is on your side, He will give you another opportunity (and another one and another one). The Lord will stand up and protect and defend you like a loving Father.

Live it out: When you see someone who needs support and help, stick up for them. Do that for someone else, because God has done it for you.

Pray about it: Thank God for always standing up for you and giving you another chance.

Bringing Everything to Light

When Jesus spoke again to the people, he said, "I am the light of the world.
Whoever follows me will never walk in darkness, but will have the light of life."
John 8:12.

When we hide dark secrets, we think we have them locked away—but really they have *us* imprisoned. Trapped by those shameful, dark experiences or habits, we desperately try to keep them suppressed, because we would be embarrassed or ashamed if anyone found out. Hiding them seems like the best way to deal with them.

However, the Christian life is all about bringing things from darkness into light. The purpose isn't to shame or condemn, but to heal and restore. You can't heal what you don't feel. You can't repair what you don't share. Jesus said, "The truth will set you free" (John 8:32). When you open up and are truthful about those hidden secrets, you will feel a sense of freedom and surrender. Whether you were abused, did something regrettable in the past, or have a habit or fantasy life you are ashamed of—you will not be free of the burden until you bring the problem to light.

Jesus said, "I have come into the world as a light, so that no one who believes in me should stay in darkness" (John 12:46). Not wanting any of us to be locked in a dark prison, He promises to redeem those dark spots and transform them into places of light: "I will turn the darkness into light before them and make the rough places smooth" (Isaiah 42:16).

So how do you bring things from darkness into light? By being honest and open about them. Begin by talking to God about them. Cry, scream, journal, pray—whatever it takes to tell Him how you feel about it. If you need further support, talk to a trustworthy adult.

God promises that His light and love will always be more powerful than any dark secret or habit. "The light shines in the darkness, and the darkness has not overcome it" (John 1:5). Just like flipping a light switch floods a dark room with light, God's light will flood the dark places of your heart with love and brightness.

Live it out: If you have something hidden in your heart, confess it to God and talk to a Christian adult about it. For those times in life when your friends share their dark secrets with you, show them love not condemnation.

Pray about it: Confide all your secrets to God. Ask for forgiveness, and accept His love.

Sammy "Stay Out of Trouble" Smith's Plan of Action

I will help this widow because she keeps on bothering me. Luke 18:5, CEV.

At Far Away High School the administration had one simple rule about discipline: The Principal is always right. When students got in trouble, he decided who would be punished and what the punishment would be. Everyone feared him, because he seemed so heartless.

You can imagine how scared little Sammy "Stay Out of Trouble" Smith felt when Polly "Pick a Fight" Peterson beat him up. (Sure, Polly was a girl, but she was a big, tough one—much taller and stronger than scrawny little Sammy.) The only thing scarier to Sammy than being beaten up by Polly was facing The Principal.

It was The Principal's habit to announce the punishment of all the troublemakers at the end of each month. So Sammy had two whole weeks to wait.

Sammy couldn't take all the worry anymore. He decided to do something. Every day he got to school early and waited by The Principal's designated parking spot. As soon as The Principal parked his car and started walking toward the school building, Sammy would run after him, begging (sometimes crying!), "Please don't punish me! It wasn't my fault. I got beat up by a girl. Isn't that punishment enough? Please, oh, please!" OK, so begging and crying isn't a great plan of action, but Sammy thought it was better than nothing. He continued this for two whole weeks. And on weekends he even stood outside The Principal's house shouting, "Please, Mr. Principal, please don't punish me! I'll never get in a fight again."

Sammy's plan was persistent (by that I mean *annoying*), and it paid off. The Principal got so fed up with the begging and pleading that he decided not to punish Sammy after all.

Jesus told a similar story of a widow who kept begging a heartless judge. The official finally gave her what she wanted, just so that she would stop bothering him. Christ used the story to illustrate one simple point: If mean people are willing to do nice things if you keep asking, just imagine how much more willing a loving God is to do nice things if you keep asking Him.

Live it out: Read Jesus' story of the widow and the judge in Luke 18:1-8.
Pray about it: Choose something or someone to pray about every day this month. Be persistent!

Live It Out!

Taste and see that the Lord is good; blessed is the one who takes refuge in him.
Psalm 34:8.

An idea that stood out to me from this week's devotional readings:

_____

_____

_____

A verse from this week's devotions that was powerful to me:

_____

_____

_____

A "Live it out" challenge I tried this week:

_____

_____

_____

Something that happened this week that was a blessing:

_____

_____

_____

My prayer today (thanks, requests, praises):

_____

_____

_____

104

Messing Up and Asking for Forgiveness

Then I acknowledged my sin to you and did not cover up my iniquity. I said, "I will confess my transgressions to the Lord." And you forgave the guilt of my sin.
Psalm 32:5.

It takes guts to say, "I messed up. I'm sorry." Those can be some of the most difficult words to force out of your mouth. When you speak them, though, you'll always be glad you did. Apologizing and confessing your sins is an important part of following God.

The great thing about it, though, is that He promises to forgive us if we honestly ask. "If we confess our sins, he is faithful and just and will forgive us our sins and purify us from all unrighteousness" (1 John 1:9).

Sometimes we ask for forgiveness from Him, but we don't actually *accept* it. Although we confess, we still feel guilty, dragging the sin and shame around like a bag of rocks. When Satan tries to make you feel guilty after you have confessed a sin, read 1 John 1:9 again. Claim it. Tell yourself, *I have confessed my sins, and God is faithful and just to forgive me and purify me of all my unrighteousness.* Don't let Satan steal the sense of freedom and forgiveness that Christ wants to give you.

Once you have confessed to God and accepted His forgiveness, you must do one more thing: forgive yourself. If the perfect God of the universe can forgive you, you can do the same with yourself. Accept God's grace, and give yourself a little grace too.

Live it out: Make it a regular part of your prayer life to ask for God's forgiveness. After you have done so, accept His forgiveness and move forward with your life.
Pray about it: Instead of praying, "Forgive me for my sins," tell God the specific things for which you are requesting forgiveness. Name them even though it may be embarrassing, and then leave them behind with God.

Shaking the Dust Off Your Feet

If anyone will not welcome you or listen to your words, leave that home or town and shake the dust off your feet. Matthew 10:14.

The fear of rejection can tie you up and hold you down by bullying its way into your brain and crowding out all your confidence. It keeps you from getting to know people and being yourself. And it causes you to stay quiet or distant from others.

If the fear of rejection is controlling you, you won't be able to live the exciting life that God has planned for you. He calls you to be bold, so that there's no time to worry about rejection.

When Jesus was on earth, He put together a crew of 12 men to be His disciples and helpers. He "gave them authority to drive out impure spirits and to heal every disease and sickness" (Matthew 10:1). Then He dispatched them out to preach the gospel, expel demons, raise the dead, and heal the sick. As He sent them out to nearby towns and villages, He gave them this very important advice: "If anyone will not welcome you or listen to your words, leave that home or town and shake the dust off your feet" (verse 14). In other words: "If anyone rejects you, just shake it off. Don't let it get you down. Hold your head up high, and keep on keeping on." Jesus wanted His disciples to have holy boldness, not a fear of rejection. If they were always worried what people would think of them, they would never be able to achieve the great things God had in store for them.

A friend of mine always says, "The one thing all really cool people have in common is they're not worried if people think they're cool or not." They just live their life confidently without fear of rejection or criticism. In a way, that's what Jesus was telling His followers to do: follow God without worrying what people might say or think. The only opinion that really matters is God's. When you courageously follow Him, you can hold your head high. If people reject you or what you say when you are serving as His disciple, then just shake it off, move on, and see what God has in store for you next.

Live it out: Ask yourself, *What would I do if I knew I wouldn't be rejected?* Then do those things! Don't let the fear of rejection hold you back from the amazing life God has for you.

Pray about it: Ask for the God-given confidence to do what He wants you to do.

Hug It Out Right Now

Go at once and make peace with your brother. Matthew 5:24, TEV.

According to Jesus, if you owe someone an apology, you need to tell the person "I'm sorry" before you and God can move on. In His most famous sermon, Jesus said it this way: "Therefore, if you are offering your gift at the altar and there remember that your brother or sister has something against you, leave your gift there in front of the altar. First go and be reconciled to them; then come and offer your gift" (Matthew 5:23, 24).

Before Jesus' death on the cross, people would ask for God's forgiveness by bringing sacrifices to an altar to symbolize Jesus' future sacrifice. In this passage, Jesus was telling people that before they tried to make things right with God, they need to make them right with other people.

Let's think about the modern-day equivalent. Before you go to God and ask Him for forgiveness, you need to ask forgiveness from those you have wronged. To take it to another level, before you offer any act of worship to God (such as leading out in your youth group, doing special music, or reading Scripture for church service), make sure you have made things right with anyone you have wronged. That way there will be nothing blocking you from receiving God's forgiveness and blessing.

So if you're fighting with someone, go and hug it out right now! Apologize and talk it through. Don't wait any longer. Otherwise, you'll have a broken relationship with that individual—and with God!

Live it out: If you owe anyone an apology, contact them today. Ask forgiveness, even if you think they wronged you too. Say, "I'm sorry." Don't add any disclaimers or jabs, such as "I was wrong, but so were you!" or "I'm sorry. Are you happy now?"
Pray about it: Pray, "Please show me if there is anything I need to set right—if there is anything blocking your power and forgiveness in my life."

Money, Money, Money, Money

People who have wealth but lack understanding are like the beasts that perish.
Psalm 49:20.

Nicknamed "the Witch of Wall Street," Hetty Green was the first American woman to make an impact on Wall Street. Famous for her wealth—and her stinginess—she became the richest woman in the world, but she remained miserly and cruel.

Hetty made her own children wear rags. She sent her daughter away to live in a convent and become a nun so that the child's living expenses would be paid.

But wait, the story gets worse. When her son developed an infection in his leg, Hetty wouldn't take him to the doctor because she didn't want to pay a medical bill. Instead, she brought him to the local hospital's charity ward intended for poor people unable to pay. When the hospital employees recognized Hetty, she took her son home without treatment. As a result, the boy's leg had to be amputated. Even then Hetty wouldn't pay for a hospital stay and insisted the surgery be done at home.

This miserly multimillionaire didn't spend money on herself, either. She ate cold food because she didn't want to purchase fuel to heat her meals. Instead of renting an office and furniture, she worked sitting in the middle of the floor in her bank building.

Hetty's story proves just what the Bible says: If you are always chasing after money, you won't be able to pursue God at the same time. "No one can serve two masters. Either you will hate the one and love the other, or you will be devoted to the one and despise the other. You cannot serve both God and money" (Matthew 6:24).

The Bible doesn't say that money is evil, but it does say that "the love of money is a root of all kinds of evil" (1 Timothy 6:10). Hetty let her love of money get in the way of loving people. If your love of money and things is blocking your *love* for people, step back and take a reality check. Should you have piles and piles of cash but no friends or loved ones, you'll just end up miserable. The Witch of Wall Street learned that lesson the hard way.

Live it out: Think about your relationship with money. What does it reveal about your priorities? Do you spend all of your money on yourself? Or on other people? Do you return tithe or give to charity or ministry?

Pray about it: Ask God to help you have a biblical—not a worldly—perspective on money.

A God Who Never Gives Up

A bruised reed he will not break, and a smoldering wick he will not snuff out.
Isaiah 42:3.

About 15 years ago I started to make a quilt. I began enthusiastically, selecting the fabrics from a craft store, hand-stitching the little squares. It was all going quite nicely, that is, until I got tired of it and gave up. Those hand-stitched squares now rest in a box in my closet.

When Rollerblades were all the rage, I gave that a try. I had never ice-skated or roller-skated, so I was starting at the ground level on this. Literally. I actually had to learn the basics to keep myself from repeatedly landing on the ground. After one intense lesson with my athletic husband as my instructor, I abandoned the idea.

It's tempting to give up on things when they start to look hopeless. But God isn't like us. In fact, the Bible says that He doesn't quit. He never ceases to see potential in situations.

A prophecy describes this characteristic of Jesus. It sounds poetic and almost cryptic: "A bruised reed he will not break, and a smoldering wick he will not snuff out" (Isaiah 42:3). Isaiah was using images that would make sense to people at that time. For example, a bruised reed referred to a large piece of grass that had been bent. Perhaps it was by the water's edge and an animal had stepped on it or the wind had blown it down. Most people would think it would be crushed and broken from then on. But according to this prophecy, Jesus wouldn't see it that way.

A smoldering wick is also an image that was relatable to people at that time. To picture it yourself, think of a candle that is just about to go out. It has more smoke than flame, and it looks as if it won't ignite again. Most people would expect the flame to completely die out, but, according to the prophecy, Jesus would view it differently.

Isaiah used these images to explain that Jesus won't give up on situations that appear hopeless. He won't break off a bruised reed, because He wants it to grow back healthy. Nor will He snuff out a smoldering wick, because He expects the flame to ignite again. When you face a seemingly hopeless situation, remember that God doesn't consider it hopeless.

Live it out: Is there a situation in your life in which you have given up hope? After reading Isaiah 42:3, do you think God has abandoned any hope? What can you do to reignite your hope?

Pray about it: Ask God to help you see things how He does—full of potential!

Never Too Cool for School

Teach me your way, Lord. Psalm 27:11.

Every day of high school is filled with new information—and another chance to learn something, whether it's a history fact or how to solve a math problem. That's why some parents often ask, "What did you learn in school today?" They know there must have been *something* you picked up in all of those classes.

However, the school classroom isn't life's *only* classroom. Life itself is a big classroom. Every single day, God will present occasions for you to acquire important knowledge—even when you aren't in school. You will have an opportunity to learn on those lazy Sundays when you sleep in. When you are mowing the lawn. When someone starts a nasty rumor about you during summer break. When you are working in an office at age 35, and even when you are retired and living in Florida.

Whenever you come face to face with a challenging situation, you are being given an opportunity to learn. And every time you learn, you become stronger, wiser, and more confident. Jesus said, "Learn from me, for I am gentle and humble in heart, and you will find rest for your souls" (Matthew 11:29). God designed us to learn. Jesus promises that we'll be at peace when we learn what He is trying to teach us. Life will be better if we are willing to learn.

As you face difficult situations, ask yourself, "What can I learn from this?" If someone says something mean about you, you have a chance to discover how to be kind, how to keep your cool. Or if your parents are getting on your last nerve, you can acquire patience and learn how to be loving even when you don't feel like it. Should you mess up and betray a friend, you can learn how to apologize and restore a friendship. Losing a ball game provides opportunity to be a good sport—and what to do differently next time.

Next time your parents ask you, "What did you learn in school today?" tell them what you learned—and then ask them, "What did *you* learn today?" Because no one should ever stop learning. Life is a school. Learn everything that you can.

Live it out: When faced with a challenging situation, ask yourself, "What can I learn from this?"

Pray about it: Ask God to help you have a teachable spirit.

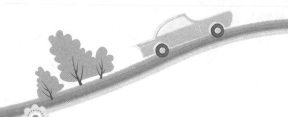

Live It Out!

Ask and it will be given to you; seek and you will find; knock and the door will be opened to you. For everyone who asks receives; the one who seeks finds; and to the one who knocks, the door will be opened. Matthew 7:7, 8.

An idea that stood out to me from this week's devotional readings:

_____

_____

_____

A verse from this week's devotions that was powerful to me:

_____

_____

_____

A "Live it out" challenge I tried this week:

_____

_____

_____

Something that happened this week that was a blessing:

_____

_____

_____

My prayer today (thanks, requests, praises):

_____

_____

_____

What Nicknames Reveal

Lord, you are my God; I will exalt you and praise your name. Isaiah 25:1.

Like many of you, I had a few childhood nicknames. And if you promise not to call me any of them, I'll even tell you a few.

I grew up on a ranch in Oklahoma, where cows surrounded our house in every direction. So I guess it shouldn't have come as any surprise, then, when my name—Heather—got replaced with Heifer (the name of a young cow that hasn't had a calf yet). And then there was the string of spice nicknames. Since my sisters are named Cinnamon and Ginger (yes, really), I often was called Nutmeg, Pepper, or All-Spice. And how could I forget the Bible term that became my nickname. When my little churchgoing friends learned the word "heathen," it became an easy replacement for Heather since it was just one letter different. Heathen stuck for a while, even though I like to think it was a completely undeserved label.

My nicknames were all pretty silly, but the Bible indicates that names—even nicknames—have a lot of meaning. The names of God, for example, are very significant. They reveal His character to us. If you want to know what God is like, look at some of His nicknames: Advocate, Almighty, Comforter, Deliverer, Desire of Nations, Everlasting Father, Guide, Prince of Peace, Redeemer, Savior, Servant, Teacher, Wonderful Counselor.

Just reading a list of God's nicknames reminds us how magnificent He is! It's no wonder David declared, "I will praise you, Lord my God, with all my heart; I will glorify your name forever" (Psalm 86:12). God's names reveal how loving and wonderful He is.

Live it out: When you pray or talk about God, what do you call Him? Start using a variety of God's nicknames to remind you of how amazing He is. (You can use the list above, or do an Internet search for "names of God in the Bible" to find more.)

Pray about it: Use at least three of God's names in your prayer today. Talk to Him about what those names mean to you.

The Names of God

Some trust in chariots and some in horses, but we trust in the name of the Lord our God. Psalm 20:7.

Each of the names of God reveals something amazing about Him. Look at some of these meaning-rich names for Him. As you read them, take time to reflect on what they indicate to you. Which of them speaks to your heart?

Elohim: the Strong One
El Shaddai: God Almighty
El Elyon: the Most High God
El Olam: the Everlasting God
Immanuel: God with us
Yahweh Jireh: the Lord will provide
Yahweh Shalom: the Lord is Peace
Yahweh Ro'i: the Lord my Shepherd
Yahweh Tsidkenu: the Lord our Righteousness

Each name holds a promise that you can claim. Should you feel alone, remember that God is *Immanuel*, the God who is with you. When you are worried or upset, remember that God is *Yahweh Shalom*, the Lord who can give you peace. And when you feel as if you'll never measure up and can't be good enough, remember God is *Yahweh Tsidkenu*, the Lord who is righteous on your behalf. Let the names of God bring you hope and encouragement.

Live it out: Choose one of the names from the list that is especially meaningful to you. Memorize it, and use it in prayer when you need a reminder of God's love for you.

Pray about it: Choose one of the names from the list, and pray about its significance. For instance, if you select Immanuel, your prayer may go something like this: "God, Immanuel, sometimes I feel so lonely, as though no one even notices me or cares about me. That's why I am so happy to know You are Immanuel, God with us. Help me to feel Your presence and to remember You are with me all the time. Thank You for not leaving me alone."

APR 16

Justice Is Served at the Waffle House

"Who can hide in secret places so that I cannot see them?" declares the Lord. "Do not I fill heaven and earth?" declares the Lord. Jeremiah 23:24.

You can't hide from God. Not even in a Waffle House in Georgia.

Before we get into the story, we first have to establish just how annoying and embarrassing it is to accidentally "pocket-dial" someone. You know, when your phone is in your pocket or purse, gets bumped, and unbeknownst to you accidentally calls a number. Yes, that's always annoying, but for one Georgia teen, it changed his life.

The teenager, a Waffle House employee, was discussing a drug deal when his phone accidentally dialed 9-1-1. Of all the numbers his pocket could have triggered, that was the absolute worst one. The dispatcher could overhear several people talking about illegal drugs, so a deputy went to the Waffle House to check into the matter.

The deputy arrived to find the teen boy making more than just waffles. He was also making a drug deal and even had drugs on him at the time.

Even when you feel as if no one knows what you are doing or can track you down, God is with you. The psalmist said it this way: "Where can I go from your Spirit? Where can I flee from your presence? . . . If I say, 'Surely the darkness will hide me and the light become night around me,' even the darkness will not be dark to you" (Psalm 139:7-12).

Don't let those words scare you, though. Even though God sees everything—good and bad—He loves you extravagantly anyway. He wants to be with you during your darkest moments to help turn things around and give you an even better life.

"If I go up to the heavens, you are there; if I make my bed in the depths, you are there. If I rise on the wings of the dawn, if I settle on the far side of the sea, even there your hand will guide me, your right hand will hold me fast" (verses 8-10). In His loving pursuit of you, God will find you anywhere, even in a Waffle House in Georgia.

Live it out: Be open with God about your struggles and secrets. Your honesty will feel freeing. For additional support, confide in a Christlike adult.

Pray about it: Pray about the secrets you keep. God knows them anyway.

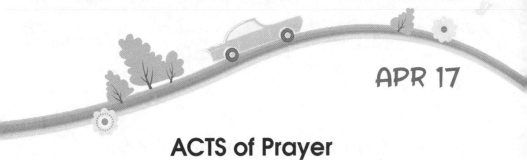

ACTS of Prayer

Hear my prayer, Lord. Psalm 86:6.

One day Jesus was praying in a certain place. When he finished, one of his disciples said to him, 'Lord, teach us to pray, just as John taught his disciples'" (Luke 11:1). Jesus' disciples wanted to learn more about how to talk to God. Just as it is possible to learn how to communicate better with other human beings, so also we can do the same with God.

If you, like the disciples, would like to pray more successfully, start by trying a new approach, such as the ACTS prayer. ACTS is an acronym that stands for adoration, confession, thanksgiving, and supplication. Here's what each component represents:

- **Adoration** involves worshipping God. Praise Him for who He is—your Creator, Savior, and Shepherd. This isn't about specific thanks (we'll get to that later). It's more about worshipping and adoring God just for who He is: almighty, loving, wise, merciful. Take time to really think about Him as the creator of the universe and redeemer of the world.
- **Confession** allows you to clear away the things blocking your relationship with God. All of us have sinned and need to confess. First John 1:8, 9 says, "If we claim to be without sin, we deceive ourselves and the truth is not in us. If we confess our sins, he is faithful and just and will forgive us our sins and purify us from all unrighteousness." Since we've all messed up—and God already knows about it, anyway—we might as well admit it and get it all out in the open. He promises to forgive us and give us a fresh start.
- **Thanksgiving** is one of the fun parts of prayer. Thank God for anything and everything—for the good grade on your math test or your fun family vacation. James 1:17 says every good thing in your life is from God: "Every good and perfect gift is from above, coming down from the Father of the heavenly lights."
- **Supplication** means to ask. Here is your chance to take to God all the things and people you're concerned about. Ask Him specifically to be with your grandmother who is sick or your best friend whose parents are getting a divorce. He wants to help and be involved.

Live it out: Set aside five minutes every day this week to pray.
Pray about it: Pray an ACTS prayer right now. Include each of the four parts of the prayer.

Do I Have News for You?

Jesus said, "...Go instead to my brothers and tell them,'I am ascending to my Father and your Father, to my God and your God.'" John 20:17.

During biblical times the world operated as a patriarchal system (in other words, as a man's world). In many ways men considered women inferior. Jesus, however, was no ordinary man. He treated women as though they were just as valuable as men.

Here's an example. With few exceptions, women could not serve as witnesses in court. Men didn't think women could be trusted to give accurate, useful testimonies. However—check this out—Jesus chose a woman to be the witness who gave testimony to arguably the most important event in the history of the planet: His resurrection.

After Jesus was raised from the dead, He could have gone and knocked on Pilate's front door and announced, "I'm alive!" He could have done an extravagant do-over of the triumphal entry, with a loud, elaborate parade announcing His resurrection. Or He could have appeared in the sky so that everyone for miles and miles could see Him up there. But He didn't choose any of those ways. Instead, He asked a woman to be the witness who would give the life-changing testimony.

Here's how it happened. After the Resurrection, Jesus found Mary Magdalene crying outside of the tomb. When she finally realized who it was in front of her, He gave her a very important job. "Jesus said, 'Do not hold on to me, for I have not yet ascended to the Father. Go instead to my brothers and tell them, "I am ascending to my Father and your Father, to my God and your God."' Mary Magdalene went to the disciples with the news: 'I have seen the Lord!' And she told them that he had said these things to her" (John 20:17, 18).

Jesus gave an important mission and ministry to a person no one else believed could do it. He sees amazing potential and value in every individual—male or female. Don't worry about what people think you can or cannot do. If God wants you to do something, He'll give you the opportunity and ability to do it!

Live it out: If you sense God calling you to do something, don't hesitate. He believes in you and will help you accomplish what He calls you to do.

Pray about it: Thank God for placing value and opportunity into your life.

The Day I Was Told to Poke Out a Bear's Eyes

He will command his angels concerning you to guard you in all your ways.
Psalm 91:11.

Several years ago my husband and I went with a group of friends to Glacier National Park. Just a few weeks before, a bear had tragically mauled a young couple, and so the park had amped up warnings to tourists.

The rangers were just trying to be responsible, but to our group of invincible skeptics, it all seemed a little like overkill. Everywhere we turned, someone was selling bear bells or bear spray. Neon signs abounded, warning tourists to hike at their own risk. Tourists prattled nonstop about what to do if you came across a bear (poke out its eyes was a commonly discussed idea) and how to avoid attracting bears (don't wear red, because it will draw them to you, they said).

We hadn't come all the way from Michigan to talk about poking out a bear's eyes—we had come to experience the park! So off we went on a hike, to which I wore a red shirt (what a daredevil). Soon my husband and I got separated from the group. As we walked along the trail, trying to catch up, we heard something in the bushes that sounded as if it were as big as a hippopotamus. Suddenly, inches (yes, inches!) in front of us, out stomped a grizzly bear so big that we *wished* it had been a hippopotamus. It turned its massive head and looked straight at me, my husband, and my daredevil red shirt. I thought it would kill us. I also thought anyone who suggested poking out a bear's eyes had never seen how tiny they are.

By God's protection, we didn't get mauled, and once that bear left, we ran as though our life depended on it (because I'm pretty sure it did). Breathless and scared, we told our friends what had happened. "Did you get a picture?" they asked. My husband and I looked at each other and laughed, because obviously they didn't understand how close we had been.

Even when we (or our friends) don't realize the danger we're in, God protects us, "He will command his angels concerning you to guard you in all your ways" (Psalm 91:11).

Live it out: Think back to a time you were in danger, and thank God for keeping you safe.

Pray about it: Thank God for protecting you even when you don't realize the danger.

APR 20

Live It Out!

But seek first his kingdom and his righteousness, and all these things will be given to you as well. Matthew 6:33.

An idea that stood out to me from this week's devotional readings:

_____

_____

_____

A verse from this week's devotions that was powerful to me:

_____

_____

_____

A "Live it out" challenge I tried this week:

_____

_____

_____

Something that happened this week that was a blessing:

_____

_____

_____

My prayer today (thanks, requests, praises):

_____

_____

_____

Kindergarten Day

A little child will lead them. Isaiah 11:6.

Pull out your crayons, your sidewalk chalk, and your finger paints, because today is Kindergarten Day! That's right, today's holiday honors Friedrich Froebel, the creator of kindergarten, whose birthday was April 21.

Now that you've moved on to complicated schoolwork (geometry, physics, world history), kindergarten looks like such a breeze, doesn't it? Aren't they really just playing most of the day, anyway?

Yes, it might seem as if kindergarteners aren't up to anything significant, but Jesus said we could learn a thing or two from them. In fact, He said that we should *be* like those little people:

"At that time the disciples came to Jesus and asked, 'Who, then, is the greatest in the kingdom of heaven? He called a little child to him, and placed the child among them. And he said: 'Truly I tell you unless you change and become like little children, you will never enter the kingdom of heaven. Therefore, whoever takes the lowly position of this child is the greatest in the kingdom of heaven" (Matthew 18:1-4).

Kindergarteners and young children are innocent, trusting, and carefree. They don't worry or try to prove themselves. Instead, they leave the big decisions to the big people and trust their parents to take care of them. Likewise, God wants us to have simple faith and to trust Him to care for us. He wants us to be happy and carefree—just like those innocent little kindergarteners.

Live it out: Pull out a picture of yourself in kindergarten. How have you changed since then? Are you more worried or cynical? What can you do to become more trusting and innocent again?

Pray about it: Pray to have the faith of a child. Think of God as a perfect, loving Father, and then talk to Him about your life—everything, whether good or bad.

Prince Charming and Good Manners

Be kind and compassionate to one another. Ephesians 4:32.

I recently saw an online discussion in which a girl had posted the question "Should a guy still open doors and pull out chairs for a girl?" One girl responded, "Absolutely, unless (a) his arms are broken or (b) he is a jerk." Another girl wrote, "Yes, and if he doesn't come around and open your car door, just stay seated in the car until he gets the idea!" Some of the guys weighed in on the other side of the debate: "That's old-fashioned." "A guy shouldn't do these things unless it is his personality. If he's just being phony, he shouldn't."

You might think chivalry and rules of etiquette exist only in stories about castles, princes, and fair maidens. However, Christ calls His followers to pay attention to such things. *The Ministry of Healing* says, "Christianity will make a man a gentleman. Christ was courteous . . . and His true followers will manifest the same spirit" (p. 489). Of course, the same is true of girls, too. Christianity can transform girls into kind and courteous young women. The apostle Paul even included kindness in the list of the fruit of the Spirit, a list of the characteristics of people who have the Holy Spirit living in them (Galatians 5:22, 23).

A lot of guys and girls feel it isn't cool to be thoughtful. Instead, they act disinterested, as if they can't be bothered with such trivialities. But God doesn't want His followers just to slouch in their chairs and say "Whatever." He is calling us to a higher standard. So why not try a little politeness—and even chivalry?

Here are some ideas you might explore today. Guys, I guarantee any girl will find it endearing if you open doors for her, offer to help her if she is carrying a heavy load, stand up when she approaches the table, help her put her coat on, or open the car door for her. And girls, you can't go wrong by making eye contact, smiling, holding a door or elevator for someone, or including people into your conversations when they approach. Once you try this, you'll be convinced that courtesy and chivalry aren't just for princes in castles in faraway lands.

Live it out: When in doubt, always err on the side of being overly kind instead of inattentive.

Pray about it: Ask God to open your eyes to ways you can be courteous, and ask Him to bring courteous people into your life so that you can learn from them.

The Plan-ahead,
Never-procrastinate God

There is surely a future hope for you, and your hope will not be cut off.
Proverbs 23:18.

One of the greatest stories in the Bible—of all time, really—is the Exodus, the account of the Israelites' journey from slavery to the Promised Land. It is a tale of miracles, and more miracles, and lessons learned the hard way.

But before that amazing journey could begin, God needed to prepare a leader who could handle the massive job of leading the Israelites on such a trip. (Just think of how complicated it is to coordinate a family vacation or a class trip with a few people. Now multiply those complications by, say, a million, and you'll get an idea of what their leader was up against!)

God chose Moses to be the special leader. Now, his life was not a boring one. Drama had filled it from his birth. In fact, the day he was born there was an order to have him killed. Pharaoh had commanded that all Hebrew baby boys be thrown into the Nile River. Nevertheless, God was watching out for this little guy to make sure he lived long enough to accomplish His purposes.

Moses' newborn adventures are so unbelievable that they sound made up. His mother *technically* put her son into the Nile, but she did so in a basket—a little baby boat in which he could float away. It's a bit of a loophole, but it worked out just perfectly. Pharaoh's very own daughter found that adorable infant drifting down the river. She felt sorry for the little guy and rescued him. With timing that could be coordinated only by God Himself, Moses' big sister popped up out of the shrubs and asked Pharaoh's daughter if she would like a Hebrew woman to take care of the baby. And just like that, Moses was back with his mommy, with the blessings of Pharaoh's own daughter.

God doesn't procrastinate. He doesn't wait until the last minute to throw together a makeshift plan. Always He looks ahead and works out all the details before we humans even have a clue what He is doing. Long before the Exodus, God saved Moses so that he could be part of an enormous plan. You may not see it now, but God has a plan for your life that He will make known little by little.

Live it out: Read Psalm 139. Think about what this passage means to you.
Pray about it: Ask God for patience and faith as you follow His plan.

He Who Dies
With the Most Stuff Still Dies

Life is not measured by how much one owns. Luke 12:15, NCV.

The TV show *Hoarding: Buried Alive* tells the true stories of people who have accumulated so much stuff that their houses are literally filled to the ceiling. Such compulsive hoarders have crammed every room with clothes, dishes, knickknacks, and odds and ends collected through the years. Most of these hoarders can't cook in their kitchens because of so much stuff piled on the stove and in the fridge. They can't even sleep on a bed, because heaps of clothes and newspapers and paper towels (and anything else you can think of) cover where the pillows and sheets should be. Resigned to sleeping on a sofa and eating fast food, they live lonely, trapped lives.

Our affluent society leads us to think that more stuff brings more happiness. However, the truth is sometimes more stuff just brings more problems. In the case of extreme hoarders, their stuff has overwhelmed their lives, preventing them from having relationships, health, or balance. Because they have no room, they can't have people over. They can't get good sleep or meals or exercise, because their stuff is closing in on them. Nor can they even breathe fresh air, because they're suffocated by old, filthy stuff.

No one says they want to be a hoarder when they grow up. Nor does anyone set out to collect a houseful of junk. Nevertheless, many of us do want to have lots of *nice* things some day. We want a big house, a good car, maybe even a boat and a vacation home. God doesn't condemn owning things, but He does give us a guideline: don't love stuff so much that you lose sight of what really matters. Whether it's hoarded junk or flashy purchases, stuff can cause a lot of heartache if it distracts us from our relationship with Him and others.

Jesus said it best when He gave this instruction: "Don't collect for yourselves treasures on earth, where moth and rust destroy and where thieves break in and steal. But collect for yourselves treasures in heaven. . . . For where your treasure is, there your heart will be also" (Matthew 6:19-21, HCSB).

Live it out: Donate something to a person who could really use it. When you give things away, it breaks its hold on you.

Pray about it: Pray that you will always treasure God and people more than things.

To Know Him Is to Love Him

Now this is eternal life: that they know you, the only true God, and Jesus Christ, whom you have sent. John 17:3.

When I first started dating my husband, Robert, there were a lot of things I didn't know about him yet. I had no idea of his favorite restaurants or what I should buy him for his birthday or Christmas. Nor was I sure what kind of activities or dates he would enjoy.

However, now that we've been together for years, it's a lot easier to think of what he will and will not like. Now I know that he doesn't want a party on his birthday. Instead, he prefers to go to camping and biking stores and pick out his own present, and then eat strawberry shortcake at home with family. I know that he never puts ice in his drinks, and he hates mushrooms. I know that he stays up late, likes to travel in Europe, and wants a German shorthaired pointer for a pet. Thus there are thousands of things I know about him now, because we are in a close relationship.

When faced with a major decision, Christians often wonder, "What is God's will? What does He want for me?" They would like to know which school to attend, if they should date a certain person, or take a part-time job. In each case they want to know what God thinks about that specific situation. It's a little like me wanting to know what my husband liked before I really became acquainted with him. Once I knew *him*, I was able to make case-by-case decisions about what he would like and want. I knew *his will* once I knew *him*.

Likewise, with God, the only way to know what He will want for you in a specific situation is to know *Him*. Once you are in a relationship with Him, you'll become aware of what He values, what is important to Him, what He likes and doesn't like. And then you'll be able to know when looking at a specific situation if it matches God's values and character. If you want to know God's will, start by getting to know God.

Live it out: Grow your relationship with God by setting aside time to read the Bible, pray, and spend time with God-followers. The more you get to know Him the more clear His likes and dislikes will be known to you.

Pray about it: Ask God to reveal Himself to you day by day, so that you will know Him better.

A Gross Fashion Statement

I delight greatly in the Lord; my soul rejoices in my God. For he has clothed me with garments of salvation and arrayed me in a robe of his righteousness.
Isaiah 61:10.

For thousands of years people have worn clothing made from animal fur. While some people think fur clothing is a sign of wealth and prestige, others consider it brutal and unnecessary. Animal activists constantly protest fur clothing and fight on behalf of minks, foxes, rabbits, and all their other furry friends.

Lately, however, fashion designers are using a new kind of fur. It comes from the nutria, an animal otherwise known as a *swamp rat.* Yes, you heard me right: the clothes are made from the shiny pelt of a swamp rat. Sound gross to you? Well, that's because it is.

Those little rodents have become quite a nuisance, especially in Louisiana, where they have overrun the swamps and gobbled up plants vital to the coastal wetlands. The state of Louisiana got so fed up with the rats that they began paying hunters $5 for every nutria killed. Since no one could stand the nasty rats—and since they were going to be killed anyway—everyone agreed that they might as well turn them into some fur hats and jackets. Even people who normally avoided fur decided that they could wear nutria guilt-free, because the dead rats would have just been left to rot in the swamps if they weren't turned into fashion.

No matter how good it looks in the end, a jacket made out of swamp rats is still just a jacket made out of swamp rats. According to Isaiah 64:6, even our most righteous acts are like filthy rags—which is even grosser than a nutria jacket. Fortunately for us, God has something far better for us. When we give our lives to Him, He drapes a beautiful garment of white over us to symbolize the perfect life of Christ.

Live it out: Think about what it means to you to put on the robe of righteousness that Isaiah describes. How does it change your thoughts and actions?
Pray about it: Pray that God will take your sins (a filthy robe) and give you righteousness (a robe of white) instead. Then believe that He will do as He promised, and thank Him for His lavish gift of salvation.

Live It Out!

I will sing of the Lord's great love forever; with my mouth I will make your faithfulness known through all generations. Psalm 89:1.

An idea that stood out to me from this week's devotional readings:

_____

_____

_____

A verse from this week's devotions that was powerful to me:

_____

_____

_____

A "Live it out" challenge I tried this week:

_____

_____

_____

Something that happened this week that was a blessing:

_____

_____

_____

My prayer today (thanks, requests, praises):

_____

_____

_____

Love Like You Mean It

Love sincerely. Romans 12:9, GW.

The Bible has a whole lot to say about love. Come to think of it, we *still* hear a whole lot of talk about love. It's woven into most movies, books, and songs. And we see it all around us every day. Parents *love* their children. Teens *love* their friends (and on a really good day, maybe even their siblings). Girls *love* their boyfriends.

We think we know what it means to love, but sometimes we get it all wrong. Love isn't just a feeling that overcomes us, like love songs would lead us to believe. Rather, love is an *action* that Jesus Himself commands us to take: "A new command I give you: Love one another. As I have loved you, so you must love one another" (John 13:34).

If you want to know what the action of love looks like, check out Romans 12:9-21. The passage starts by telling us to "Love sincerely" (verse 9, GW). It then gives a list of practical ways you can show sincere love. Here are just some of them:

- "Excel in showing respect for each other" (verse 10, GW).
- "Don't be lazy in showing your devotion" (verse 11, GW).
- "Share what you have with God's people who are in need" (verse 13, GW).
- "Be happy with those who are happy. Be sad with those who are sad" (verse 15, GW).
- "Don't be arrogant. . . . Don't think that you are smarter than you really are" (verse 16, GW).
- "Don't take revenge" (verse 19, GW).

Next time you're not feeling very loving to someone, *act* loving toward them. After all, it's not an option for Christians—it's a command.

Live it out: Today show sincere love to someone who seems unlovable. Read Romans 12:9-21 for inspiring ideas on how to love sincerely.

Pray about it: Focus your prayer today on the ways God has shown you love. The more you think about His love for you, the easier it will be to love others.

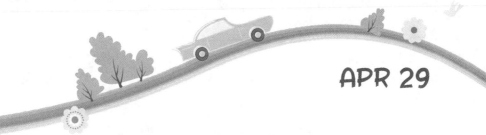

Making a Mountain Out of a Wantitump

Say to this mountain, "Move from here to there," and it will move. Matthew 17:20.

In 1702 William III of England died of pneumonia. That wasn't such a strange thing back then. After all, lots of people died of pneumonia. His death was, nevertheless, a little more complicated. It all started when he fell off a horse. That, too, was probably pretty common, considering that horses were a primary form of transportation in those days. Tumbling off a horse would have been the equivalent of having a car accident nowadays.

As William III fell off his horse, he broke his collarbone, which forced him to remain in bed. It was then, when he was feeling sickly, that he got pneumonia.

Back the story up a little more, and you'll discover why William III fell off his horse. He tumbled to the ground after his horse tripped on a wantitump. Even if you don't know what such a thing was, you recognize that it doesn't sound like anything tough enough to make someone die! A wantitump is actually a very old word for molehill, a little mound.

When people overreact to something, it's often said they are "making a mountain out of a molehill." They are creating a big deal out of something insignificant. A molehill, after all, is just a tiny little thing (yeah, try telling *that* to William III). But it is true, with the exception of William III's story, that molehills really aren't a very big deal.

Yet, sad to say, it is easy to make a mountain out of a molehill. Someone says a snide little comment, and you hold it against them . . . *forever*. You don't get invited to a party, and you ignore the birthday girl for the rest of the school year. A person bumps your shoulder in the hall, and your rage flares up and you just want to punch him or her in the face. All making mountains out of molehills.

God, on the other hand, turns mountains into molehills. He can level any difficulty and make it easy to conquer. What seems like a mountain—a very big deal—to you is just a small thing to Him. So when you face a little wantitump, just trust God and keep right on moving.

Live it out: Don't overreact and make a big deal out of things. Trust God to work things out.

Pray about it: Ask God to help you let go of any molehills that you've turned into mountains.

Fear Factor

For God has not given us a spirit of fear, but of power and of love and of a sound mind. 2 Timothy 1:7, NKJV.

Which of the following is scarier to you: Spiders or snakes? Scuba diving or skydiving? Public speaking or not being noticed? Failure or never accomplishing anything great? The future or the past? Being rejected or being alone?

Even if they don't admit it, most people are afraid of something. While one person may have arachnophobia (fear of spiders), someone else may have arachibutyrophobia (fear of peanut butter sticking to the roof of their mouth), or cyanophobia (fear of the color blue). (Check the dictionary: I couldn't make this stuff up!)

OK, so there are some extreme and unusual fears out there (such as cyanophobia). However, a lot of common fears—such as that of rejection and failure—will hold us back if left unchecked. We simply cannot live out God's will for our lives if our fears constantly get in the way. That's why the Bible repeatedly reminds us not to be afraid.

For those times when you feel fear rising, try these practical steps to build your courage:

- **Identify the fear.** Sometimes when we are worried, angry, skeptical, or defeated, those feelings are actually caused by or related to fear. Ask God to help you realize whether you might have fears holding you back. Then ask Him for the courage to live in faith, not fear.
- **Claim God's promises.** Do a Bible search to find verses about fear and courage. Choose one or two of them to memorize and repeat during difficult times.
- **Face each day with faith.** Remember that living past your fears requires risk and trust in God. When you live with Christ, He will always be pushing you to grow and to learn.

Live it out: Read Psalm 27:1; Psalm 91:5-7; Isaiah 41:10, 13; Matthew 10:29-31, and listen to what God is telling you in those verses.

Pray about it: Ask God to help grow your faith and shrink your fears.

How to Be a Singer/Songwriter

Sing to the Lord a new song. Psalm 96:1.

When God does something great in your life, what do you do to celebrate? Maybe you say a prayer of thanks or tell a friend about it. In the Bible, God followers found creative ways to honor the times that He did something wonderful.

One of those ways to honor special moments was to write a song. Moses, for example, composed a song after his many years with the Israelites in the wilderness. As he faced death, he thought back to everything that God had done, and he put all the facts and feelings into a song. But he didn't just keep it to himself. Instead, he "spoke all the words of this song in the hearing of the people" (Deuteronomy 32:44).

Deborah, a prophet and judge, also composed a song in honor of what God had done. After she led the Israelites into battle and encouraged them to live for God, she performed a duet with Barak, the army commander. If you ever thought it wasn't manly to sing about God, just consider Barak singing with Deborah after going to battle!

And then there was Mary, the mother of Jesus. She wrote an original song after she discovered she was pregnant with the Messiah, and her cousin Elizabeth was pregnant with John the Baptist. She burst out in praise, "My soul glorifies the Lord and my spirit rejoices in God my Savior" (Luke 1:46, 47).

You don't have to be a professional songwriter to turn your gratitude and love into a song. Moses was a shepherd, and he did it. Mary was a pregnant teenager, and she did it. Multiple times the Bible tells all of us—not just professional musicians—to "sing a new song to the Lord."

Live it out: Read Mary's song in Luke 1:46-55. Think of something great that God has done for you, and write a song about it—really! Even if you don't set it to music, you can compose it in the form of a poem. Keep it somewhere safe, so that you will be able to look back on it years from now.

Pray about it: Think back and praise God for the great things He has done for you.

MAY 2

Celebrate Your Individuality

I praise you because I am fearfully and wonderfully made; your works are wonderful, I know that full well. Psalm 139:14.

My dad likes to keep things simple. That's hard to do, though, when you have six children. When we kids were young, he often made executive decisions on small matters, for the sake of simplicity. For example, if we stopped to get a snack on a road trip, we all got the same thing. If he wanted an ice-cream sandwich, we all ate ice-cream sandwiches. (*What's that, you're craving a Bomb Pop instead? Ice-cream sandwich or nothing.*) If he was in the mood for a cherry limeade, we all had cherry limeades. (*Not in the mood for cherry flavor? Well, then, you're fresh out of luck. Don't enjoy tangy lime? Too bad, kiddo, because that's what we're serving up.*)

It was just six times simpler to get everyone the same thing than to take individual orders. Such occasions did not encourage individuality. It wasn't so bad, though. As an 8-year-old, I hadn't met an ice-cream sandwich or cherry limeade I didn't like.

God has about 7 billion children on this planet. You'd think He would get overwhelmed with all *7 billion* of us having our own desires, personalities, and preferences. But He doesn't. He allows individuality. In fact, He *encourages* it. Our Creator made each of us to be a unique combination of likes, dislikes, looks, talents, and personality traits.

The Lord doesn't want you to be a Christian clone. We don't have to say the same thing, wear the same thing, think the same thing, or eat the same thing. God is creativity. He likes variety, and maybe even a little quirkiness (I mean, have you *seen* some of the animals He created?) To celebrate His creativity, God wants you to live out your uniqueness while you follow Him!

Live it out: Make a list of at least 10 unique things about you. List at least three ways you can use your special characteristics to glorify God.

Pray about it: Thank God for making you unique. Ask Him to bring out the best in you as you continue to develop your personality and character.

The Mind-Body-Spirit Connection

May the God who gives us peace make you holy in every way and keep your whole being—spirit, soul, and body—free from every fault at the coming of our Lord Jesus Christ. I Thessalonians 5:23, TEV.

Your mind, body, and spirit are all connected. If you feel physically sick, you're more likely to feel down in the dumps mentally and spiritually. It makes sense, right? When you are vomiting or coughing or writhing in pain, you usually aren't laughing and happy, correct? The mind and spirit have the same kind of effect on the body. As you feel sad, your body has less energy and health. That's why the Bible says, "A cheerful heart is good medicine, but a crushed spirit dries up the bones" (Proverbs 17:22).

When you do anything to make your mind, body, or spirit healthier, all the components become healthier. Try some of these easy health boosters, and you'll benefit physically, mentally, and spiritually:

- **Keep your mind sharp.** Exercise your brain! Your mind gets stronger every time you learn something new in school, play a word game, or do a puzzle.
- **Be sappy.** According to research studies, thinking about someone you love actually improves mental and emotional well-being. Spend a couple minutes reminiscing about the people who mean the most to you, and you'll be healthier and happier.
- **Shrug it off.** Your neck and shoulders can't talk, but if they could, they would probably tell you they are tired from sitting at a computer or a school desk all day! Strengthen your trapezius muscles and reduce pain by doing simple shoulder shrugs.
- **Pray instead of worry.** When you start to worry, stop yourself. Say a prayer or read a Bible verse instead. Spiritual coping strategies will not only help lower stress but can also improve mood levels, pain levels, relationships, habits, and quality of life.

Live it out: Do at least one of these health boosters today. Pay attention to how your decisions this week affect you mentally, physically, and spiritually.

Pray about it: Praise God for creating you in His image—a complex and amazing connection of mind, body, and spirit.

MAY 4

Live It Out!

Because he turned his ear to me, I will call on him as long as I live. Psalm 116:2.

An idea that stood out to me from this week's devotional readings:

_____

_____

_____

A verse from this week's devotions that was powerful to me:

_____

_____

_____

A "Live it out" challenge I tried this week:

_____

_____

_____

Something that happened this week that was a blessing:

_____

_____

_____

My prayer today (thanks, requests, praises):

_____

_____

_____

What Can I Do to Help?

Carry each other's burdens, and in this way you will fulfill the law of Christ.
Galatians 6:2.

The Bible has an interesting message about your life. You ready for it?

Here it is: Your life isn't all about you.

God has called us to look up, look around, and think about other people. *How can we help them? How can we show them love?* Most of us spend most of our time dwelling on ourselves. However, the Bible gives us a challenge: "Do not forget to do good and to share with others, for with such sacrifices God is pleased" (Hebrews 13:16).

If you start watching for opportunities, you'll discover new ways every day. You can make a big difference in someone's life even with a small gesture. For example, if you invite a lonely student to have lunch with your group of friends, it might have a major impact on that individual.

There are lots of other ways you can focus on other people. Why not try one of these, or think of one of your own?

- Help teach a young child to read.
- Offer to do yard work or housework for an elderly neighbor.
- Make care packages for people at the homeless shelter.
- Volunteer to help with the Special Olympics or a children's sports team.
- Teach an older person how to use a computer and the Internet.
- Don't text or check your phone while driving. Being a responsible driver protects the people around you (not to mention yourself).
- Set up a recycling system for your home.
- Donate your old computer to a school or student who could use it.

Live it out: Do a kind act for someone else. Think of a way you would like to help others, and go for it!

Pray about it: Spend your prayer time today praying only for others. Make it all about other people—not yourself.

MAY 6

Failure Is Why I Succeed

Lord, save us; Lord, grant us success! Psalm 118:25.

In an old Nike commercial, basketball legend Michael Jordan talked about his career failures:

"I've missed more than 9,000 shots in my career.

"I've lost almost 300 games.

"Twenty-six times I've been trusted to take the game-winning shot . . . and missed.

"I've failed over and over and over again in my life.

"And that is why I succeed."

Michael Jordan, like many other great achievers, realized that failure is not the opposite of success. It is *part* of success. Failure teaches us the lessons and gives us the strength that we need on our way to success. If you try to avoid failure, you're going to end up avoiding success too. Failure, after all, teaches us more than success does.

Many people don't attempt hard things because they're afraid to fail. You've got to try anyway. So what if you fail? You'll learn something, and you'll be one step closer to success. Don't let your fears hold you back. God doesn't want you to live a small, scared life, because you're afraid of failure. He has called you to live boldly and confidently. If He is leading you to try something, He will be with you the entire time—no matter the outcome.

Want to play a song on the guitar at the next school talent show? Go ahead. Want to be friends with the new kid? Give it a try. Wish you could be confident enough to speak up in class, tell a joke, or invite someone to go on a hike? Well, by all means—do not fear failure any longer. Take a step of faith. Even if things don't go the way you wanted, you'll learn something and will grow stronger with every attempt.

Live it out: Search on YouTube for "Michael Jordan failure Nike commercial" to hear his inspiring words about the role of failure in life. Now make a list of things you would attempt if you knew that you would not fail. Pray over the list, and ask God which you should try.

Pray about it: Ask God for the courage and faith to attempt hard things, even if it means possible failure. Thank God for turning every failure into part of your success.

The Day the Lord Listened to a Human Being

Surely the Lord was fighting for Israel! Joshua 10:14.

It was epic, one of the greatest days of all times. The Bible describes it this way: "There has never been a day like it before or since, a day when the Lord listened to a human being" (Joshua 10:14).

Let me back up for a minute and tell the story behind it.

It all started when Joshua led the Israelites into battle against the Amorites. (The Amorites were standing in the Israelites' way of starting their new life in the Promised Land.) After marching all night, Joshua's army surprised the Amorites, causing them to scatter in all directions. To help the Israelites beat down the enemy, God sent such massive hailstones that "more of them died from the hail than were killed by the swords of the Israelites" (verse 11).

But the victory wasn't complete yet. Joshua knew he needed more time. The sun was going to set, and the enemy would escape in the darkness. So Israel's leader sent up a huge prayer: he asked God to make the sun stand still so that there would be continued daylight for the battle. And, amazingly, God answered that prayer! "The sun stopped in the middle of the sky and delayed going down about a full day" (verse 13).

Not only was it a great day—it was a long day. In fact, it lasted two days! God actually kept the sun shining in the sky so that the enemies of His people could not escape in the dark.

Before the battle had even begun, God told Joshua that he would win. If the Lord has summoned you to do something, He will give you what you need. If He calls you to be a lawyer, He'll help you get the tuition money. Or if He wants you to be president of your senior class, He will give you the wisdom and ability to do it. Like Joshua, ask for what you need to accomplish what He desires for you to do. He may not turn one day into two again, but He will give you just what you need!

Live it out: Instead of taking your plans into your own hands, surrender your life to God. Spend time in prayer asking Him to lead you and to provide what you must have along the way.

Pray about it: Instead of praying in large, vague terms (such as "Bless this day"), pray in specifics, just as Joshua did. Tell God your needs and desires, and see how He responds.

MAY 8

How to Deal With a Frenemy

But to you who are listening I say: Love your enemies, do good to those who hate you. Luke 6:27.

An old saying declares, "Keep your friends close and your enemies closer" (so that you can keep an eye on those enemies, that is). If that's the case, how close should you keep your frenemies, those enemies disguised as friends? You know the type, the ones who rival you while also behaving like your friend. You've had good times with them, but they've betrayed you more times than you care to admit.

The Bible has a few things to say about frenemies. For starters, you have to be selective about whom you hang out with and whom you really let close. "The righteous choose their friends carefully," advises Proverbs 12:26. With that in mind, you have to consider prayerfully into which relationships you should put your time and effort.

But even if you are selective about your circle of friends, a frenemy or two is still likely to sneak in. After all, it happened even to Jesus when His friend Judas betrayed Him like an enemy. For those cases, here are a few words about frenemies:
- "But to you who are listening I say: Love your enemies, do good to those who hate you" (Luke 6:27).
- "For the Lord your God is the one who goes with you to fight for you against your enemies to give you victory" (Deuteronomy 20:4).
- "When the Lord takes pleasure in anyone's way, he causes their enemies to make peace with them" (Proverbs 16:7).
- "Rather, worship the Lord your God; it is he who will deliver you from the hand of all your enemies" (2 Kings 17:39).

Live it out: Are you acting like a frenemy toward someone? Is someone behaving like a frenemy toward you? If so, carefully begin to make adjustments to those relationships this week.

Pray about it: Thank God for loving you even when you've been more like His frenemy than His friend.

Waiting for the Vultures to Circle

Be alert and of sober mind. Your enemy the devil prowls around like a roaring lion looking for someone to devour. I Peter 5:8.

I grew up in wide open spaces on a ranch in Oklahoma. My sisters and I would roam around fields and ponds, building hideouts and kicking cow chips (why, yes, those are dried cow manure, and yes, it's gross now that I think about it).

One day we noticed vultures circling in a nearby meadow. We'd been around long enough to know that the massive birds were attracted to dead animals lying on the ground. It must have been a slow day on the ranch, because we couldn't think of anything more exciting to do than to create what I'll simply refer to as the Vulture Experiment. We decided to lie on the ground in the tall grass as if we were dead to see how long it took the vultures to start circling. Our anticipation and excitement was still high as we giggled and plopped down. *They will be here any second,* we thought. Time passed. The grass was starting to make us itch, but we would wait it out. Although we didn't want to open our eyes entirely, in case they noticed we were alive, we did peek out of squinted eyes to check the vultures' status. *H'mmm, still not circling,* we noticed. Even when we resituated ourselves into positions that looked more convincingly dead, that didn't work either. Finally our stomachs started growling, so we went back home and circled the dining room table like vultures looking for something to eat.

The Vulture Experiment ended up being a total drag. We never tried it again, since we concluded that those birdbrains weren't even smart enough to find us.

Those vultures never swooped down looking for us, but the Bible says we do have a predator after us. "Be alert and of sober mind. Your enemy the devil prowls around like a roaring lion looking for someone to devour" (1 Peter 5:8). Satan is circling us all the time, trying to take us down. Fortunately, God is right beside us and will hurl Satan away every time we ask. Whenever you feel Satan hovering overhead, call on God for protection.

Live it out: Have you put yourself in any situations that invite Satan's temptations? What can you do to escape them?
Pray about it: Thank God for protecting you against Satan's attacks.

Anger Management

He who is slow to anger is better than the mighty, and he who rules his spirit than he who takes a city. Proverbs 16:32, NKJV.

Have you ever lost your temper? Perhaps you have yelled at someone, or just wanted to hit something—or someone. Maybe your little brother just wouldn't leave you alone, or your teacher gave you too much homework.

The Bible gives some advice for those times you are about to lose your cool. For a crash course in anger management, check out what the Bible has to say:

- **God is extremely loving and doesn't get angry as easily as we do.** "The Lord is gracious and compassionate, slow to anger and rich in love" (Psalm 145:8).
- **When you're tempted to get angry, slow down.** "He who is quickly angry will do what is foolish" (Proverbs 14:17, BBE).
- **It's OK to feel angry, but it's not OK to do or say something terrible because of it.** "In your anger do not sin" (Ephesians 4:26).
- **Forgive and forget.** Instead of holding on to things that make you angry, try a little kindness and forgiveness. "Get rid of all bitterness, rage and anger, brawling and slander, along with every form of malice. Be kind and compassionate to one another, forgiving each other, just as in Christ God forgave you" (verses 31, 32).

Live it out: If you lose your cool a little more often than you'd like, follow the Bible's advice and try to slow down before you have an angry outburst. When you feel anger rising up in you, take several deep breaths and pray silently. If you need to, clench your fist or walk away. Just be sure to give yourself time to gain your composure before you say or do something you will regret.

Pray about it: Ask God to help you stay calm, cool, and collected.

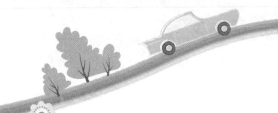

Live It Out!

How can a young person stay on the path of purity? By living according to your word. Psalm 119:9.

An idea that stood out to me from this week's devotional readings:

_____

_____

_____

A verse from this week's devotions that was powerful to me:

_____

_____

_____

A "Live it out" challenge I tried this week:

_____

_____

_____

Something that happened this week that was a blessing:

_____

_____

_____

My prayer today (thanks, requests, praises):

_____

_____

_____

Death by Loneliness

Turn to me, Lord, and be merciful to me, because I am lonely and weak.
Psalm 25:16, TEV.

Suicide is the third-leading cause of death for teenagers. Those who actually commit suicide aren't the only ones hurting, though. Fifteen percent of students say they have seriously considered suicide, and more than one out of 10 teens reported creating a suicide plan.

Those statistics are heartbreaking. Fifteen percent of teens seriously think their life isn't worth living? If you or one of your friends is a part of that 15 percent, you need to believe me: You (yes, *you!*) are valuable. Every one of you are precious to God, because you are one of a kind. There has never been and never will be another you. God has a plan for your life. He wants to see you successful and happy, and He can make that happen if you have patience and faith. And remember, Jesus understands what it is like to be lonely and rejected. Not only does He feel compassion for you— He wants to give you the strength and wisdom to face your difficult circumstances.

One of the main contributors to suicide is a sense of loneliness. If you feel lonely, even when surrounded by people, soak in what the Bible has to say especially to the lonely:

- "I will never leave you. I will never desert you" (Joshua 1:5, NIrV).
- "Even if my father and mother abandon me, the Lord cares for me" (Psalm 27:10, HCSB).
- "Then you will call, and the Lord will answer; you will cry for help, and he will say: Here am I" (Isaiah 58:9).
- "Be strong and of good courage, do not fear nor be afraid of them; for the Lord your God, He is the One who goes with you. He will not leave you nor forsake you" (Deuteronomy 31:6, NKJV).

Live it out: If you are struggling with suicidal thoughts, talk to an *adult* today. Go to a teacher or your school counselor, or call a person from your church. If you have a friend who has confided about having suicidal thoughts, you have to tell an adult. You may think it is a betrayal to reveal your friend's secret, but the true betrayal would be to let your friend consider suicide without doing everything possible to stop him or her.

Pray about it: Thank God for comforting you when you feel lonely. Pray that you will sense His presence and comfort.

Taking His Own Sweet Time

Jesus said to her, "I am the resurrection and the life." John 11:25.

Recently my friend Jennie got a flat tire while driving on the interstate. She called our mutual friend Greg to help her change the tire. Now, it just so happened that Greg and I were at the same event that evening, so I heard him take the call. He hung up and said he was going to assist Jennie. Forty minutes later I glanced around the room and spotted him. When I asked if he was still planning on going, he said, "Yeah, yeah, I'm on my way. I'm going to leave right now." It was growing dark, and I knew Jennie was probably getting frightened on the side of the road. Nevertheless, laid-back, worry-free Greg was taking his own sweet time.

I wanted Greg to respond quickly—and I'm sure Jennie did too. *If he cared, why didn't he leave immediately?* I wondered.

That must have been how Martha and Mary felt when their brother Lazarus was sick and they asked Jesus for help. Jesus got word of the crisis . . . and then He took His own sweet time.

Eventually He did go to Lazarus' home. But by the time He arrived, Lazarus was dead—and had already been in the grave four days. Mary went out to meet Jesus and said, "Lord, if you had been here, my brother would not have died" (John 11:32).

Then Jesus did a couple things worth noticing. First, as John 11:35 records, "Jesus wept." He grieved with His friends. Second, He did one of the most amazing acts of His earthly ministry: He raised Lazarus from the dead. As if it was no big deal, nothing to it. By the power of God, He called His friend from death back into life. Jesus said to His followers, "Did I not tell you that if you believe, you will see the glory of God?" (verse 40).

If He had arrived soon enough to heal Lazarus, the people would never have seen the miracle of resurrection. Even before arriving at Lazarus' house, Jesus had told His disciples, "Lazarus is dead, and for your sake I am glad I was not there, so that you may believe" (verses 14, 15). Jesus' timing wasn't late. It was perfect. According to Him, it was the exact timing needed to reveal God's amazing power.

Now, about my friend Greg's timing? I think he was just late.

Live it out: Is there an area in your life in which you need to trust God's timing?
Pray about it: Praise God for His power and tenderheartedness.

141

Google Brain

I have hidden your word in my heart. Psalm 119:11.

When I need to see a map of Maryland, I google it. Or when I want to know the lyrics to a song, I google it. And when I want to read about a certain topic or buy an item, yes, I google. I've even googled my own name, just to find out what people are seeing about me. (Oh, come on, don't act as if you've never done that!)

According to research, our habit of using Internet search engines has actually changed the way we think. Before Google, our brains worked harder to retain information once we discovered it. However, now that we can easily retrieve information online, our brains don't try so hard to remember the facts. If we forget the info, we know we can just look it up again within a few seconds. Our brains, as a result, have gotten lazy about retaining things. We let data come into our brain and slide right back out. Instead, we store it on our phones rather than in our minds.

Even though we can access information anytime anywhere, we still need to store some things in our minds. The Bible is one of them. Here are just a few reasons to keep Bible verses in your brain instead of just on your computer:

- **Bible verses help us fight temptation.** "I have hidden your word in my heart that I might not sin against you" (Psalm 119:11).
- **Bible verses give us hope.** "For whatever was written before was written for our instruction, so that through our endurance and through the encouragement of the Scriptures we may have hope" (Romans 15:4, HCSB).
- **Bible verses teach us, correct us, and equip us.** "All Scripture is God-breathed and is useful for teaching, rebuking, correcting and training in righteousness, so that the servant of God may be thoroughly equipped for every good work" (2 Timothy 3:16, 17).
- **Bible verses give us joy and wisdom.** "The law of the Lord is perfect, refreshing the soul. The statutes of the Lord are trustworthy, making wise the simple. The precepts of the Lord are right, giving joy to the heart" (Psalm 19:7, 8).

Live it out: Store a Bible verse in your brain this week! Pick one you like, and memorize it.

Pray about it: Ask God to help you understand and memorize scriptures.

A Different 100 Percent

He who was seated on the throne said, "I am making everything new!"
Revelation 21:5.

Rob McGovern was a hard-driving, high-achieving, successful businessman who was the founder of popular job-search Web sites.

In 2009, while driving down a country road, Rob had a head-on collision with a 17-year-old who was passing a car illegally. Rob was on his cell phone with one of his vice presidents at the time. The VP heard the crash through the phone. Because the phone stayed live when it fell from Rob's hand, the VP continued to hear everything else: the ambulance; the paramedics using the jaws of life and then saying that Rob had no vital signs.

Suffering a severe brain injury, Rob was in a coma for weeks. His body was crushed, and doctors predicted that he would be vegetative. He would never walk again or be able to take care of himself. The physicians told Rob's mother that the best-case scenario would be that her son would be able to feed himself someday.

Six months after the accident Rob asked his neurologist if he would ever be 100 percent again. The doctor said, "Yes, you will. But a different 100 percent."

McGovern set out to achieve that new but different 100 percent. He wanted to be strong and accomplished again. His brain wasn't operating as quickly as before, but he worked at retraining the pathways of his brain. The trauma caused a rewiring of his brain, and he had to learn to think in new ways. Now he is back at work and has mastered that new way of life. "I'm fine with the new 100 percent," he says.

Sometimes when you go through a difficult time—your parents' divorce, a broken heart, abuse, or a major disappointment—you feel as if you've lost part of yourself. It seems as if you'll never be 100 percent again. But you will. It will just be a different 100 percent. If you allow Him to, God will use that experience to build you back stronger, wiser, and more compassionate. Here is God's promise: "Forget the former things; do not dwell on the past. See, I am doing a new thing!" (Isaiah 43:18, 19). He is making you into a new 100 percent.

Live it out: By journaling or talking to a friend, reflect on a bad experience from your life. Focus on how God can use (or already has used) it to make you stronger and different.

Pray about it: Ask God to remake you into something new and better than you've ever been.

A Lying, Cheating, Murderous God Follower

Have mercy on me, O God, according to your unfailing love; according to your great compassion blot out my transgressions. Wash away all my iniquity and cleanse me from my sin. Psalm 51:1, 2.

King David cheated on his wife, had a man killed, and lied about it all. You would expect God to write him off as a selfish jerk. But look at what the Lord said about him instead: "I have found David son of Jesse, a man after my own heart; he will do everything I want him to do" (Acts 13:22).

If a lying, cheating murderer is a man after God's own heart, then there's hope for us all! David wasn't in good standing because of all the things he had done wrong—he was in good standing *despite* all of those things. He was a man after God's own heart, because he asked for forgiveness when he messed up, sincerely tried to change, and kept following God.

As a result, David set a beautiful example: if you mess up, ask for forgiveness and a fresh start. Here is part of one of his prayers for forgiveness:

> "Cleanse me with hyssop, and I will be clean;
>> wash me, and I will be whiter than snow.
> Let me hear joy and gladness;
>> let the bones you have crushed rejoice.
> Hide your face from my sins
>> and blot out all my iniquity.
> Create in me a pure heart, O God,
>> and renew a steadfast spirit within me.
> Do not cast me from your presence
>> or take your Holy Spirit from me.
> Restore to me the joy of your salvation
>> and grant me a willing spirit, to sustain me" (Psalm 51:7-12).

Live it out: Read all of Psalm 51. Include some of the verses in your own prayers. Ask for God's forgiveness, and then accept it.

Pray about it: Say a prayer of confession for any specific things you've never confessed before.

Will This Make You Bitter or Better?

When you have many kinds of troubles, you should be full of joy, because you know that these troubles test your faith, and this will give you patience. Let your patience show itself perfectly in what you do. Then you will be perfect and complete and will have everything you need. James 1:2-4, NCV.

Hard times will either make you bitter or better. It's your choice, really. You can't avoid difficulties (they happen to everyone), but you can decide how you'll respond. For example, you can get angry and feel cheated, or you can keep your faith and grow stronger.

Paul explains that with the right faith-filled attitude, we really can become better because of life's hard times: "Since we have been made right with God by our faith, we have peace with God. This happened through our Lord Jesus Christ, who through our faith has brought us into that blessing of God's grace that we now enjoy. And we are happy because of the hope we have of sharing God's glory. We also have joy with our troubles, because we know that these troubles produce patience. And patience produces character, and character produces hope. And this hope will never disappoint us, because God has poured out his love to fill our hearts. He gave us his love through the Holy Spirit, whom God has given to us" (Romans 5:1-5, NCV).

It's a domino effect. Our troubles build patience. Patience builds character. Character builds hope. You would think that troubles steal our hope, but Paul says the exact opposite is true. When you keep a good attitude, your troubles will end up giving you more hope than ever before!

Live it out: Are you facing a difficult situation? Don't let it get you down. Claim the promise in Romans 5:1-5, and let your troubles make you better, not bitter.

Pray about it: Ask God to help you maintain a positive attitude even when things aren't going well.

Live It Out!

"Then you will know the truth, and the truth will set you free." John 8:32.

An idea that stood out to me from this week's devotional readings:

_____

_____

_____

A verse from this week's devotions that was powerful to me:

_____

_____

_____

A "Live it out" challenge I tried this week:

_____

_____

_____

Something that happened this week that was a blessing:

_____

_____

_____

My prayer today (thanks, requests, praises):

_____

_____

_____

Sending Silent Messages

Now you are the body of Christ, and each one of you is a part of it.
I Corinthians 12:27.

Before you even open your mouth, your body language has already sent a message. But is it the one that you want to give?

Research shows that people make a lot of decisions about you based on your body language. Even before they have a conversation with you, they decide if they like you, believe you, or want to hang out with you. For example, let's say there's a new girl at school with whom you've never had a conversation. You see her several times a day though, and she is always smiling. When you pass her in the hall, she always looks you in the eye and smiles. Even though you've never talked to her, you probably conclude that she is friendly. Her body language spoke for her.

Here's another example. A new guy shows up in school. Although you've never talked to him, he is in three of your classes. He constantly rolls his eyes at the teachers, and he smirks when students raise their hand to answer a question. Other times he slumps his shoulders, keeps his eyes on the ground, and bumps people just a little too hard when he's passing them in the hallway. No words necessary—you probably don't want to spend a lot of time with this guy. His body language spoke for him.

Jesus' body language sent a message too. He used body language to welcome people and show their value. As He healed sick people, He touched them—even though He didn't have to. When little children were brought to Him, He put His hands on them and blessed them. Jesus knew His body language sent a message, and He wanted it to be a loving, accepting one.

Jesus isn't walking around on earth anymore, but the Bible says His body is still here. "Now you are the body of Christ, and each one of you is a part of it" (1 Corinthians 12:27). Now *we* represent Christ to the people around us! That makes our body language even more important. What kind of signals are you sending?

Live it out: Pay attention to your body language today. Are you making yourself approachable? Are you standoffish? When you catch yourself sending an unfriendly message, change your body language.

Pray about it: Ask God to guide and teach you how to represent Him well.

What Message Are You Sending?

So we are the representatives of Christ. 2 Corinthians 5:20, BBE.

Since God has asked us to be His representatives on earth, He wants us to present a warm and inviting message to the people around us. Before we even speak a word, we can project a sense of acceptance through our body language. Here are some practical ways to communicate positive messages with body language:

- **Look people in the eye.** Make eye contact 100 percent of the time when someone is talking to you, and about 50 percent of the time when you are speaking. It makes people feel valued when you look at them with undivided attention when they talk. It can, however, be a little uncomfortable or threatening for them if you stare at them the entire time *you* are speaking. In those cases, it's good to look away now and then to create healthy boundaries.
- **Get on their level.** If you are talking to someone who is standing, then stand up. When speaking to someone sitting on the floor, get down on the floor on eye level with them. Meet them where they are.
- **Don't tease.** Body language is a big part of flirting, and out-of-control flirting can lead to hurt feelings or behavior you'll regret later. Don't misuse the power of body language to lead someone on or to spark something that shouldn't be ignited. Seriously think about the message you're sending with both your body and your words.
- **Don't create barriers.** When you have your arms and legs crossed, you suggest that you are closed off or unapproachable. Instead of creating a physical barrier, use gestures that will draw people in. When people approach, wave them toward you, or give them a fist bump. Invite them into your space. And above all: stop texting and looking at your phone. Give your undivided attention to the real-life people standing right beside you.

Live it out: Try one of these body language techniques today. When you come in contact with people, use body language to show they matter. And when all else fails, just smile! That's a body language signal that always works.

Pray about it: Ask God to help you make people feel valued and important. Thank Him for placing value and importance on you.

God's Pet Peeves

There are six things the Lord hates, seven that are detestable to him.
Proverbs 6:16.

I don't like it when people lick their fingers while eating food. It's one of my pet peeves.

I also get a little annoyed when people say, "Have a good one!" Does it really take any more effort to identify the "one" you're talking about? *Have a good day! Have a good afternoon! Have a good dinner! Have a good trip!* See, that's not so hard.

Oh, and I don't like it when highway drivers don't move over to the left lane to let merging traffic onto the highway. Share the road, I say!

Those are my pet peeves. Everybody has one or two. According to Proverbs 6:16-19, even God has a few. Six to be exact. Well, make that seven:

"There are six things the Lord hates,
seven that are detestable to him:
haughty eyes,
a lying tongue,
hands that shed innocent blood,
a heart that devises wicked schemes,
feet that are quick to rush into evil,
a false witness who pours out lies
and a person who stirs up conflict in the community."

So let me get that right: the six things God can't stand are a cocky look, dishonesty, the death of innocent people, wicked plans, people who are quick to do evil, and a witness who lies. But, to be very clear, He adds a seventh item to the list—the thing that *really* upsets Him. His greatest frustration is people stirring up trouble among others.

When you're tempted to start a rumor, spread gossip, be cliquish, or say something that could start a fight, remember God's list. He hates our causing division among people. No good will come from it. It will just upset you, God, and everyone else involved.

Live it out: Before you say or do something questionable, ask yourself, *Will this cause conflict or division?* If the answer is yes, don't do it.

Pray about it: Ask God to help you build a sense of community instead of tearing it down.

MAY 22

Baby Talk

For it was You who created my inward parts; You knit me together in my mother's womb. Psalm 139:13, HCSB.

The birth of a baby is supposed to be a happy occasion. But when the child is, well, an accident, and the mom and dad are teenagers—then it may not seem so happy.

In such situations as these, some teenagers think an abortion is the easiest solution. It seems like a quick fix, but it doesn't solve the problem. Instead, it just causes *different* problems. Both the mother and father risk emotional and spiritual problems after an abortion, including guilt, flashbacks, nightmares, depression, anger, and spiritual numbness. For the mother, there can also be physical complications.

An unplanned pregnancy can feel terrifying and embarrassing. It is not easy to face, but ending it in a panic isn't the only option. For instance, thousands of loving families are even now praying for the opportunity to adopt and raise a child, to give a little one a lifetime of opportunities.

The very moment of conception determines a baby's gender, eye color, and height. At just three weeks the heart is beating and the brain is in place. By five weeks the fingers appear, and at nine weeks the little one can smile, kick, and somersault. After 12 weeks the baby can feel pain. If God can put all of that in place within the first few weeks, He can definitely help a teenager figure out how to handle an unexpected pregnancy.

Live it out: If you or someone you know is considering abortion, talk to a trusted adult immediately. You may feel shame and embarrassment to admit it, but you have to ask for help to face the situation.

Pray about it: Thank God for the miracle of life. Thank Him that you were given the opportunity to live.

Symptoms of Spiritual Sickness

Heal me, Lord, and I will be healed; save me and I will be saved, for you are the one I praise. Jeremiah 17:14.

When your body isn't healthy, it gives you warning signs—symptoms such as a headache, stomachache, sore throat, or fever. Similarly, when your spirit isn't healthy, you'll experience symptoms. Here are a few that indicate your spiritual life needs a little extra attention:

- I'm having a hard time getting along with people.
- I have a habit or relationship of which I feel that God and others wouldn't approve.
- I am guilty of stirring up desires I could not righteously fulfill.
- My language, jokes, and conversations often have crude or negative undertones.
- I struggle with feelings of jealousy.
- I have a hard time forgiving myself or others.
- I am haunted by past mistakes.
- I don't have a desire to slow down and pray.
- I do not sense God's love and acceptance in my daily life.

If you're experiencing any of these symptoms, you need to plan some extra time with God. It's possible to improve your spiritual health (and become more peaceful and happy) by spending more quiet interaction with God.

Live it out: Disconnect from media and friends for a little while each day. Try talking to God, journaling your prayers, or reading a chapter or two from Psalms.
Pray about it: If you could relate to any of the symptoms on the list above, talk it through with God. Tell Him specifically how you are struggling and ask Him what you should do to become spiritually healthier.

MAY 24

What a Lame Excuse

All you need to say is simply "Yes" or "No"; anything beyond this comes from the evil one. Matthew 5:37.

Ever had one of those days when you just didn't feel like going to school? Adults have those times too, when they just want to stay home and call in sick. On such days, even adults can be tempted to make up an excuse to get out of work. Check out these real excuses people gave their bosses about why they couldn't make it in to work:

- "I'm calling from my cell phone. I was accidently locked in a restroom stall, and there is no one around to let me out."
- "I have a very bad case of hiccups, so I can't come to work today."
- "A buffalo escaped from the nearby game reserve. Every time I try to get in my car, the buffalo charges me!"
- "I blew my nose so hard that my back went out."

The bosses who got those calls definitely thought those were lame (or made-up) excuses!

Have you ever given a lame excuse when you didn't want to do something? Maybe you promised friends that you would do something with them, but when the time came you were tired and didn't want to do it. Or maybe your parents asked you to go somewhere you are dreading. If you feel a lame excuse coming on, stop yourself before you say it. Instead, face the day with confidence. God knows what it will hold for you, and He'll be with you through it all. Not to mention that everyone can spot a lame excuse when they hear it, so don't even waste your time trying to come up with one.

Live it out: Eliminate lame excuses from your life. When one is about to escape your mouth, stop and think, *Is this a real reason?* If it's lame, just don't say it.
Pray about it: Pray that the Holy Spirit will help you nix lame excuses from your life. Ask for the courage to do hard things instead of avoiding them.

MAY 25

Live It Out!

If you declare with your mouth, "Jesus is Lord," and believe in your heart that God raised him from the dead, you will be saved. Romans 10:9.

An idea that stood out to me from this week's devotional readings:

_____

_____

_____

A verse from this week's devotions that was powerful to me:

_____

_____

_____

A "Live it out" challenge I tried this week:

_____

_____

_____

Something that happened this week that was a blessing:

_____

_____

_____

My prayer today (thanks, requests, praises):

_____

_____

_____

MAY 26

I Can't Hear You—the TV Is Too Loud!

I am like the deaf, who cannot hear. Psalm 38:13.

Some days I wish that God would send me a text or ring me up on Skype, or meet me for dinner. I think the whole idea of following Him would be a lot easier if He and I could just sit down and talk it over a little bit. It's like the ultimate long-distance relationship—He's way out there, and I'm right here.

Of course, God finds lots of ways to speak to us—through prayer and reflection, Scripture, nature, godly people, the Holy Spirit. When I don't hear Him, the problem usually isn't that He is quiet, but that my life is loud. Like a lot of people, I have to fight against a noise addiction: the temptation to fill every quiet minute with some kind of stimulation, such as music, Internet, or television. That can definitely become a problem when I'm trying to hear from God: how could I possibly hear Him when I have racket blaring all the time?

First Kings 19 depicts the prophet Elijah running for his life after a scary encounter with Jezebel. He ended up in the wilderness, feeling depressed and even suicidal. God told him to go out and stand on the mountain, because the Lord was going to pass by. There came a powerful wind, next an earthquake, and then a fire—but Elijah didn't hear God in any of those things. However, the Bible says, "And after the fire came a gentle whisper" (1 Kings 19:12). It was then, in the whisper (rather than in all the chaos and noise), that Elijah heard the Lord's voice.

If you want to hear from God, the first step is to turn all the dials to the left and put the noise on mute, so that He doesn't have to shout.

Live it out: Set aside some time for silence every day. Add a little quiet time while you're getting ready for school, taking a shower, or ending your day.
Pray about it: Turn down all the noise and start praying. Instead of just talking, be sure to listen too.

What to Do When You Feel Down

He ate and drank and then lay down again. I Kings 19:6.

Sometimes depression and discouragement hit at the most unlikely times. Things are fantastic, and then all of a sudden you feel down. That's what happened to Elijah. After an amazing victory in a showdown against false prophets, you would think that he would be thrilled and excited. However, just the opposite happened. When Jezebel found out that he had defeated her supporters, she was infuriated—and that left him shaking in his boots. Even though he had just seen God do miraculous things (such as bring fire down from heaven!), he was still scared and anxious. He became so frightened that he hightailed it right out of town and headed straight for the middle of nowhere. First Kings 19:3 says, "Elijah was afraid and he ran for his life."

The prophet was so depressed that he wanted to die. "He came to a broom bush, sat down under it and prayed that he might die. 'I have had enough, Lord,' he said. 'Take my life'" (verse 4). God could have swooped down right then and given Elijah a pep talk. The Lord could have reminded him of all the great things that Elijah just witnessed. Or He could have sent an angel to pat him on the back and say, "Come on, boy, keep going. Don't give up now!"

Instead, God let Elijah sleep. Once the depressed guy got some rest, an angel woke him up to eat some bread and water. Elijah ate, then he slept some more. A second time the angel awakened him and told him to have some food. After another meal and a lot of rest, Elijah was strengthened. It was only then that God started leading him on to the next phase of his journey.

Whenever you feel defeated or depressed, start with the simple things, just like God did with Elijah. Have you gotten plenty of rest? Have you had a good meal? Fatigue and hunger make everything worse, so make sure you meet those needs. A great night's sleep and a warm meal can often give you the energy to get up and face another day. Simple strategies—such as rest and nourishment—can help you feel stronger, more peaceful, and ready to conquer those crushing waves of discouragement.

Live it out: When feeling down, power up by going to bed early and never skipping meals.

Pray about it: Turn your worries and fears into prayers. Thank God for taking care of you.

MAY 28

Books-a-Million

The fear of the Lord is the beginning of wisdom, and knowledge of the Holy One is understanding. Proverbs 9:10.

Sir Thomas Phillipps had a case of bibliomania. (Yes, believe it or not, that's a real word. It means he had an obsessive-compulsive tendency to collect and hoard books.) Unfortunately, he lived during the 1800s before e-books were an option, so his house was literally crammed full of printed books from floor to ceiling.

Phillipps had the largest private collection of manuscripts and books in the world at the time. He spent all of his inheritance on books, and when he ran out of money he went into debt to buy more books. When he ran out of room for the books in his house (and the floors actually began to sag because of their weight), he moved into a new home with more space for books. It took 230 horses, 103 wagons, and 160 men to move them all. Even then they had to leave some of the books behind, because some of the wagons began breaking under the weight. After Sir Phillipps died, it took his family nearly 100 years to sell his massive collection.

Solomon, the wisest person in the world, had a thing or two to say about books and wisdom: "Of making many books there is no end, and much study wearies the body. Now all has been heard; here is the conclusion of the matter: Fear God and keep his commandments, for this is the duty of all mankind" (Ecclesiastes 12:12, 13).

According to Solomon, we don't get true wisdom by studying thousands of books. Instead, true wisdom begins when we fear—that is, when we stand in awe—of God and follow after Him. We learn more by doing what He commands than by collecting a house full of books. Too bad Sir Phillipps didn't know that.

Live it out: If you want true wisdom, get to know more about God, not just facts and figures. An education is very important, but the most vital thing you'll ever learn is how to follow God.

Pray about it: Pray for wisdom and guidance.

Taking Jesus at His Word

The man took Jesus at his word and departed. John 4:50.

This guy was important. The Bible doesn't say his name—it only calls him a "certain royal official." He was probably used to giving orders instead of asking for help. But this time he was desperate. His son was dying, and no physician could turn things around. The royal official could think of only one last thing to try: ask Jesus for help.

The man arrived in the town where Jesus was, and he pushed through the crowds. The Bible says he "begged him to come and heal his son, who was close to death" (John 4:47). Did you catch that? He *begged*. Someone used to people pleading with him now had become the beggar.

When he asked a second time, Jesus looked him in the eye and said, "Go, . . . your son will live" (verse 50). Christ didn't have to be in the same home to heal the boy—He didn't even have to be in the same town! Instead, Jesus sent healing power from a distance. And the royal official believed Him. "The man took Jesus at his word and departed" (verse 50). He just *took Jesus at His Word* and went on his way.

As the royal official traveled home, his servants met him on the road to tell him the boy was alive and well. Maybe they intended to urge him not to bother Jesus, that everything was OK after all. But the official didn't think the healing was a coincidence. He asked the servants for details. "When he inquired as to the time when his son got better, they said to him, 'Yesterday, at one in the afternoon, the fever left him.' Then the father realized that this was the exact time at which Jesus had said to him, 'Your son will live.' So he and his whole household believed" (verses 52, 53).

If I had to summarize this story, it would be this: "Boy was dying. Man had faith. He took Jesus at His word. Boy was healed. Everybody believed." At the center of the story is an individual who took Jesus at His word.

In the Bible Jesus has told you what He can do for you. Do you take Him at His word?

Live it out: Take God at His word. Choose a promise from the Bible and claim it as your own. Memorize it, repeat it when you're discouraged, and include it in your prayers.

Pray about it: Tell God that you take Him at His word. Thank Him for being trustworthy.

MAY 30

Dinner Is Served

And so we know and rely on the love God has for us. God is love. I John 4:16.

I have some friends who have adopted several neglected, abused, and abandoned children. The children have had very difficult lives. Abandoned by their birth parents, they got passed from foster home to foster home. After years of neglect, the children were finally swept into my friends' home and lavished with love and attention. You would think they would respond with appreciation and joy, right? Well, it's not that simple.

One 10-year-old girl the couple adopted had previously been forced to scavenge for her own food. She had never had family meals, and she had had to get her food anywhere she could find it. Long after living in her new home she refused to eat the meals served at the table. Instead, her parents would find her later in the day digging through the kitchen trash, pulling out the meal scraps, and eating them. Used to taking care of herself and not relying on anyone, she wasn't comfortable accepting love, and didn't understand it. She resorted to what she was familiar with: taking care of herself and not trusting anyone.

Can you relate in any way to this adopted girl? Maybe you feel as if it's just you against the world. Or perhaps it's hard for you to accept unconditional love. Just like her adoptive parents, God wants to lavish love on you. He will never deny you love because you've had a rough past. God will not force you to take care of everything by yourself, even though you feel unworthy of His help. His love is unconditional. No matter what the circumstances or conditions, He will show you love. So instead of digging through the trash trying to find scraps of what you need, pull up a chair and feast on God's love.

Live it out: Read Psalm 136. Reflect on the message God wants you to learn from the verses.
Pray about it: Thank God for the unconditional love He has lavished on you. Ask Him to help you receive it and share it with others.

Hello? Is Anyone Listening?

Praise be to the Lord, for he has heard my cry for mercy. Psalm 28:6.

There's nothing worse than talking and then feeling as if no one is listening. When you've got an incredible story, a killer joke, or sad news, you want someone to stop and really hear you out. It's the same whether you're speaking to a friend or to God: if you're talking, you want to make sure they're listening!

At times even the spiritual heroes of the Bible wondered if God was out there hearing them. All throughout the Psalms, David pleads with God to listen to him. Look at just a few of his pleas:

- "Hear, Lord, and be merciful to me" (Psalm 30:10).
- "Lord, hear my voice. Let your ears be attentive to my cry for mercy" (Psalm 130:2).
- "Hear my prayer, Lord; listen to my cry for mercy" (Psalm 86:6).
- "I call to you, Lord, come quickly to me; hear me when I call to you" (Psalm 141:1).
- "Hear my prayer, O God; listen to the words of my mouth" (Psalm 54:2).

Can you relate? Ever said a prayer and wondered if it made it past your bedroom ceiling? Fortunately, God promises to be listening before the words even tumble from your mouth: "Before they call I will answer; while they are still speaking I will hear" (Isaiah 65:24). He is waiting with eager anticipation to listen to you. In fact, He can hardly wait for you to talk to Him, because it brings Him such delight.

Tell God what makes you happy, sad, excited, or scared. He's all ears.

Live it out: When something good happens, send up a prayer. And when something bad happens, send up a prayer. Once you truly believe God is listening, you'll want to pray more than ever before.

Pray about it: Pray with the confidence that God hears you. Acknowledge this confidence by including in your prayers phrases such as "I know You hear me" or "Thank You for hearing me now as I pray."

Live It Out!

Create in me a pure heart, O God, and renew a steadfast spirit within me.
Psalm 51:10.

An idea that stood out to me from this week's devotional readings:

_____

_____

_____

A verse from this week's devotions that was powerful to me:

_____

_____

_____

A "Live it out" challenge I tried this week:

_____

_____

_____

Something that happened this week that was a blessing:

_____

_____

_____

My prayer today (thanks, requests, praises):

_____

_____

_____

Now, That's a BFF

A friend loves at all times. Proverbs 17:17.

Paralyzed, he couldn't walk or work. All he could do was lie in bed day and night. The unfortunate man did, however, have one thing going for him: he had four great friends. When those four men found out that Jesus was in town, they were determined to do whatever it took to get their paralyzed friend to Him to be healed.

I can't tell the story any better than Mark did, so read what he wrote about the creative and forceful way those individuals got their friend through the crowds to Jesus:

"A few days later, when Jesus again entered Capernaum, the people heard that he had come home. They gathered in such large numbers that there was no room left, not even outside the door, and he preached the word to them. Some men came, bringing to him a paralyzed man, carried by four of them. Since they could not get him to Jesus because of the crowd, they made an opening in the roof above Jesus by digging through it and then lowered the mat the man was lying on. When Jesus saw their faith, he said to the paralyzed man, 'Son, your sins are forgiven.' . . . 'I tell you, get up, take your mat and go home.' He got up, took his mat and walked out in full view of them all. This amazed everyone and they praised God, saying, 'We have never seen anything like this!'" (Mark 2:1-12).

The four buddies hacked open the roof of the building Jesus was in, and they deposited their friend right in front of Him! Imagine how shocked the people must have been to see someone pulling back the roof. No one likes it when someone cuts in line, but maybe they didn't mind in this case. The passionate desperation of these friends must have stirred the hearts of the crowd, because instead of making him wait his turn, they praised God that Jesus healed him.

That's the kind of friend we all want. Make it your goal to be that kind of individual. When your friends are in need, pray for them, encourage them, and be there for them. Your acts of kindness will be like opening up the roof and taking them to Jesus.

Live it out: Do you have a friend who could use a little help right now? Do something about it.

Pray about it: Thank God for being a friend to you. Thank Him for the friends in your life.

It's Repeat Day. It's Repeat Day.

As a dog goes back to its vomit, [so] a fool repeats his stupidity.
Proverbs 26:11, GW.

Repeat Day, which falls on June 3, is a chance to repeat what you do and say all day. Repeat Day, which falls on June 3, is a chance to repeat what you do and say all day. (All right, I know, that was funny for a split second, but it's going to get old fast. I promise not to do it again. I promise not to do it again . . . *Starting now.*)

To really enjoy Repeat Day, you must carefully select your activities for it. Remember you're going to have to do everything twice, so if you get stuck doing things you don't enjoy, you're *really* not going to like them a second time around. For example, to truly honor the spirit of the day, if you watch a video on Repeat Day you would have to go back and watch it again. See what I mean? You really have to be selective!

If anyone really tried to celebrate Repeat Day (and I've never known anyone who has), I'm sure they—and all the people around them—would be sick of it within the first hour. Repeating really isn't much fun after a while. In fact, the Bible tells us that we should never repeat some things.

For instance, if someone has done something wrong, don't continually talk about it. "Whoever would foster love covers over an offense, but whoever *repeats* the matter separates close friends" (Proverbs 17:9). Wise King Solomon warns that you'll risk losing your friends if you keep reciting your complaints about them.

To put it bluntly, another thing never to repeat is *stupid stuff.* Proverbs 26:11 says, "As a dog goes back to its vomit, [so] a fool *repeats* his stupidity" (GW). When you do something foolish, don't beat yourself up—but don't do it again. Ask for forgiveness, forgive yourself, and then move on. The imagery is totally gross: a dog returning to its vomit! Who wants to be like that?

All right, so maybe Repeat Day is a bad idea. So is bringing up other people's mistakes or constantly doing stupid stuff.

Let's just forget about Repeat Day. Let's just forget about Repeat Day.

Live it out: Is there something negative in your life you want to stop repeating? Talk to God about it or ask an adult for help. You don't have to be stuck in an endless cycle.

Pray about it: Ask God to help you break the negative cycles you have fallen into.

What Is God's Will for My Life?

Who is the man who fears the Lord? He will instruct him in the way he should choose. Psalm 25:12, ASV.

One of the most common questions that Christians ask, whether they are 16 or 96, is "What is God's will for my life?" They wonder about such things as *Whom should I date? Whom should I marry? What kind of job should I have? What school should I attend? How should I spend my money?*

Although we sometimes feel as if we're left to make such decisions on our own, the Bible repeatedly assures us that God wants to help us make good choices. Psalm 32:8 says, "I will instruct you and teach you in the way you should go; I will counsel you with my loving eye on you."

When you seek to know the will of God, the first thing to remember is that His primary desire for your life is that you accept Jesus as your Savior. All the other stuff falls somewhere far lower on God's list of important stuff. When you are making all of life's other decisions, always keep in mind that your salvation is His number one priority. Remembering this will help you make decisions, because you can ask yourself right away, "Will this choice lead me closer to God or further away from Him?" If the answer is "further away," then you know for sure it is not God's will.

The next thing always to keep in mind is this: God wants you to know His will as much as—or more than—you want to know it. Sometimes we feel as if He doesn't care and isn't even trying to talk to us about what to do. However, He is eager to be a part of your decisions and daily life. Always assume He is trying to speak to you. It will make you more receptive to hearing His voice.

Live it out: Make a list of all the decisions you would like God to help you make. Pray about them every day until you feel God's peace and leading.

Pray about it: Think about people you know who are making important decisions, and pray specifically that God will lead and guide them.

How Do I Know God's Will?

A man's heart plans his way, but the Lord directs his steps. Proverbs 16:9, NKJV.

OK, so God has a special plan for your life, and you're ready to start following it. Just one problem—you're not sure what the plan is!

Fortunately, God reveals His will to us in lots of ways so that we won't miss it. When you face a major decision, here are some of the channels your Creator may use to communicate with you:

- **The Bible.** In Psalm 119:105 David says, "Your word is a lamp to my feet and a light to my path" (NKJV). You might think those old verses have nothing to do with your life, but they do! The more you read the Bible, the more it will lead you. If you're not sure where to begin, start with Proverbs and the Gospels. You'll soon begin to pick up principles that will guide you in decision-making.

- **Circumstances.** Sometimes doors open, and sometimes they close. If you're struggling to knock a door down or wedge a door open, then stop for a minute and consider that God might be trying to tell you something. Forcing a particular situation may not be God's will.

- **Godly people.** God uses His faith-filled followers to help others. When making an important decision, talk it over with a Christlike pastor, parent, or teacher. Proverbs 15:22, ASV reminds us, "Without consultation, plans are frustrated, but with many counselors they succeed."

- **The Holy Spirit.** If you feel convicted about something that lines up with Scripture, then follow the Spirit's leading. The Bible teaches us that the Holy Spirit can actually teach us and help us to understand God and His ways.

The will of God may not jolt you like a bolt of lightning, but His guidance will come. Keep praying, watching, and listening—and He'll lead you all along the way.

Live it out: Consider whether God has been trying to speak to you through circumstances, people, the Bible, or the Holy Spirit. How will you respond?
Pray about it: Ask God to help you understand and follow His will.

Like Putty in His Hands

We are the clay, you are the potter; we are all the work of your hand. Isaiah 64:8.

What better way to pass the summer months than working at summer camp? *It's like one long slumber party—even for the staff,* I thought. As soon as I was old enough, I set my sights on punching the clock at the nearby camp. Now all I had to do was figure out for which job I would apply. Lifeguard? No, I couldn't swim well enough to guard anybody's life. Kitchen staff? No, I couldn't stomach the thought of spraying down heaps of plastic trays smeared with leftover food. Counselor? No, it took all my teen powers to keep myself safe and sound. I shouldn't be responsible for dozens of people younger than I.

As my list of job options got shorter, one job title jumped out at me: ceramics teacher. How hard could that be, right? I had *made* ceramics as a camper; and that had gone well (if I do say so myself). Ceramics was going to be my gig. I just knew it.

Apparently everyone else applied for the cooler, yet riskier, jobs of lifeguard and counselor, because I landed in the ceramics room without facing any formidable opponents. They must have been impressed with my résumé of childhood ceramics experience, because they didn't give me much on-the-job training and just left me in the classroom to start teaching.

My coteacher and I scraped our way through that crafty summer, only one time dashing the dreams of children by announcing that their toothbrush holders, mugs, and decorative ladybug paperweights had melted during the night. (The meltdown resulted from some malfunction related to a cone and a kiln, but I don't understand it well enough to explain it—which is probably why it happened on my watch in the first place.)

The Bible says that God is a potter and we are the clay. It's not up to us to turn ourselves into something special. We, as lumps of clay, just have to let Him shape us into a work of art. "Then the word of the Lord came to me. He said, 'Can I not do with you, Israel, as this potter does?' . . . 'Like clay in the hand of the potter, so are you in my hand'" (Jeremiah 18:5, 6). God is a much better potter than I am a ceramics teacher, so He can be completely trusted.

Live it out: Write out some of your dreams for your life. Pray about the list, asking God to shape your life into a masterpiece—even if it ends up looking different than you imagined.

Pray about it: Ask God to turn you from a lump of clay into a work of art!

Good-Mood Music

Sing and make music from your heart to the Lord. Ephesians 5:19.

Recently 16-year-old Jay told me he just couldn't shake the feeling of depression. He felt down, tired, and discouraged all the time, and he just couldn't find any happiness in daily life. But he couldn't trace the depression to anything in particular: there hadn't been a major crisis or problem in his life. Nevertheless, life just seemed dark and discouraging to him.

Since he couldn't trace his low, junky mood to anything specific, I suggested that Jay conduct an experiment. I challenged him to do just one thing: replace his secular music with Christian music. Reluctantly he agreed to give it a try. After just three weeks he came to see me with a smile on his face. "I honestly can't believe it, but that one change made a major difference. I feel so much lighter and happier now."

The tunes you listen to can have a major impact on your mood (not to mention your worldview and values). In the Bible, when a dark, depressing spirit tormented King Saul, his attendants came up with a solution. They offered to find someone who could play soothing, uplifting music for him. Explaining their plan to the ruler, they described the musician they would bring: "He will play when the evil spirit from God comes on you, and you will feel better" (1 Samuel 16:16). It actually did the trick. Nice music improved Saul's mood.

In modern times, when you're feeling a little blue, you don't have to call for a harpist as Saul did. You can get the same results by loading your iPod with positive music or listening to Christian CDs or radio. Don't think for a second that Christian music is just for grandmas and preachers! The world is full of incredible songs with positive, biblical messages. To find something to match your taste, ask friends for recommendations, search online, or listen to demos at a Christian bookstore.

The messages you repeatedly hear in music will either make you feel better or worse about life. If you want to change your mood, start by changing the radio station.

Live it out: Experiment and see for yourself the impact of music. If you normally listen to secular music, replace it with contemporary Christian, praise songs, or hymns for a few weeks.

Pray about it: Let music be your prayer. Listen to Christian songs, and let those lyrics inspire your prayer time with God.

Live It Out!

Do not fear, for I have redeemed you; I have summoned you by name;
you are mine. Isaiah 43:1.

An idea that stood out to me from this week's devotional readings:

_____

_____

_____

A verse from this week's devotions that was powerful to me:

_____

_____

_____

A "Live it out" challenge I tried this week:

_____

_____

_____

Something that happened this week that was a blessing:

_____

_____

_____

My prayer today (thanks, requests, praises):

_____

_____

_____

A Magical Switcheroo

"For I know the plans I have for you," declares the Lord, "plans to prosper you and not to harm you, plans to give you hope and a future." Jeremiah 29:11.

Have you ever wished you could trade lives with someone else? You know, just snap your fingers and have their life instead of your own? When I was a teenager, there were a few people whom I thought had it a lot better than I did. If given the chance, I definitely would have gone for any magical switcheroo that could have landed me in their lives with their looks, personality, money, and popularity.

Now I see things differently. There's not a person in the world with whom I would change places. That's not because my life is perfect or better than everyone else's. I have blessings, but I also have problems and challenges. The difference is that I now completely believe God has an ultimate design for my life. He is weaving together my personalized good times and bad times to make me exactly what He wants me to be. I would rather have His unique plan for my life than anyone else's, because I trust Him to give me exactly what is best for me.

God sees things with a far wider perspective than we do. Think of it this way: imagine your life as a story written in a book. Right now you have the book right up to your eye—so close that all you can see is just a word or two of one sentence. God, however, is holding that book in His hands and is flipping through it from beginning to end. He knows what is happening in this chapter, and He knows what will take place in the next. And He knows there will be a happy ending if you stick with Him through all the ups and downs.

Now, when I see someone who appears to have a perfect life, I remember the bigger picture. God is leading them through blessings and challenges, just like He is doing with me. You have a special life designed just for you by God Himself. Don't waste a minute of it by wishing you had someone else's.

Live it out: If you catch yourself thinking someone else has it better than you, stop and remind yourself that God has unique plans for both that person and for you. Remember that He will use all the experiences in your story to create your very own personalized happy ending.

Pray about it: Thank God for having an exciting, special plan just for you.

Jesus' Rule of Etiquette

For all those who exalt themselves will be humbled, and those who humble themselves will be exalted. Luke 14:11.

There are certain unspoken rules of etiquette we're expected to follow. It's not polite, for example, to say, "It looks like you're packing on the pounds there, buddy" to someone who is gaining weight. Nor is it considered acceptable to eat spaghetti with your hands, or to take a sip out of someone's drink without their permission.

When Jesus was on earth, He shared some important but unexpected rules of etiquette. Here's just one of them: *don't try to prove anything.* In other words, don't seek to make yourself look like the coolest, most important person in the room. Your coolness and importance will come out if you stop trying so hard to prove it. Check out how Jesus explained this social rule: "When he noticed how the guests picked the places of honor at the table, he told them this parable: 'When someone invites you to a wedding feast, do not take the place of honor, for a person more distinguished than you may have been invited. If so, the host who invited both of you will come and say to you, "Give this person your seat." Then, humiliated, you will have to take the least important place. But when you are invited, take the lowest place, so that when your host comes, he will say to you, "Friend, move up to a better place." Then you will be honored in the presence of all the other guests. For all those who exalt themselves will be humbled, and those who humble themselves will be exalted'" (Luke 14:7-11).

At parties during the time of Jesus, honored guests would sit closest to the host. Jesus warned against assuming that *you* were that honored guest. It's better to sit at a lower station and be invited to a more prestigious seat than to think you're the greatest guy in the room and end up embarrassed when the host asks you to move on down the row.

Don't try to prove anything. Focus on the importance of others. As Philippians 2:3 says: "Do nothing from rivalry or conceit, but in humility count others more significant than yourselves" (ESV).

Live it out: Today treat others as if *they* are the most important people in the room.

Pray about it: Pray that God will help you remember to focus on others, not just yourself.

Party Planning Rules by Jesus

Be kind and compassionate to one another. Ephesians 4:32.

Jesus had another unexpected rule of etiquette: *when you throw a party, invite people who often get left out, instead of your friends.* Well that's strange, since parties are for friends, right? According to Jesus, it's fine to hang out with your friends, but it's even better to do it with people who might not have any friends of their own.

Here's how Jesus explained it:

"Then Jesus said to his host, 'When you give a luncheon or dinner, do not invite your friends, your brothers or sisters, your relatives, or your rich neighbors; if you do, they may invite you back and so you will be repaid. But when you give a banquet, invite the poor, the crippled, the lame, the blind, and you will be blessed. Although they cannot repay you, you will be repaid at the resurrection of the righteous'" (Luke 14:12-14).

When you throw an amazing party and invite all your friends, you benefit from it. Everybody has fun, and they think you're cool for having such a great bash. Plus, all the people whom you invited will probably now ask you to *their* parties.

However, when you invite people who are often left out, it is truly an act of kindness. You won't necessarily impress anyone or look like the coolest kid. But you will make a big difference in people's lives. You will make them feel special and important.

This doesn't just apply to parties. Jesus' rule works in every setting. If you're in the school cafeteria, don't just talk to your friends. Speak to people who are left out too. Or if you're at a church event, don't just laugh and joke with your buddies. Instead, break away from your crowd and give a little love and attention to people who really need it. Don't worry about what's in it for you. Just do it to be nice.

Live it out: This week extend friendship to someone who could use a friend.
Pray about it: Ask God to place you to situations in which you can make a difference by being friendly and accepting.

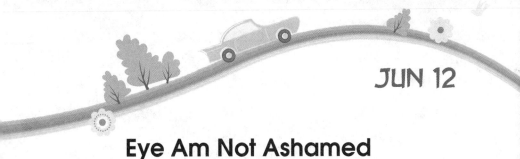

Eye Am Not Ashamed

For I am not ashamed of the gospel, because it is the power of God that brings salvation to everyone who believes. Romans 1:16.

Tim Tebow, one of the best college quarterbacks of recent time, was born in the Philippines, the son of Christian missionaries. His mother homeschooled him and worked to instill Christian principles in the family. As his fame increased, the public and the media took note of how conservative Tim's background was compared to other professional athletes.

His Christian values got even more attention when someone asked him during a press conference if he was saving sex for marriage. Completely confident and without hesitation, Tim answered yes. It stunned the reporters. Tim just laughed and casually joked that the reporters were more uncomfortable with that answer than he was.

Tebow has never been ashamed to speak up about his belief in God. In fact, during his college football career, he often wore references to Bible verses on his eye black, the paint or grease applied beneath the eye to prevent glare. In the 2009 Bowl Championship Series Game, Tim wore "John 3:16" on his eye paint. As a result, millions of people googled "John 3:16" during or shortly after the game. Similarly, when he wore "Proverbs 3:5, 6" on his eye black during another game, it produced 3.43 million Internet searches for that verse.

"It just goes to show you the influence and the platform that you have as a student athlete and as a quarterback at Florida," Tim said about those Internet inquiries.

He could have kept his beliefs quiet, but because he was not ashamed millions of people looked up Bible verses. His confidence about his belief made a huge impact on millions of people he had never even met.

In fact, Tim's eye-paint messages had such a huge impact that a new rule, dubbed "The Tebow Rule," banned messages on eye black! Even the Tebow Rule didn't quiet him, though. He continued to speak openly about God, thus having a positive impact on countless people across the nation.

Live it out: If Tim Tebow can speak out about God, so can you! The next time you have the chance, confidently share your belief in God.

Pray about it: Ask God to help you be prepared for opportunities to share your faith.

JUN 13

A Baby Story

For it was You who created my inward parts; You knit me together in my mother's womb. Psalm 139:13, HCSB.

When Pam Tebow was pregnant with her son, she suffered a life-threatening infection. It plunged her into a coma, causing doctors to use heavy medication to help her gain consciousness. She experienced a number of serious health problems that led to major trauma to the fetus. Doctors didn't think it was possible for the baby to be born alive, so they encouraged her to have an abortion.

Pam believed God had a special plan for her baby. Despite the doctors' advice, she decided to have the child, even though it was risky.

The baby grew up healthy and strong—very strong, in fact. That baby was Tim Tebow, who went on to become one of the greatest college football players of his time.

Tim, who has never shied away from sharing his beliefs, has openly talked about how brave his mother was to choose to have him. At a press conference in 2010 he said, "That's the reason I'm here, because my mom was a very courageous woman."

His mother wasn't the only woman to make this difficult—but rewarding— decision. She says the story isn't about her, but about God's plans for her baby: "The story of our youngest son Timmy is a God story." He was writing Tim's life story even before Tebow was born.

Live it out: Read Psalm 139 as a reminder that God loved you and had a plan for you before you were even born. If you or someone you know is considering an abortion, talk to a trusted, Christian adult. Do not let shame or fear determine the future.

Pray about it: Thank God for lovingly knitting you together in your mother's womb, as Psalm 139 says. Thank Him for designing you to be a special one-of-a-kind.

A Friendly Ghost

May the grace of the Lord Jesus Christ, and the love of God, and the fellowship of the Holy Spirit be with you all. 2 Corinthians 13:14.

Anyone with "Ghost" as a part of His name is destined to be mysterious. It's no wonder, then, that the Holy Ghost—or Holy Spirit—is often misunderstood.

Many people refer to the Holy Spirit as an "It," but the Holy Spirit is actually the Spirit of God dwelling among us. As a result, it's actually more accurate to call the Holy Spirit "He." He isn't just an eerie phantom floating around, but the very presence of God among us.

Even though we can't see Him, the Holy Spirit is doing amazing things all around. If you're not quite sure what He's up to, check out this list of just a few of the things He does:

- **He gives us power to do what God has called us to do.** "But you will receive power when the Holy Spirit comes on you; and you will be my witnesses" (Acts 1:8).
- **He teaches us and reminds us what God has told us before.** In John 14:26 Jesus promised, "But the Advocate, the Holy Spirit, whom the Father will send in my name, will teach you all things and will remind you of everything I have said to you."
- **He comforts us.** In that same verse, John 14:26, the word for Advocate is sometimes translated "Comforter," representing the Spirit's role of comforting us during hard times.
- **He showers God's love onto us.** Romans 5:5 says, "And hope does not put us to shame, because God's love has been poured out into our hears through the Holy Spirit, who has been given to us."

Do a search through Scripture for "Holy Spirit" or "Holy Ghost," and you'll discover many other ways the Spirit of God is trying to cooperate with you and help you. When you sense Him nudging you to do something, remember He is on your side. He wants you to feel loved and to be led by God. He is the very Spirit of God sent down to be with you.

Live it out: Think about it: how will you live differently knowing what the Holy Spirit is doing all around you? Do you feel as if He is on your side?

Pray about it: Offer a prayer of thanks that the Holy Spirit is your teacher, comforter, and guide. Ask for the clarity of mind to hear and respond to Him.

JUN 15

Live It Out!

Blessed is the one who perseveres under trial because, having stood the test, that person will receive the crown of life that the Lord has promised to those who love him. James 1:12

An idea that stood out to me from this week's devotional readings:

_____

_____

_____

A verse from this week's devotions that was powerful to me:

_____

_____

_____

A "Live it out" challenge I tried this week:

_____

_____

_____

Something that happened this week that was a blessing:

_____

_____

_____

My prayer today (thanks, requests, praises):

_____

_____

_____

Bad-mannered Pranksters

Be strong, and let us fight bravely for our people and the cities of our God. The Lord will do what is good in his sight. 2 Samuel 10:12.

Invitations to slumber parties, lock-ins, and summer camp should come with a warning label: "Attendance at this event will put you at high risk for becoming the victim of a prank."

The first slumber party I attended, a roomful of sleeping girls awoke to faces covered with toothpaste and lipstick (jokingly applied by the host's older brother). A couple summers later at camp a friend of mine awakened to find his buddies hysterically shaving off his eyebrows. And don't even get me started about the year at summer camp when pulling down people's shorts in public was all the rage.

Pranks almost always are funnier to the prankster than the pranked. But pranksters, beware! The humiliated victim might just get payback. That's what happened with King David and his messengers. It all started when David sent men to Hanun, a newly appointed king, to bring condolences because Hanun's father had died. Hanun's inner circle was skeptical, though, and they thought David's real intention was to spy out their land. Their cynicism was so strong that they seriously pranked David's well-intended messengers: "So Hanun seized David's envoys, shaved off half of each man's beard, cut off their garments at the buttocks, and sent them away" (2 Samuel 10:4). Oh, that's so bad. These guys were walking around with one side of their beard cut off and a hole in the rear of their robes! No surprise that the Bible says the victims were "greatly humiliated" (verse 5).

But, as in all great comeback stories, the underdog gained strength. Not too long after the embarrassing event, David and his humiliated men massively defeated the Ammonite pranksters in battle. The Ammonites lost the battle, their pride, and more than 40,000 people—all because of their skepticism and one rude trick. David and his troops fought confidently against the Ammonites, knowing that God is on the side of the person who does the right thing—not the degrading, prankster thing.

Live it out: Refuse to do any prank or behavior that could humiliate someone.
Pray about it: Pray for someone in particular who has been picked on or humiliated by others.

What Would You Do for an iPad 2?

Keep your lives free from the love of money and be content with what you have, because God has said, "Never will I leave you; never will I forsake you." Hebrews 13:5.

The iPad 2 was pretty cool, right? What would you have given to have one? Would you have saved your allowance for a year? Would you have gotten an after-school job? Would you have sold some of your belongings? What about selling one of your organs? Yes, you heard me right. One of your organs?

A 17-year-old boy in China sold one of his kidneys on the black market so that he could buy an iPad 2. The boy, known only by his last name Zheng, received 22,000 yuan ($3,400) for the organ.

Without telling his plans to his family, he traveled to a hospital in Chenzhou, in which he was operated on under the supervision of the shifty kidney-selling agent with whom he had made the agreement. Such a transaction, by the way, was a crime, because selling an organ on the black market is illegal.

When he returned home with an iPad and an iPhone, his mother was suspicious. Zheng, bearing a deep-red scar from the surgery, was forced to admit what he had done.

Keeping up with the latest trends can be expensive. What will Zheng sell the next time he wants a hot item? The consumerism cycle is vicious. Once you get caught up chasing after the next big thing, you lose sight of what really matters. You also lose appreciation for what you already have. Hebrews 13:5 sums it up perfectly: "Keep your lives free from the love of money and be content with what you have, because God has said, 'Never will I leave you; never will I forsake you.'"

Live it out: Don't lose your cool chasing after the latest big trend. Make a commitment never to risk your health or your relationship with God or with others in order to get stuff.

Pray about it: Thank God for all the things He has already given you.

Rescue Plan

Flee for your lives! Don't look back, and don't stop anywhere in the plain!
Genesis 19:17.

When the Lord tries to save you from something terrible, it's a really good idea to *let Him* rescue you. Repeatedly in the Bible, God attempts to deliver people from destruction, but even with fair warning some people wouldn't let Him.

Take the story of Lot's family, for example. Angels came to him with insider information: God was going to destroy the cities of Sodom and Gomorrah. If Lot had any family members in the cities, he should tell them to get out immediately. And he did indeed. He wanted to make sure his wife, two daughters, and two sons-in-law all made it out of town alive.

Right away he went to his sons-in-law for a man-to-man conversation. Panicked, he told them, "Hurry and get out of this place, because the Lord is about to destroy the city!" (Genesis 19:14). Even though it was no laughing matter, "his sons-in-law thought he was joking" (verse 14).

Giving up on those two young men, Lot went on to get his daughters and his wife out of harm's way. Two angels helped him rescue the women by taking them by the hand and leading them to safety. As soon as they were in the clear, one of the angels warned, "Flee for your lives! Don't look back, and don't stop anywhere in the plain! Flee to the mountains or you will be swept away!" (verse 17).

You would think the heat of the flames on their back and the sounds and smell of their hometown going up in a blaze would be enough to keep them moving. But Lot's wife didn't follow their guidance. She wanted one more glance of her former home—her former life. In one tiny sentence the Bible tells an enormous story: "But Lot's wife looked back, and she became a pillar of salt" (verse 26).

When the Lord tries to deliver you from something terrible, don't be like Lot's sons-in-law and wife. Instead, take it seriously and keep your gaze forward.

Live it out: Do you sense God trying to rescue you from an unhealthy relationship, circumstance, or habit? Are you resisting or cooperating? What do you need to do to cooperate with Him so that He can free you?

Pray about it: Thank God for always working to give you a fresh start.

If Wishes Come True

The Lord appeared to Solomon during the night in a dream, and God said, "Ask for whatever you want me to give you." I Kings 3:5.

If you could make three wishes that would all come true, what would you choose? Go ahead, think about it. Now, what if you could have only *one* wish, what would it be?

Many people fantasize that, just like in fictional stories, they might discover a genie in a bottle who could grant their very heart's desire. In make-believe tales the lucky person often wishes for money, the affection of a person they love, or power and fame. (I'd probably make that third wish some version of "I wish for 1,000 more wishes.")

Although I've heard lots of fantasy tales about wild wishes coming true, I've only heard one *true* story about it. After Solomon became king, God told him in a dream, "Ask for whatever you want me to give you" (1 Kings 3:5). The all-powerful, mighty God of the universe told a simple man that he could ask for absolutely anything! Solomon could have sought power to conquer the world or to live for hundreds of years. Instead, he requested wisdom. "Give your servant, then, a wise heart for judging your people, able to see what is good and what evil" (verse 9, BBE).

The young king must have been a pretty smart guy already, because that was a wise thing to request. It so pleased the Lord that He promised to give Solomon even more blessings: "So God said to him, 'Since you have asked for this and not for long life or wealth for yourself, nor have asked for the death of your enemies but for discernment in administering justice, I will do what you have asked. I will give you a wise and discerning heart, so that there will never have been anyone like you, nor will there ever be. Moreover, I will give you what you have not asked for— both wealth and honor—so that in your lifetime you will have no equal among kings. And if you walk in obedience to me and keep my decrees and commands as David your father did, I will give you a long life" (verses 11-14). When Solomon asked for wisdom to do God's will, God gave him wisdom—plus everything else that he could ever need.

Live it out: Instead of focusing on wealth or fame, spend time in the Bible pursuing wisdom.

Pray about it: Follow Solomon's example and ask God for wisdom.

The One That (Almost) Got Away

Don't be afraid; from now on you will fish for people. Luke 5:10.

John Goldfinch loved to fish for mackerel on the beaches near his home in England. He always enjoyed the sport; but like most fishers, he especially loved the thrill of the big catch. You can imagine his excitement, then, when he felt a huge bite on his line. It was so massive and powerful that John knew it was going to be the biggest catch of his life.

John struggled to reel in the catch, but finally managed to pull it to the surface. When he caught a glimpse of what was on his hook, his excitement turned to shock. John had caught a scuba diver!

Attached to his hook was an unsuspecting man who had been out for a dive with his girlfriend. Stunned, John looked at his catch and mumbled, "Sorry, mate, I didn't see you there."

Going fishing for a person sounds ridiculous, but Jesus told His followers to do just that. Speaking to the disciples who had been lifelong fishers, He said it was time to stop reeling in fish and time to start reeling in people:

"As Jesus was walking beside the Sea of Galilee, he saw two brothers, Simon called Peter and his brother Andrew. They were casting a net into the lake, for they were fishermen. 'Come, follow me,' Jesus said, 'and I will send you out to fish for people.' At once they left their nets and followed him" (Matthew 4:18-20).

Fishers always talk about "the one that got away"—the huge catch they *almost* reeled in. They look back with regret, thinking it would have been theirs with just a little more time, effort, and luck.

When it comes to fishing for people, you never want to look back with regret. If God impresses you to talk to someone, you don't want them to be "the one that got away" because you didn't do your part. You're not called to hook someone and drag them kicking and screaming to Jesus. No, fishing for people simply means you reach out, talk to them, show them love, and help draw them closer to Jesus.

Live it out: Reach out to someone this week. Invite someone to church or to a youth activity.
Pray about it: Ask God to help you be attentive to people.

A Poisonous Treat

Be alert and of sober mind. Your enemy the devil prowls around like a roaring lion looking for someone to devour. 1 Peter 5:8.

My father-in-law lived in Communist Cuba much of his life. Because he had very limited resources there, he learned to be extremely creative. When he moved to the United States, he became an exterminator and used some of the tricks he had discovered in Cuba to eliminate mice, termites, and, of course, *la cucarachas.*

One of his homemade exterminator specialties was peanut butter squares— guaranteed to attract and eliminate rats and mice. He would grind pellets of poison into powder, mix in a little bit of the powder with a large amount of peanut butter, and mold the combination into small cubes.

One day when my husband, Robert, was only 8 years old, he watched his dad make the concoction. Protesting loudly, he asked his dad why he was wasting so much perfectly good peanut butter on rats. Robert suggested he just put out the poison by itself instead. Smiling, his father told him, "Son, rats don't like poison, but they love peanut butter. If you put just enough poison with something they love, they'll be fooled into eating the deadly poison every time."

Just like the exterminator, when Satan brought sin to this earth, he didn't introduce it in all its destructiveness. Instead, he combined a little poison along with something very appealing to us. Like a mad scientist, Satan continues to grind up lies, feeding them to us in small but deadly doses, mixing poison with things we love. He introduces a little poison into song lyrics, movies, books, or Web sites. Beware if something doesn't line up with what the Bible says (even in a little way), because it could be Satan's way of sneaking a little poison into the peanut butter.

Live it out: Identify areas in your life that are like the exterminator's peanut butter squares—attractive but poisonous. What can you do to avoid such temptations?

Pray about it: Ask God to help you detect when Satan is trying to sneak lies into your life.

Live It Out!

Come to me, all you who are weary and burdened, and I will give you rest. Take my yoke upon you and learn from me, for I am gentle and humble in heart, and you will find rest for your souls. For my yoke is easy and my burden is light. Matthew 11:28-30.

An idea that stood out to me from this week's devotional readings:

_____

_____

_____

A verse from this week's devotions that was powerful to me:

_____

_____

_____

A "Live it out" challenge I tried this week:

_____

_____

_____

Something that happened this week that was a blessing:

_____

_____

_____

My prayer today (thanks, requests, praises):

_____

_____

_____

Liar, Liar, Pants on Fire

The Lord detests lying lips, but he delights in people who are trustworthy.
Proverbs 12:22.

Ever wondered if someone was telling you a lie? Maybe your friend said he couldn't come to your party because he had to visit his grandma. (But wait, you thought his grandma lived in a nursing home in *Ohio*. How could he be visiting her *tonight*?) Or perhaps you walked up to a group of friends who were talking, but as soon as they saw you they went quiet. When you asked what they were talking about, someone mumbled without looking at you that they were discussing a new movie that just came out. (But wait, someone else started to say that they were deciding where to go for lunch. Which is it?) Seem suspicious?

Sometimes it is possible to determine whether someone is trying to pass off a lie to you. Here are some telltale signs that someone is lying:

- If their story sounds vague, it's probably because there aren't any real details, and the person is making things up as they go.
- Liars usually avoid eye contact. They may also appear uncooperative or on edge.
- Sometimes the voices of liars will rise and sound higher than usual when they are telling a fib. When making up a story on the spot, they also end up pausing more than usual so they can create the lie one step at a time.
- It might be a giveaway if the person keeps saying things such as "I promise," "I'm not kidding, that really happened," or "I'm being honest." Such statements are ways of trying to make the lie seem more credible.

Now you know some of the tricks that cops, detectives, and psychologists use to tell when people are lying. Sure, you can use them on others, but you have to remember that others can employ them on you, too! If you want to keep your story straight—and keep your friends—just tell the truth instead of trying to spin a deceitful story.

Live it out: Avoid the temptation to make up a story. Instead, follow God's plan and speak the truth in love (see Ephesians 4:15). Telling the truth may seem difficult at the moment, but everything always goes better when you are honest.

Pray about it: Aim to be honest with God in your prayer life. Are there things you haven't been straightforward with Him or even yourself? If so, pray openly about those things.

I'll Let You Know
When You Get There

So Abram went. Genesis 12:4.

Abraham (known as Abram before God changed his name) was a successful and wealthy man who believed in God. The Lord had special plans for him, but not because he was successful and wealthy. God handpicked Abraham because he believed.

The Lord promised to make Abraham's descendents a great nation. All Abraham had to do was follow God.

Turns out, Abraham *literally* had to follow Him.

God asked Abraham to pack up, journey to a new land, and start his life afresh. This took a double dose of faith. Abraham was being asked to head out without even knowing where he was headed. Nope, the Lord didn't give him an address to enter into his GPS. He just said (not exactly in these words), "I'll let you know when you get there." Genesis 12:1 records, "The Lord had said to Abram, 'Go from your country, your people and your father's household to the land I will show you.'"

God promised that the reward for following would be great. He told Abraham:
"I will make you into a great nation,
        and I will bless you;
I will make your name great,
        and you will be a blessing.
I will bless those who bless you,
        and whoever curses you I will curse;
and all peoples on earth
        will be blessed through you" (verses 2, 3).

And here's what happened next: "So Abram went" (verse 4). Those three little words tell a huge story. Abraham stepped out in faith. And he became a part of God's amazing plan.

Live it out: Is God calling you to step out in faith? Be like Abraham, and do it!

Pray about it: Ask God to help you have the wisdom, faith, and courage to follow Him.

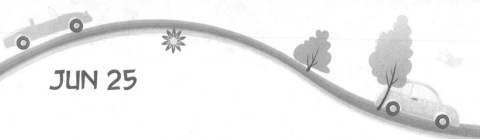

One Thing I Know

I will not venture to speak of anything except what Christ has accomplished through me. Romans 15:18.

Christians constantly discuss the importance of "witnessing," "sharing your faith," and "evangelizing." Sure, we hear about it all the time, but few teens (or adults!) actually want to do it. Maybe you feel as if you don't know enough about the Bible to talk about it. Perhaps you feel that you'll come across as fanatical or dorky if you really do it. Or maybe you fear you'll be rejected, excluded, or ridiculed as a "Jesus Freak."

One very cool story in the Bible will ease all of those fears. In John 9 Jesus restored the sight of a man who had been blind since birth. The Jewish leaders at the time hated Jesus and wanted to put Him out of the business of saving people. When they heard about the incident (that had happened on the Sabbath), they started quizzing the excited, healed man.

The leaders hoped to trap him into saying something incriminating about Jesus. They wanted him to admit that Jesus was a sinner, but the man wouldn't fall for it. He responded, "Whether he is a sinner or not, I don't know. One thing I do know. I was blind but now I see!" (John 9:25). So they kept grilling him: *Where did Jesus come from? What did He do to you? How did He open your eyes? How can a sinner do such miraculous signs?*

The simple man didn't know the answers to all of their questions and admitted it. "One thing I do know. I was blind but now I see!"

That is the very best model for witnessing: just tell what you do know. Explain what God has done for you. That is the best way to be a powerful representative for Him. If He helped you through your parents' divorce, relate that. Perhaps He gave you a wonderful friend or family, so share that. Or if He led you to a great summer job, say that. Like the healed man, just tell the "one thing" you know. Your personal story of what He has done for you is the most powerful thing you can offer.

Live it out: Tell what God has done for you. Don't worry that you can't explain every Bible verse or doctrine. Just start with your personal story of what the Lord has done in your life.

Pray about it: Thank God for the things He has done in your life.

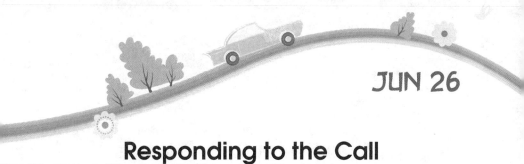

Responding to the Call

Then I heard the voice of the Lord saying, "Whom shall I send? And who will go for us?" And I said, "Here am I. Send me!" Isaiah 6:8.

In most places political races are heated and competitive. Not in Tar Heel, North Carolina. In 2011 no one—not one person—ran for mayor or three commission seats. As a result, the election authorities printed the ballots with blank spaces for voters to write in their choices. Even though the town has only 117 residents, no one wanted to take on the tough jobs. The previous mayor admitted that it had been a lot of work but not much pay.

Tar Heel isn't the only place people dodge tough jobs. In the vision of Isaiah 6 the Lord is looking for someone to be a messenger for Him. Like the mayoral position of Tar Heel, that job was probably a lot of work.

Isaiah describes the scene: "Then I heard the voice of the Lord saying, 'Whom shall I send? And who will go for us?" (Isaiah 6:8).

In response, the prophet didn't hesitate. No matter how difficult the task, he would do it. When he heard the call, he responded, "Here am I. Send me!" (verse 8).

The next time you hear God calling you to do something for Him, will you be like the people of Tar Heel, North Carolina? Or will you be like Isaiah?

Live it out: Is there something you sense that God wants you to do? If so, spend time praying about it. Should it be a big task, discuss it with a spiritual adult who can help you make a plan of action. So if you are hearing God's call, don't hesitate any longer.

Pray about it: Offer the prayer: "Here am I. Send me!" And see where God leads you.

JUN 27

Life Is Better With Friends

A friend loves at all times. Proverbs 17:17.

Life is better shared. Every aspect of it is greater if you have a friend to celebrate with you, cry with you, cheer you on, and make you laugh. The Bible says it this way: "Two are better than one, because they have a good return for their labor" (Ecclesiastes 4:9).

If you have great friends, say a prayer of thanks for that gift from God. And if you want more friends (and who couldn't use more of them?), there's no time like the present to find them. Most people start their hunt for friends with the question *How can I make more friends?* But there's an even better question. Instead, ask yourself, *How can I be a friend to someone?* Once you phrase it that way, you won't just think selfishly about what's in it for you. If you start thinking about how you can *be* a better friend, you will attract people to you.

Begin by finding ways to help, encourage, and share experiences with people. Friendship is all about showing love to people as you go through life together. Proverbs 17:17 says, "A friend loves at all times." Galatians 5:13 states it this way: "Serve one another humbly in love."

Jesus was the ultimate example of friendship. He came and gave everything He had to help us. After serving and loving the people all around Him, He said, "I have called you friends" (John 15:15).

God doesn't just *suggest* this approach to friendship, He *commands* it. "My command is this: Love each other as I have loved you. Greater love has no one than this: to lay down one's life for one's friends" (John 15:12, 13). Jesus showed that the very best, regret-free way to live is to love your friends with everything you've got. When you do that, you'll be doing exactly what God wants, and He will reward you with all the love your life can hold.

Live it out: Find a way today to extend love and friendship to someone you don't know very well. It might just be the beginning of a new friendship.
Pray about it: Ask God to bring people into your life today who need a friend. Ask for the guidance to know whom to befriend and how to show love and friendship to them.

Walking on Eggshells

Great peace have they which love thy law: and nothing shall offend them.
Psalm 119:165, KJV.

Trista is touchy. She gets offended by almost everything. (Actually, the girl I'm talking about isn't really named Trista. I've changed her name to protect her privacy—and to protect *me*, because if she knew I was writing about her, she would definitely be offended!)

If I laugh at something Trista says, she gets upset, because she hadn't *meant* it to be funny. But should I not laugh at something, she gets offended because it *was* meant to be funny. As soon as I make an innocent comment, I can tell by the look on her face that she's taken it the wrong way. I offend her without meaning to—and sometimes without even realizing it.

As a result, Trista leaves everyone around her walking on eggshells—tiptoeing around every conversation so that we don't disturb her. She assumes everyone is out to get her, so she's always on edge assuming the worst. I feel compassion for her, because she has obviously been hurt in the past, which leaves her feeling as if she has to keep her guard up to protect herself.

If you know a Trista—someone easily offended—don't give up on them. Keep showing them love and kindness; and no matter what, don't let yourself be hurt if they are mean to you. No one wins when everyone is offended!

Perhaps if you can relate to Trista, it may be because people may feel as if they are walking on eggshells around *you*. You may not sense it, but others might be afraid you're going to explode or sulk at any moment. First Corinthians 13 reminds us that love is not easily offended: "it is not easily angered, it keeps no record of wrongs" (verse 5). It is a choice to be not offended. Also it is an act of love.

With each interaction, stop yourself from coiling up in offense. You can't take yourself too seriously. Even though it might *feel* like it sometimes, God and people aren't out to get you. Focus on God's love and acceptance, and you'll slowly begin to become less sensitive and more open and welcoming to others.

Live it out: Next time you feel offended, remind yourself that love is not easily upset. Make the choice to let it go and not get angry.

Pray about it: Ask the Lord to help you not to be easily offended. Pray also for patience with those who are touchy.

JUN 29

Live It Out!

For it is by grace you have been saved, through faith—and this is not from yourselves, it is the gift of God. Ephesians 2:8.

An idea that stood out to me from this week's devotional readings:

_____

_____

_____

A verse from this week's devotions that was powerful to me:

_____

_____

_____

A "Live it out" challenge I tried this week:

_____

_____

_____

Something that happened this week that was a blessing:

_____

_____

_____

My prayer today (thanks, requests, praises):

_____

_____

_____

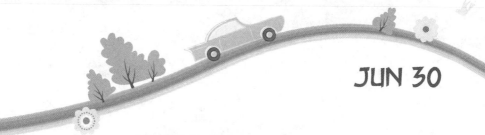

43,800 Sunny Days

By faith Noah, when warned about things not yet seen, in holy fear built an ark to save his family. Hebrews 11:7.

If the weather forecast says there is a zero percent chance of rain, do you carry an umbrella to school? What about if the forecast calls for sunshine and 98 degrees Fahrenheit—do you take your rain jacket *just in case*? No way. If you have no reason to believe it's going to rain, why bother planning for it?

Imagine what it must have been like for the people during the time of Noah. They had never seen rain and had no idea what it would be like to have water fall from the sky. But there they were, with one wild man telling them they had better get ready, because God was going to flood the planet with water.

Here you've got massive amounts of people being told to prepare for rain, and they've never even *seen* rain. I can understand why they would be skeptical.

God had given Noah a special message and a special mission: there would be a flood, so Noah should build an ark. Funny thing was, the flood wasn't going to come for another 120 years. That means he went around for 43,800 sunny days talking about a boat, a flood, and a sky full of rain. It was as crazy as walking around for 43,800 sunny days wearing a raincoat, galoshes/boots, and an open umbrella. The people saw no sign of rain, so it all seemed ridiculous to them. That is, well, until it started raining. *Then* they believed Noah.

Noah, however, had believed God. He had seen no evidence for years—not even a tiny little drizzle of rain—but he trusted the Lord.

If God says He will do something, He will do it. Living by faith means you just believe Him, even if there's no immediate proof. Jesus Himself said, "Blessed are those who have not seen and yet have believed" (John 20:29). Faith doesn't have to see rain to believe it exists—it just puts on galoshes and heads out the door, ready for anything.

Live it out: Have confidence that God can do amazing things—even if you can't see how.

Pray about it: Ask God to help you believe Him, come rain or shine.

JUL 1

Google Maps
and Bad Directions

Listen, my son, and be wise, and set your heart on the right path. Proverbs 23:19.

If you're trying to get to Round Valley State Park, don't use Google Maps. Apparently the Web site keeps sending boaters, campers, and hikers to the wrong place: the home of Laurie Gneiding and Michael Brady. The couple have a steady stream of visitors knocking on their door demanding entrance into the New Jersey State Park.

Their home is a log cabin marked with signs that read "No Trespassing, Private Road." Nevertheless, some parkgoers won't be turned away. They insist they are in the right place—because Google Maps told them it was the spot.

Laurie explains her serious (but still a little funny) concerns: "My biggest fear is coming home someday and having 'visitors' in my backyard pool."

Those eager tourists aren't the only ones who get their directions mixed up. Proverbs 14:12 says, "What you think is the right road may lead to death" (TEV). When we start out on a path without asking God for directions, we could be headed straight for trouble. Fortunately, the Bible promises that He has a great sense of direction. He will help us get to the place where we would be happiest.

The psalmist describes God's route several ways. It is a nice path on which we can stay strong: "You provide a broad path for my feet, so that my ankles do not give way" (Psalm 18:36). Also it is one on which we will be happy: "Direct me in the path of your commands, for there I find delight" (Psalm 119:35).

Following God's route will ultimately lead us to life, joy, and pleasure: "You make known to me the path of life; you will fill me with joy in your presence, with eternal pleasures at your right hand" (Psalm 16:11).

Live it out: When you make decisions this week, stop and ask God for directions. Make sure you're headed the right way before you take the next step.
Pray about it: Ask God if you're headed in the right direction. Invite Him to guide you down the best path.

The Waiting Game

I wait for the Lord, my whole being waits, and in his word I put my hope.
Psalm 130:5.

Some people hate to wait, but I usually don't mind it. If I have to stand in line at a grocery store, I flip through a magazine off the rack. Should I have to wait for a plane, I surf the Internet, read a book, or eat a snack. And until someone arrives, I will make calls or send overdue texts or messages.

When you think about it, though, those examples are the *easy* kind of waiting—such as for your food in a restaurant or a friend to phone.

There is, however, a much more difficult type of waiting—the kind mentioned throughout the Bible. The difficult waiting comes when you are going through a hard time, and you're waiting for God to clear things up. The difficult waiting comes when your reputation has been damaged and you're waiting for God (or anyone!) to step in and help you. The difficult waiting comes when you're waiting to hear the results of your mom's medical tests to see if she has cancer. The difficult waiting comes when you feel as if you just don't belong and maybe never will.

Waiting is a big part of the Christian's life. God never panics or rushes things. He takes His time and does things perfectly. We, however, are naturally impatient creatures, so the Bible has to warn us time and time again that following God will require some waiting.

If you are waiting on God right now in your life, remember that God will make it worth the wait. He will bring out a good result. In the meantime, take these verses to heart:

- "We wait in hope for the Lord; he is our help and our shield" (Psalm 33:20).
- "Lord, I wait for you; you will answer, Lord my God" (Psalm 38:15).
- "Wait for the Lord; be strong and take heart and wait for the Lord" (Psalm 27:14).

Live it out: Is there an area in your life in which you are waiting on God? Write one of these verses about waiting somewhere you can see and read it every day.
Pray about it: Tell God you are waiting on Him. Talk things out with Him, and tell Him you're putting your trust in Him.

JUL 3

Time Flies When You're in Love

Jacob was in love with Rachel. Genesis 29:18.

Jacob would say that true love is worth the wait. He should know: he worked 14 years to marry Rachel, the woman of his dreams.

It's a great love story. But before we get to the *love* part of the story, we have to back up and talk about its deceitful, not-so-loving aspect.

Here's how it went down. Jacob told Rachel's father, Laban, that he would work seven years in exchange for marrying Rachel. Laban agreed, and Jacob went to work. Genesis 29:20 says: "So Jacob served seven years to get Rachel, but they seemed like only a few days to him because of his love for her." The time flew by, because Jacob was so in love. Even a skeptic of true love has to admit how sweet that is.

The love birds must have been so excited when their wedding day finally arrived. But Laban wasn't much of a romantic. He didn't really care that Jacob loved Rachel. According to custom, he needed someone to marry his older daughter, Leah, before little sister Rachel could get hitched. So Laban did a heartless switcharoo and gave Leah as a wife to Jacob instead.

The groom's heart sank. His new wife wasn't the woman he loved. What a disappointment to everyone involved! Jacob got conned into marrying someone he didn't love. Leah was pawned off on a man who didn't appreciate her. And Rachel had been cheated out of her dream marriage by her own father.

But love doesn't give up that easily. Jacob and Laban struck another deal. The father would allow Jacob to marry Rachel (in addition to Leah) in exchange for another seven years of work. That's 14 years total. And Jacob agreed.

If your parents have said you can't date until a certain age (or you're feeling the desire to rush a relationship), remember Jacob's story. True love can wait—even for years! When it's true love, the time will fly by, and it will be worth the wait.

Live it out: Are you trying to rush a relationship? Slow down and remember that love is patient.
Pray about it: Ask God to help you to trust His timing in your relationships.

192

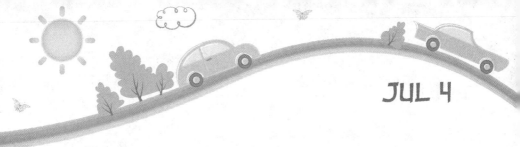

A Promise You Can Count On

The Lord is trustworthy in all he promises and faithful in all he does. Psalm 145:13.

Someone has counted 1,260 promises in the Bible. That's enough to have a new promise from God every day for nearly three and a half years!

The cool thing about God's promises is that they are different from human ones. We may say such things as "I'll never do that again. I promise!" (and then we end up doing that very thing again). Or we announce, "I promise I will be there" (and then we get busy or tired and don't show up). Sometimes our promises aren't really worth much.

God, however, is good on His word. If He promised it, He will do it. Psalm 145:13 declares, "The Lord is trustworthy in all he promises and faithful in all he does." That means you can claim any promise God has made to you in the Bible—and you can have complete confidence that He will keep His word.

If you want your Christian experience—and the Word of God—to spark into something extraordinary, then start claiming His promises. You'll quickly realize that God is active, involved, and faithful. Explore the promises in the Bible, and choose one or two to claim as a personal promise just for you. For example, if you have a broken heart, claim God's promise to be near you and help you: "The Lord is close to the brokenhearted and saves those who are crushed in spirit" (Psalm 34:18).

The promise may not get answered as quickly as you like, but you can be certain it will be answered. Just keep believing that God will keep His word. As Hebrews 10:23 urges us: "Let us hold unswervingly to the hope we profess, for he who promised is faithful." What's really amazing is that once you've seen one promise fulfilled, you still have 1,259 more to claim for your very own.

Live it out: Choose a promise to claim by searching the Bible or doing an Internet search for "promises in the Bible." Underline the promise in your Bible, or write it somewhere you'll see it often. Read it regularly and pray, "God, I believe You will keep Your word and do this for me. Thank You."

Pray about it: Thank God for keeping His promises. Tell Him you believe He will do it for you.

Crushing Those Terrible Temptations

And God is faithful; he will not let you be tempted beyond what you can bear.
1 Corinthians 10:13.

Do you have a temptation that always seems to get the best of you? Some people wrestle with food. That sandwich, ice cream, or bag of chips just won't stop calling their name. For other people, it's the temptation to drink, smoke, ignore curfew, or break the law. Other teens struggle with sexual enticement.

Sometimes temptations make us feel as if it is impossible to overcome them. When a temptation grabs hold of us, we start the same old battle again—trying to ignore the temptation, but being drawn to it at the same time. It seems that the longer we attempt to avoid that familiar temptation, the stronger it gets.

Here's the good news about temptations, though. Even though it *feels* as if the temptation will keep intensifying until you cave in, that isn't the truth. Yes, it may get stronger as you battle it out, but if you stay tough, the temptation will eventually fade away. Think of fighting a temptation as like climbing a steep, rugged mountain. It just keeps getting steeper and more intense as you struggle up. But just when you think you're going to have to give in because you can't hold on any longer, you've reached the mountain's peak, and the path starts going back downhill. The moment you think you have to give in is actually the moment you're about to gain victory. Don't believe that when temptation grows stronger, you have no other choice but to surrender to it. The truth is, when the temptation is at its very strongest, you have two choices: (1) cave in (and end up feeling guilty afterward), or (2) prayerfully hold on just a little bit longer and watch the temptation subside.

Many people don't know that a temptation will eventually weaken, because they always surrender to it before that happens. The Bible promises, however, that you can fight against a temptation and win. "No temptation has overtaken you except what is common to mankind. And God is faithful; he will not let you be tempted beyond what you can bear. But when you are tempted, he will also provide a way out so that you can endure it" (1 Corinthians 10:13).

Live it out: Read Jesus' advice in Luke 22:46 and make God your partner in overcoming.

Pray about it: Be honest with God about your temptations, struggles, and need for help.

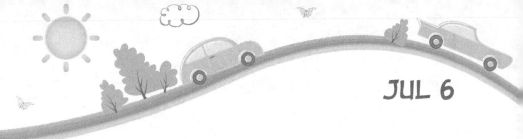

Live It Out!

The Lord is good, a refuge in times of trouble. He cares for those who trust in him. Nahum 1:7.

An idea that stood out to me from this week's devotional readings:

_____

_____

_____

A verse from this week's devotions that was powerful to me:

_____

_____

_____

A "Live it out" challenge I tried this week:

_____

_____

_____

Something that happened this week that was a blessing:

_____

_____

_____

My prayer today (thanks, requests, praises):

_____

_____

_____

Parents Just Don't Understand
(or Maybe They Do)

No temptation has overtaken you except what is common to mankind.
1 Corinthians 10:13.

Parents just don't understand!" It's a common complaint among teens everywhere. In a way, you're right. Parents and other adults don't completely understand what you're up against. You are exposed to situations they never faced at your age. However, you might be surprised to know that parents, in many ways, *do* realize what you're going through. They understand more than you think, for a couple of reasons. First, they were young once (hard to believe, huh?), and some temptations are timeless and universal. Satan has only so many tricks in his bag. If he tried a temptation on you, don't be surprised if he employed it on one of your parents too. Although it's hard to imagine, even if your parents seem like the most straight-and-narrow folks on the earth, Satan might have tempted them to drink, curse, have premarital sex, cheat on a test, or even scream "You just don't understand!" at their parents.

The second reason your parents understand more than you might think: they *still* have temptations similar to yours, just different versions of them. In many ways, adults and teens struggle with a lot of the same issues: fitting in, wanting more money, being accepted, desiring to be attractive, making friends, overcoming sexual temptations, fighting depression and insecurity, and knowing what to do with their lives. The common temptations and struggles that we all share (no matter our age) are what Paul was talking about when he wrote, "No temptation has overtaken you except what is common to mankind" (1 Corinthians 10:13).

What's even more comforting (and even harder to believe) is that Jesus Himself understands what we're going through too. Hebrews 4:15 says that Satan threw all these common temptations at Jesus too: "For we do not have a high priest who is unable to empathize with our weaknesses, but we have one who has been tempted in every way, just as we are—yet he did not sin." If you're struggling with a temptation, take comfort knowing that your compassionate Savior completely understands.

Live it out: Don't assume the adults in your life wouldn't understand what you're going through. Talk about your life with a parent, teacher, or pastor. Ask them what they learned when faced with the same temptations as you.

Pray about it: Pray openly and honestly about your struggles, knowing that God understands.

Jesus on a Walmart Receipt

Such is the generation of those who seek him, who seek your face, God of Jacob.
Psalm 24:6.

In June 2011 Jacob Simmons and Gentry Lee Sutherland went to a church service that challenged listeners, "Would you know God if you saw Him?" Apparently, for Jacob and Gentry, the answer was yes. When they arrived at Gentry's apartment after the church service, they noticed a Walmart receipt on the floor. The ink on the receipt had smeared into an image that looked shockingly like a face of Jesus. They immediately wondered whether God was revealing Himself to them. Yes, to repeat, *on a Walmart receipt.*

Jacob and Gentry aren't the only ones who claim to have spotted the face of Jesus in unlikely places. There's also the 22-year-old man who claims an image of Jesus appeared in the burned bacon fat at the bottom of his frying pan. (The image, he says, showed up after he fell asleep while cooking bacon. The fact that he fell asleep while cooking bacon seems almost as strange as an image of Jesus manifesting itself in the bacon fat, but that's beside the point.) And then there's the array of people who have thought they have seen the face of Jesus in all kinds of food, from fish sticks to grilled cheese sandwiches (the latter resulting in what cynics have nicknamed a Grilled Chessus).

The Bible promises that people who seek to see God's face will be blessed (although I don't think it means hoping to see His face in Walmart receipts and fried fish sticks). Here's what it says: "They will receive blessing from the Lord and vindication from God their Savior. Such is the generation of those who seek him, who seek your face, God of Jacob" (Psalm 24:5, 6). When we look for Him, we will find Him everywhere. We will come face to face with Him in the nice things people do, in beautiful skies and massive trees, and in our parents' selflessness or our pastor's sermon.

God guarantees that we will see Him when we look for Him: "You will seek me and find me when you seek me with all your heart" (Jeremiah 29:13). Open your eyes, and you will indeed observe God all around you. Just be sure to look somewhere other than your grilled cheese sandwich.

Live it out: Look for God today. Try to perceive Him in people, nature, or circumstances.

Pray about it: Open up to God in prayer and seek Him with all your heart.

We're All in This Together

Don't look out only for your own interests, but take an interest in others, too.
Philippians 2:4, NLT.

Listen up, all you Lone Rangers out there, those of you who like to go it alone in life. The Bible has an important message: God designed us to live in a community. We need friends, family, and a church family in order to thrive. Even if some of the people at church seem hypocritical or your big brother sometimes acts like a jerk, God has brought all of you together for a reason.

Proverbs, the ultimate book of wisdom, says, "As iron sharpens iron, so one person sharpens another" (Proverbs 27:17). In other words, we learn from each other. Coming into close contact with each other will smooth our rough edges off. When we're all alone in our room, it's easy to think we're perfectly nice, easygoing people. However, when we get into relationships with others, we start learning what we're *really* like. Sure, you can be patient when by yourself and there's nothing to be impatient about. But what about when you are around someone who is getting on your last nerve? There's only one way to learn to be patient in that situation, and that is to *be* in that situation.

Our encounters with others make us better people. We learn acceptance by meeting people who are flawed or different than we are. Spending time with those struggling with a problem will teach us compassion. And we learn about life through individuals who have different temperaments, personalities, and life experiences than ours.

No one is perfect—including you—but don't let that keep you from getting close to others. Life is more beautiful and fun when all of us imperfect people take the journey together. We will learn from each other along the way.

Live it out: Find opportunities to spend time with people you might have otherwise avoided. Ask them questions, and get to know them.
Pray about it: Thank God for wanting a relationship with you. Ask Him to help you have healthy relationships with others.

Shout Even Louder!

The crowd rebuked them and told them to be quiet, but they shouted all the louder, "Lord, Son of David, have mercy on us!" Matthew 20:31.

One day, as Jesus and His disciples left Jericho, a large crowd followed Him. Nothing new about that. It seemed as if crowds accompanied Jesus wherever He went. Everyone wanted to ask Him for something or to touch Him or talk to Him.

On this day two blind men were sitting by the roadside when Jesus passed by. They shouted to Him, "Lord, Son of David, have mercy on us!" (Matthew 20:30). Apparently the crowd thought Jesus had more important people and things to address than two blind beggars, so they told the men to pipe down. "The crowd rebuked them and told them to be quiet, but they shouted all the louder, 'Lord, Son of David, have mercy on us!'" (verse 31).

Did you catch what those rebel beggars did? Ordered to stop crying out to Jesus, they "shouted all the louder"! The Bible says that Jesus noticed them and inquired what they wanted. When they asked for sight, "Jesus had compassion on them and touched their eyes. Immediately they received their sight and followed him" (verse 34).

If you are desperately crying out for God, keep shouting. And when someone tells you to quiet down, shout even louder! God will hear you and have compassion on you, just as Jesus did with the blind beggars. Should your friends not think it's cool to search for God, don't let that silence you. Shout even louder!

Live it out: Are you embarrassed for people to know you are searching for God? Don't let others quiet you or stop your pursuit of Him. Find a way this week to shout even louder in your search for Jesus!

Pray about it: Shout even louder in your prayers this week. Is there something you've been praying about but haven't sensed an answer yet? Keep praying about it, believing that God will hear and have compassion.

JUL 11

If You Have Something Nice to Say, Then Say It!

But encourage one another daily, as long as it is called "Today." Hebrews 3:13.

It has been years since I graduated from high school, but I can still remember some of the nice things my classmates wrote in my yearbook my senior year. I've lived in seven states since high school, and I haven't even seen that yearbook in the past five or six states. While it may not have survived all of those moves, the kind words people wrote in it are still with me.

I also remember a few insults spoken to me during those years. I carried the sting of those cruel words long afterward.

You rarely know the impact your words will have on someone. The words you say—whether cruel or kind—will often remain with people for years. Something you blurt out without thinking can become lodged in their heart. That's why it is important to speak words that will build them up instead of tearing them down. Even people who don't seem to require affirmation (or who don't seem bothered by insults) need to hear kind words.

Scripture tells us not to miss an opportunity to say nice things. If you have anything nice to say, go ahead and speak it now: "But encourage one another daily, as long as it is called 'Today'" (Hebrews 3:13).

Compliment someone's work, affirm their talent, tell them they are funny or smart. It won't hurt a thing, and it can only do good. First Thessalonians 5:11 urges, "Therefore encourage one another and build each other up, just as in fact you are doing."

Live it out: Say kind words to three people today. Tell them in person, or send them a message. It will make their day.

Pray about it: Thank God for the people who have said kind things to you. Ask Him to give you the right words to encourage those who cross your path today.

The Voices in Your Head

We demolish arguments and every pretension that sets itself up against the knowledge of God, and we take captive every thought to make it obedient to Christ. 2 Corinthians 10:5.

You're not crazy if you hear voices in your head. An old saying claims that we're crazy only if we start talking back to them. The Bible, however, says something a little different. Scripture tells us that we have to get in our heads and show our thoughts who's boss—even if that means talking back to them.

According to 2 Corinthians 10:5, every time we have a thought that doesn't agree with the Bible, we have to take that thought prisoner and remove it from our brain: "We demolish arguments and every pretension that sets itself up against the knowledge of God, and we take captive every thought to make it obedient to Christ."

Let's assume that you have a negative thought that keeps creeping into your mind, something such as *I'm such an idiot* or *I'm so stupid*. Those thoughts don't line up with what the Bible says, so you need to stop yourself every time Satan tries to sneak them into your mind. Then, as 2 Corinthians 10:5 says, you have to take that imprisoned thought and change it to something that is "obedient to Christ." The best way to do that is to replace the downer thought with something straight out of Scripture. In this case, when you catch yourself thinking, *I'm such an idiot*, you could replace it with the verse, "I am fearfully and wonderfully made; your works are wonderful" (Psalm 139:14).

Here's what it comes down to: Satan and God are both trying to tell you something about yourself. One or the other of these forces constantly seeks to influence your thoughts. Satan will try to tear you down and make you feel hopeless and inadequate. Whenever you catch yourself with one of his thoughts in your mind, take it prisoner. Replace it with the gracious, uplifting words of God.

Live it out: Start today to take your negative thoughts captive. As soon as a defeating, negative thought comes to mind, replace it with something from Scripture. Tell yourself, "I will believe God instead of Satan."

Pray about it: Ask God to help you spot the lies that Satan has slipped into your mind. Ask for help retraining your thoughts, so that you won't be trapped by negativity.

JUL 13

Live It Out!

And we know that in all things God works for the good of those who love him,
who have been called according to his purpose. Romans 8:28.

An idea that stood out to me from this week's devotional readings:

_____

_____

_____

A verse from this week's devotions that was powerful to me:

_____

_____

_____

A "Live it out" challenge I tried this week:

_____

_____

_____

Something that happened this week that was a blessing:

_____

_____

_____

My prayer today (thanks, requests, praises):

_____

_____

_____

Living by the Golden Rule

Do to others as you would have them do to you. Luke 6:31.

Called the golden rule for a reason, it really is the gold standard for how to treat other people: "Do to others as you would have them do to you" (Luke 6:31). Excellent advice . . . but easier said than done.

If there were a silver rule (a second-place, runner-up rule), it would probably be something like "Do to your friends and family as you would have them do to you." That is, be nice to the people you like. However, when Jesus gave the golden rule, He said it really isn't enough to be nice just to nice people. "If you love those who love you, what credit is that to you? Even sinners love those who love them. And if you do good to those who are good to you, what credit is that to you? Even sinners do that" (verses 32, 33).

Jesus goes on to explain that while the rest of the world may be living by the silver rule (being nice to nice people), God calls Christians to live by the golden rule. "Love your enemies, do good to them, and lend to them without expecting to get anything back. Then your reward will be great, and you will be children of the Most High, because he is kind to the ungrateful and wicked" (verse 35).

Are there those in your life who you think don't *deserve* kindness? They are the very people to whom Jesus said you should be nice. Or is there someone you ignore, avoid, or insult? Jesus says you'll be happier if you change your ways and treat them as you would want to be treated. Has someone been cruel to you? Jesus says that you should love them and do nice things for them. Proverbs 25:21, 22 explains it this way: "If your enemy is hungry, give him food to eat; if he is thirsty, give him water to drink. In doing this, you will heap burning coals on his head, and the Lord will reward you."

According to Jesus, that silver rule of being nice to nice people just won't cut it. The real reward—and real happiness—will come only when we love others as extravagantly as He loves us. Luckily for us, He follows His own advice and treats us a lot better than we deserve.

Live it out: Find at least one way this week to live out the golden rule.
Pray about it: Thank God for treating you with extravagant love and kindness.

An Unbelievable Free-Throw Contest

And do not forget to do good and to share with others, for with such sacrifices God is pleased. Hebrews 13:16.

Allan Guei was an 18-year-old student with great basketball skills *and* great grades. The combination made him eligible for Compton High School's free-throw contest, in which the top prize was $40,000 in scholarship money.

Allan knew the money would make a big difference for his family, who had immigrated to the United States from the Ivory Coast. Although under high pressure, he didn't crack—and beat the other seven finalists and netted the $40,000!

Now, this is where the story gets really interesting. A few weeks after the competition, Allan found out he'd scored a full-ride basketball scholarship to California State University-Northridge. And to make things even better, Allan was eligible to accept the full-ride scholarship *and* keep most of the $40,000 free-throw prize.

But he couldn't stop thinking about the seven other talented competitors from the free-throw contest. They too had dreams to go to college—and very real needs for financial assistance. So Allan decided to donate his $40,000 winnings to the other seven students.

"I've already been blessed so much, and I know we're living with a bad economy, so I know this money can really help my classmates," he said. "It was the right decision."

Having earned that money, he had every right to hang on to it. No one would have blamed him if he had kept the prize. But he chose to be generous and thoughtful. As a result, seven other lives changed.

The Bible encourages us to look out for others, and not just ourselves: "Do nothing out of selfish ambition or vain conceit. Rather, in humility value others above yourselves, not looking to your own interests but each of you to the interests of the others" (Philippians 2:3, 4). That's exactly what Allan did.

Live it out: Look out for someone else's interests this week. Find a way to help someone with an act of generosity or kindness.

Pray about it: Ask God to enable you to have the humility to value others above yourself.

The Poison of Not Forgiving

Forgive, and you will be forgiven. Luke 6:37.

Not forgiving someone is like drinking poison and hoping the other person dies. You think you're getting back at them, but you really are only killing yourself.

When someone has hurt or disappointed you, it is hard to forgive them. We fear that if we forgive them, we would then be letting them off the hook. Or that forgiving them would be acknowledging that what they did was OK. Perhaps they will hurt us again if we forgive them. None of this, however, is true.

Rather, forgiveness means you will not carry around resentment and hatred anymore. Instead, you trust God to take care of your life—and the other person's life. Because He has forgiven you for a ton of things, you have no right not to forgive someone else.

Forgiveness doesn't mean you forget what happened to you or that you put yourself back in a situation that will injure you again. It just allows you to release the pain to God, and you tell Him that you don't want the grudge to eat away at you anymore.

Forgiveness usually doesn't happen immediately. The memory and negative feelings may return, so you may have to repeatedly say, "I forgive that person." Each time you sincerely say this and give the pain to God, the hurt will fade a little more.

Check out this interaction between Peter and Jesus: "Then Peter came to Jesus and asked, 'Lord, how many times shall I forgive my brother or sister who sins against me? Up to seven times?' Jesus answered, 'I tell you, not seven times, but seventy-seven times'" (Matthew 18:21, 22). Jesus wants us to forgive again and again.

He promises that He will forgive us, as we forgive others. Mark 11:25 says, "And when you stand praying, if you hold anything against anyone, forgive them, so that your Father in heaven may forgive you your sins."

Live it out: Is there someone you need to forgive? Close your eyes and imagine dragging that person to the foot of the cross! Tell God you want to be released from the pain and hurt of what happened. Let Him know that you forgive the person and are surrendering the situation—and the outcome—to Him.

Pray about it: Ask God for forgiveness. Be specific. Thank Him for forgiving you.

JUL 17

Facing Crazy, Impossible Stuff

With man this is impossible, but not with God; all things are possible with God.
Mark 10:27.

Have you ever faced a situation that looks impossible? If so, probably one of two thoughts ran through your mind: "What was I thinking? There's no way this can be done" or "You know what? This looks crazy, but I can do anything (anything!) that God wants me to do."

The Israelites faced a situation that seemed impossible, and they were torn between those two responses. Here's how it all went down. The Israelites had been miraculously freed from slavery in Egypt. After that enormous version of a prison break, God had them wander around in the desert for a while, to give them time to have an attitude adjustment. Apparently almost everyone in the whole lot was a cranky, unappreciative complainer. After about 15 months out in the desert, the Lord led them to the border of Canaan, the Promised Land.

But before they could move into the neighborhood, they faced just one small problem: people already lived there. So the Israelites chose 12 of their bravest leaders to scope out the place.

Five weeks later the 12 men arrived back at camp, announcing that Canaan was everything they'd imagined—and more. But after they talked it up, 10 of the exploring spies declared, "We can't attack those people; they are stronger than we are" (Numbers 13:31). They thought it was definitely impossible to take the land.

However, two of the spies felt that the Israelites should go for it. Caleb, for example, said, "We should go up and take possession of the land, for we can certainly do it" (verse 30). And the great leader Joshua agreed: "The land we passed through is exceedingly good. If the Lord is pleased with us, he will lead us into that land, a land flowing with milk and honey, and will give it to us. . . . And do not be afraid of the people of the land" (Numbers 14:7-9).

All of those 12 men saw the same situation. Ten of them thought it was hopeless, and two of them regarded it as possible with God's help. When you face a situation that seems impossible, look at it like Caleb and Joshua would: if God's on your side, it can be done!

Live it out: Have a refreshing, faith-filled attitude about things that seem impossible.
Pray about it: Ask God to increase your courage and faith.

The Language Barrier

Why is my language not clear to you? John 8:43.

A few years ago my husband—who is a pastor—and I went on a trip to Germany with a group of other pastors. It was a Reformation tour, in which we traced the steps of some truly influential God followers.

One evening after a day of learning about Martin Luther, a group of us stopped in a little German restaurant for dinner. Nestled in a tiny town, the restaurant probably didn't get many tourists. No one on the staff spoke even a word of English. No problem, said one of the pastors. He had studied German back in the day, he assured us, so he would easily place our order in German.

With great confidence he started off our order with a glass of water for everyone. His German sounded just fine to me, so I was impressed. That is, until five minutes later when our waiter returned with a round of beers for all of us. (By the way, my husband did take a photo of that pastor with all those beers, just in case he ever needed it for blackmail purposes . . .)

Honestly, it is very difficult to communicate across a language barrier. Even if you think you're getting your message through, it may be completely misunderstood. When Jesus was on earth, He found a language barrier between Him and His disciples. They couldn't understand what He was saying, so He used stories, or parables, to get His point across. In Matthew 13:13 Jesus explains, "This is why I speak to them in parables: Though seeing, they do not see; though hearing, they do not hear or understand."

Fortunately, the more we talk and listen to God, the more we come to understand His language. Jesus told His disciples that eventually they would grasp Him and His language so clearly that He could communicate more directly with them. John 16:25 records His words to them: "Though I have been speaking figuratively, a time is coming when I will no longer use this kind of language but will tell you plainly about my Father."

If there's a language barrier between you and God, just keep talking and listening. The more you communicate with each other, the more you'll understand.

Live it out: Break down the language barrier. Listen to God by reading His words in the Bible.
Pray about it: Talk to God as if you were speaking to a friend.

JUL 19

Going Out on an Anti-Date

Flee from sexual immorality. I Corinthians 6:18.

In 1997 Pastor Josh Harris wrote *I Kissed Dating Goodbye*, a book about the advantages of courting instead of dating. The idea of courtship seemed totally old-fashioned to most people until this young, hip pastor brought the idea into the modern dating scene. During the next few years 1 million people bought that book—and many young Christians across the nation decided they too would try courtship instead of traditional dating.

As you make decisions about your approach to dating, take a look at the differences between dating and courting. Dating is, well, you know what it is. You ask someone out, or they ask you out, and the two of you head out to, say, Olive Garden or some other activity. People who date might end up playing the field, going on a date with one person this weekend and a different one the next weekend.

Courting, on the other hand, is considered anti-dating by some people. Don't get me wrong. By anti-dating, I don't mean staying in your room alone doing geometry on a Saturday night. No, this kind of anti-dating just means you are more intentional and focused than casual dating. For example, courtship usually involves group activities, little or no physical touch, and high parental involvement (yes, that means the person you are courting comes over to your house and gets to know your family). The goal is to take it slow and really become acquainted with the person to discover whether you two would make a good married couple.

In a world that glamorizes a hot dating scene, courtship may sound boring. However, thousands of teens and young adults have happily opted out of the pressure-filled dating game to try a new approach. As you and your parents talk about what your dating/courting future might hold, consider the options. Most important, don't rush. Trust God to work out the very best plan for your relationships.

Live it out: Ask a married couple you admire to tell you about how they met and dated (or courted). Listen to their stories, and learn from their successes and mistakes.

Pray about it: Ask God to give you the patience and wisdom to follow His lead when it comes to dating, courtship, and marriage.

Live It Out!

Whoever does not love does not know God, because God is love. I John 4:8.

An idea that stood out to me from this week's devotional readings:

_____

_____

_____

A verse from this week's devotions that was powerful to me:

_____

_____

_____

A "Live it out" challenge I tried this week:

_____

_____

_____

Something that happened this week that was a blessing:

_____

_____

_____

My prayer today (thanks, requests, praises):

_____

_____

_____

How Much Money Is *Enough*?

Whoever loves money never has enough; whoever loves wealth is never satisfied with their income. Ecclesiastes 5:10.

Some things in life it seems you just can't have too much of. Happiness, for example. *You can't have too much of that, right?* What about good looks? *You can't be too good-looking, can you?* And then there's money. *The more, the better, right?* Wrong. When it comes to cash, you actually can have too much—according to the Bible.

Proverbs 30:7-9 records the prayer of Agur, in which he asks God to give him neither too *much* nor too *little* money:

"Two things I ask of you, Lord; do not refuse me before I die:

Keep falsehood and lies far from me; give me neither poverty nor riches,

but give me only my daily bread.

Otherwise, I may have too much and disown you and say, 'Who is the Lord?'

Or I may become poor and steal, and so dishonor the name of my God."

According to this passage, if you have too little money, you'll be tempted to steal. But if you have too much, you may forget your need of God.

Don't spend all your life and energy trying to pile up more money. Instead, pray Agur's prayer and ask for enough—but not so much that you forget all about God.

Live it out: Take time to evaluate carefully your beliefs about money. Do you think it is possible to have too much money? If you were a billionaire, do you think you would still feel a need for God? In what ways can you honor Him with your money—no matter how much or how little you have?

Pray about it: Ask God to provide your "daily bread" (Proverbs 30:8)—what you need to survive each day. Pray that you will always honor and remember God, no matter how much or how little money you have.

Stuck in the Mud

He lifted me out of the slimy pit, out of the mud and mire. Psalm 40:2.

Kathleen Shino was a stick-in-the-mud. Literally. In 2011 the 62-year-old grandmother took a walk one evening near her Florida home, and she got stuck in the mud—for four days!

For unexplained medical reasons, Kathleen had blacked out while taking a walk and had fallen into a swampy area. After she had spent 90 long hours in the heat and mud—without food or water—one of her neighbors heard her faint cry and called 911.

When rescuers spotted her, all they could see was her face peeking out of the watery mess. Rescuers used chain saws to hack through vines and branches to pull her to safety.

During those torturous four days, Kathleen managed to laugh a few times when she thought about the people who pay money to sit in mud spas. She would chuckle, concluding that sitting in mud isn't all it's cracked up to be. Apart from those few laughs, though, her time in the pit was miserable. She kept wondering if she would die—or if she already had.

Chances are you'll never get stuck in a muddy swamp. Yet the odds are that you *will* get trapped in a muddy, discouraging situation. For those times in muddy pits, take comfort in Psalm 40:1-3, verses especially about being in the pits:

"I waited patiently for the Lord;
     he turned to me and heard my cry.
He lifted me out of the slimy pit,
     out of the mud and mire;
he set my feet on a rock
     and gave me a firm place to stand.
He put a new song in my mouth,
     a hymn of praise to our God.
Many will see and fear the Lord
     and put their trust in him."

Live it out: When you feel down in the pits, do what the psalmist did: wait for the Lord, cry out to Him, and sing songs of praise. Don't give up. Let God pull you out.
Pray about it: Talk to God about whatever has you down. Ask Him to pull you out of the pit.

Bored With Church

Now you are the body of Christ, and each one of you is a part of it.
1 Corinthians 12:27.

"Church is boring!" is one of the most common complaints I hear from teenagers, and to be perfectly honest, from adults too. Before you groan those words again, take a minute to think about the church.

Ask yourself, *Who is the church?* According to the Bible, we—you and I—are the church: "Now you are the body of Christ, and each one of you is a part of it" (1 Corinthians 12:27). Do you think *you* are boring? If not, what can you do to make church more interesting? Since you are the church, then you are as responsible as the next person for making it less boring.

Here are a few things you can do to take the boring and snoring out of your church experience:

- **Don't think of church as entertainment.** It isn't a movie but an opportunity to worship. Instead of questioning "What's in this for me?" ask "What can I do in this to worship God?" Sing as a way to worship Him. Listen as a way to worship Him. Give offerings as a way to worship Him. Think of ways you can go from a spectator to a participant.
- **Be the change.** Talk to your youth leader and your peers about what you can do to contribute to the church service. Maybe you would focus better on the sermon if you were running the church's video camera or tweeting key thoughts. Find a fresh, new way to change your church experience. It will make church less boring for you—and for others.
- **Come prepared.** Bring your Bible, study the lesson for the day, or take notes during the sermon. The more involved you get, the less boring it will feel. Ask what the leader or pastor will be speaking about next week, and read about it ahead of time. That way you'll already have sparked some interest and knowledge about the subject.

Live it out: Do one thing this week that will make your church experience less boring.

Pray about it: Ask God for guidance on how you can help wake up your church and make it more interesting for teens.

A Ridiculously Simple Strategy

Then the Lord said to Joshua, "See, I have delivered Jericho into your hands."
Joshua 6:2.

Sometimes problems seem bigger the more you think about them. Take, for example, the argument you had with your friend. The more you replay it in your mind, the angrier you get and the more irreparable your friendship seems. The SAT exam you're scheduled to take is another example. The more you think about it, the more pressure you feel to do well so that you can get a scholarship, because if you don't get a scholarship, you won't be able to go to college, and then you won't be able to get a job, and then you won't be able to afford to have a home or a spouse or a car or children. See how that goes? The more you dwell upon it, the worse it seems.

Joshua may have felt that way when he looked out over Jericho. He knew the Israelites needed to conquer it, but how could their makeshift army ever match up against Jericho's? Maybe Joshua was thinking about this very thing when a man with a drawn sword appeared in front of him one day. But it wasn't just any man. He identified Himself as the "commander of the army of the Lord" (Joshua 5:14), and Joshua realized that He was talking to the Lord Himself!

The Commander of the heavenly army told Joshua exactly what he wanted to know: a strategy for conquering the formidable city of Jericho. When the Lord started giving directions, Joshua probably felt tempted to get out pen and paper. Surely it was going to be a complicated, intricate strategy, right? Wrong. It was absurdly simple, actually: march around the city every day for six days. On the seventh day, Israel's forces should circle the city seven times, with priests blowing trumpets. Then everyone would scream at the top of their lungs, and the walls of the city would collapse.

Now it suddenly all seemed so simple to Joshua. It had been so complicated and intimidating before, when he was trying to figure it out on his own. But when he allowed God to take over, everything became so perfectly doable and trouble-free.

Live it out: Think of something that you are trying to work out on your own. Decide today to let God be the commander of the difficulty. Set aside quiet time to pray and reflect about the situation. Ask God how He wants you to handle it.

Pray about it: Pray, "Lord, I trust You to lead me and guide me. I believe Your strategies for dealing with life are better than my own. Thank You for having a plan to help me."

JUL 25

Thread-the-Needle Day

For the love of money is a root of all kinds of evil. I Timothy 6:10.

Once again, I've uncovered a little-known holiday that no one cares about. (Drum roll, please.) Today is . . . Thread-the-Needle Day. Granted, it could be an especially fun day if you like to sew. Statistically speaking, though, there's probably only one person reading this book who enjoys doing that. But, hey, to that one crafty sewer, I send a hearty "Happy-Thread-the-Needle-Day" greeting. Nevertheless, for those of you who don't sew, don't count the day out yet. The saying "thread the needle" has another meaning that might interest you. It also refers to doing something difficult, which threading a needle can certainly be.

Even Jesus mentioned the challenge of getting an object through the eye of a needle. Listen to this: "Then Jesus said to his disciples, 'Truly I tell you, it is hard for someone who is rich to enter the kingdom of heaven. Again I tell you, it is easier for a camel to go through the eye of a needle than for someone who is rich to enter the kingdom of God'" (Matthew 19:23, 24).

If you're not busy sewing something right now, take a minute to think about what Jesus said. When we get a lot of money, it's easy to lose sight of spiritual things. The kingdom of God doesn't matter as much to us when we are busy building our own kingdom.

A lot of us dream of having tons of money. It can definitely be a real blessing when used for good. But we shouldn't love money so much that we don't love God anymore. We'll focus on either money or God: "No one can serve two masters. Either you will hate the one and love the other, or you will be devoted to the one and despise the other. You cannot serve both God and money" (Matthew 6:24).

This Thread-the-Needle Day, make the commitment: "I will love God more than money." And if you're feeling especially crafty, you can even thread a needle and cross-stitch that saying onto a pillow.

Live it out: When considering your future career, do you think about what would please God or only about what would make the most money? Always start by asking for God's guidance.

Pray about it: Ask God to help you establish a healthy relationship to money.

214

Holy Hypocrites

On the outside you appear to people as righteous but on the inside you are full of hypocrisy and wickedness. Matthew 23:28.

Like it or not, you're going to run into hypocrites. Such people pretend to be one thing in public, but are completely different in private. Jesus met lots of hypocrites. (He even called them hypocrites to their faces!) You'll also encounter droves of them too (although, since you aren't the Savior, you might not want to call them hypocrites, as He did).

Even though hypocrisy can be a major turnoff in Christianity, you can't let it ruin your spiritual experience. Sure, there are hypocrites in the church, but there are also genuine, humble people there too.

How do you handle hypocrisy? Here are a few things to keep in mind:

- **Don't be a hypocrite yourself.** Several times Jesus told people not to be like the hypocrites: "So when you give to the needy, do not announce it with trumpets, as the hypocrites do. . . . When you pray, do not be like the hypocrites, for they love to pray standing in the synagogues and on the street corners to be seen by others" (Matthew 6:2-5). "When you fast, do not look somber as the hypocrites do, for they disfigure their faces to show others they are fasting" (verse 16).
- **Mind your own business.** More good advice from Jesus about hypocrisy: don't criticize someone else if you have problems of your own. "You hypocrite, first take the plank out of your own eye, and then you will see clearly to remove the speck from your brother's eye" (Matthew 7:5).
- **Trust the Holy Spirit.** Don't give up on God or the church because of hypocrites. The Holy Spirit is still working in their lives, just as He is still doing in yours.

Live it out: Is there someone you have criticized or disliked because they seemed to be hypocrites? How does God want you to treat them? Find a way to show genuine kindness to them this week.

Pray about it: Ask God to reveal your own areas of weakness. Pray David's prayer: "Create in me a pure heart, O God" (Psalm 51:10).

Live It Out!

The Lord is my shepherd, I lack nothing. Psalm 23:1.

An idea that stood out to me from this week's devotional readings:

_____

_____

_____

A verse from this week's devotions that was powerful to me:

_____

_____

_____

A "Live it out" challenge I tried this week:

_____

_____

_____

Something that happened this week that was a blessing:

_____

_____

_____

My prayer today (thanks, requests, praises):

_____

_____

_____

The Daniel Challenge

At the end of the ten days they looked healthier and better nourished than any of the young men who ate the royal food. Daniel 1:15.

In 605 B.C. King Nebuchadnezzar of Babylon declared war on Jerusalem. He took captives and ordered the finest young men of Jerusalem brought to Babylon to learn the language and culture in preparation for service in the royal court. According to the Bible, those selected were healthy, attractive, intelligent, and well-educated. The king would provide them not only training but also the finest food and wine. In fact, they would receive the same diet as the king himself.

You would think they would consider it a privilege to have the opportunity to dine like royalty, but four men asked to be exempted from the king's fare. Daniel, Hananiah, Mishael, and Azariah (given the new names of Belteshazzar, Shadrach, Meshach, and Abednego) asked the head of the palace staff for healthier, simpler food.

The steward hesitated to agree, fearful the king would kill him if the men weren't as healthy as the others. But the four Hebrews assured him they would perform even better mentally and physically on a more natural diet.

Daniel proposed a plan: "Please test your servants for ten days: Give us nothing but vegetables to eat and water to drink. Then compare our appearance with that of the young men who eat the royal food, and treat your servants in accordance with what you see" (Daniel 1:12, 13). The steward agreed, and after just 10 days he noticed the four young men did indeed seem stronger and healthier than the others.

As a result, Daniel and his friends continued to receive exemption from the royal diet. At the end of the training period, King Nebuchadnezzar himself interviewed them. The ruler found them far superior to all the other young men.

Never be afraid to take a stand for what you believe in. God's plan for you will turn out better than the most extravagant ones of an earthly monarch.

Live it out: Take the Daniel Challenge. For 10 days, eat healthy food. See if you can tell a difference in how you feel and your ability to concentrate at school.
Pray about it: Ask for the courage to take a stand for God.

Even if He Does Not

But even if he does not, we want you to know, Your Majesty, that we will not serve your gods or worship the image of gold you have set up. Daniel 3:18.

Shadrach, Meshach, and Abednego were just pushing their luck now. It's one thing to ask for their own special food, as they did when they first arrived at the king's court. But it is an entirely different matter to refuse to bow down to his golden image. That was simply deplorable.

When it concerned his golden image, King Nebuchadnezzar wasn't joking around. He gave very clear orders: "Whoever does not fall down and worship will immediately be thrown into a blazing furnace" (Daniel 3:6).

But Shadrach, Meshach, and Abednego hadn't come this far to turn back now. They worshipped only one God and would refuse to bend the knee to Nebuchadnezzar's image. Sure, when the order went out to bow down, they could pretend to be lacing their sandals or looking at a bug on the ground—some fake-out to keep the authorities off their back. But they would not compromise in any way.

Word that the three men were not bowing down infuriated the king, and he ordered them to explain themselves. Confidently, the men declared, "We do not need to defend ourselves before you in this matter. If we are thrown into the blazing furnace, the God we serve is able to deliver us from it, and he will deliver us from Your Majesty's hand. But even if he does not, we want you to know, Your Majesty, that we will not serve your gods or worship the image of gold you have set up" (verses 16-18).

The men's simple but assertive reply says a lot: they believed that God could save them, but *"even if he does not,"* they would still follow Him. They were willing to take a stand for God—even if it meant they would die.

Live it out: Is there an area in your life in which you sense God asking you to take a stand? Will you uphold your beliefs, even if you aren't sure of the outcome?
Pray about it: Thank God for always having your back and standing up for you.

A Hot-headed King and a Hot Furnace

Look! I see four men walking around in the fire, unbound and unharmed, and the fourth looks like a son of the gods. Daniel 3:25.

Surely powerful King Nebuchadnezzar could change the mind of Shadrach, Meshach, and Abednego. Surely they would just bow down to his golden image. Surely they would come around to his way of thinking when they saw the flames and felt the heat of the furnace. Surely.

But even after the king told them, "Bow down, or else," they would not.

Now it looked as if they would die. Surely.

Their refusal to bow down made the king so angry that he ordered the men be thrown into the blazing furnace—but only after it was heated seven times hotter than usual. The Bible says, "The king's command was so urgent and the furnace so hot that the flames of the fire killed the soldiers who took up Shadrach, Meshach and Abednego" (Daniel 3:22).

The king watched the men thrown into the blazing fire. He expected them to turn to ashes within seconds. It looked as if they were walking around in there—along with a fourth individual who resembled a god.

Realizing that the three men were servants of the Most High God, Nebuchadnezzar shouted at them to leave the furnace. Out they came, just as if they'd been on a stroll through the city park: "The fire had not harmed their bodies, nor was a hair of their heads singed; their robes were not scorched, and there was no smell of fire on them" (verse 27).

The scene was so amazing that even King Nebuchadnezzar couldn't keep from extolling their God. Daniel 3:28, 29 says, "Then Nebuchadnezzar said, 'Praise be to the God of Shadrach, Meshach and Abednego, who has sent his angel and rescued his servants!'"

Live it out: When you take a stand for God, it can encourage others to believe. Think of someone in history, in the Bible, or in your life who took a stand and inspired others.

Pray about it: Thank God for the people who have inspired you by taking a stand for God.

Nice Guys Finish Last
(or Is That First?)

So the last will be first, and the first will be last. Matthew 20:16.

"Nice guys finish last," the saying goes. Ever feel as if that's true? While you're just trying to keep your nose down and do your best, troublemakers seem to catch all the breaks. The guy who cheated on the test gets the highest score. *Not cool.* The conniving girl ends up dating the nicest guy in school. *Not cool.*

Even though it may sometimes appear as if the bad guys get the happy endings, the Bible has something else to say about that. In Psalm 37 David advises us not to worry about people who are doing evil, because God will reward you for doing the right thing:

"Do not fret because of those who are evil or be envious of those who do wrong.... Trust in the Lord and do good; dwell in the land and enjoy safe pasture. Take delight in the Lord, and he will give you the desires of your heart. Commit your way to the Lord; trust in him and he will do this: He will make your righteous reward shine like the dawn, your vindication like the noonday sun" (Psalm 37: 1-6).

Jesus reinforced this idea when He said, "So the last will be first, and the first will be last" (Matthew 20:16). It may look as if someone is getting ahead, but it's all just a short-lived illusion if they aren't following God. According to Jesus, heaven plays by different rules than earth does.

The people who follow Him will have the truly happy ending. It's a bit of a riddle, but I suppose nice guys *do* finish last—which according to Jesus, is *first!* Keep on the straight and narrow, and when it's all said and done, God will make sure you come out a winner.

Live it out: Are you ever tempted to "fret because of those who are evil or be envious of those who do wrong" (Psalm 37:1)? If so, make a commitment to stick with what's right, even if it doesn't seem like the most rewarding plan. Watch and see how God sets everything in order, because He will.

Pray about it: Ask forgiveness for times you have cheated, lied, or manipulated to get ahead. Pray for the perseverance and faith to stick with God's plan—no matter what other people around you are doing.

The Tower of Babbling Babblers

I will glorify your name forever. Psalm 86:12.

"Make a name for yourself!" It's common advice to graduates and up-and-comers ready to take on the world. The message: make yourself famous, so that everyone will recognize you. But before you go out and do it, it's a good idea to read the story of the Tower of Babel first.

After the Flood, the whole world had one language. They also had one mission: "Come, let us build ourselves a city, with a tower that reaches to the heavens, so that we may make a name for ourselves" (Genesis 11:4). Pay attention to their goal: they wanted to make a name for themselves. They weren't building for God's glory or for some greater good. Instead, they sought to prove how great *they* were.

The Lord saw their towering plan and decided to break it up. God knew where it could lead: with all these evil people able to scheme and plan together, they would continue to do even more evil things. Today, a tower. Tomorrow, who could even guess?

You know how the teachers split up troublemakers when they see that they're up to no good? He or she will put one troublemaker on one side of the classroom and one on the other, so that they won't be able to talk to each other anymore. That's a little like what God did. He just did it on a grander scale.

He went down and divided the people by mixing up everyone's speech. Some began speaking one language, and others another. You can imagine what kind of confusion that caused in the middle of a massive building project! That's exactly why the tower is called the Tower of Babel, which means the Tower of Confusion.

God wants you to accomplish great, lofty things in your life. However, He never calls us to do mighty things to make a name for ourselves. When we devote our lives to God, our achievements should be to glorify Him. Otherwise things will just end in confusion, like at that old Tower of Confusion.

Live it out: Surrender your plans to God, and then watch and see what He builds in your life. You'll love what He has in mind for you more than any plan you could build on your own.

Pray about it: Pray that what you do today and every day will glorify God.

The Millionaire Janitor

But he gave up his place with God and made himself nothing. He was born as a man and became like a servant. Philippians 2:7, NCV.

Tyrone Curry was a janitor with serious money problems. But then his luck changed. In the midst of filing bankruptcy, Tyrone experienced any janitor's dream come true: he won the lottery!

His wife realized the good news first, so she called him at Evergreen High School, where he worked. When he asked how much they had won, she wasn't even sure. She tried to explain that it was a three and then a four followed by a lot of zeros. The number she was trying to describe was $3,410,000. Yes, $3.4 million, but who's counting?

You would think Tyrone would have dropped his mop bucket on the spot. Why clean toilets at a high school if you're a millionaire, after all? Yet Tyrone had other plans. He kept his dirty job—toilets and all.

Tyrone continues to work as the school's janitor and track coach. He and his wife still live simply. They don't travel much or even eat out very often. Their biggest splurges were a heat pump, vinyl siding, and a new driveway for their small home. Not too glamorous, huh?

The most spectacular thing Tyrone did with his big winnings wasn't for himself. Besides continuing to give his time to the school's track team, he also donated funds for a new state-of-the-art track.

The locals call Tyrone a hero, because he chose a simple life of helping others instead of a flashy, self-centered one. If that's the definition of hero, then Jesus is the ultimate hero. He could have stayed as king in the luxury of heaven, but He gave that up to come live on this shabby old shack of a planet. He abandoned His magnificent life to be the ultimate janitor and clean up our dirty old planet.

Live it out: Imagine what heaven might look like. Picture it as magnificent and fantastic as your imagination allows (because it's even better than that!). Now think about how much Jesus must love us to have left that behind to live on earth.
Pray about it: Say a prayer of thanks for Jesus' sacrifice to come to earth to save us.

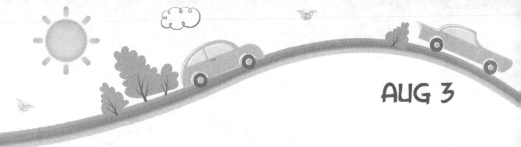

Live It Out!

Repent and be baptized, every one of you, in the name of Jesus Christ for the forgiveness of your sins. And you will receive the gift of the Holy Spirit. Acts 2:38.

An idea that stood out to me from this week's devotional readings:

_____

_____

_____

A verse from this week's devotions that was powerful to me:

_____

_____

_____

A "Live it out" challenge I tried this week:

_____

_____

_____

Something that happened this week that was a blessing:

_____

_____

_____

My prayer today (thanks, requests, praises):

_____

_____

_____

The Never-ending Prayer

Pray continually. I Thessalonians 5:17.

Apparently teens have gotten a bad rap when it comes to spiritual activities. Some adults assume they have no interest in God, but research shows that teens are actually some of the most spiritually active Americans. Their most common spiritual activity is praying, which is twice as popular as studying the Bible or attending a youth group.

What research doesn't reveal, however, is just how long or meaningful those prayers are. I did a little informal research of my own (OK, by that I mean I asked around among my teen friends). They said some of the most common times they pray are before meals and before tests at school. Prayer has become a habit (a good one!) at those times, but getting their prayer life to spark outside of those set times is a little bit of a challenge.

The Bible tells us to pray continually, or without ceasing. Is it even possible to pray all the time? If the Bible says to do it, it must be possible, right? Sure, but it requires a new way of thinking. Having a mind-set of continual prayer is a revolutionary way to live. It means that when you are thinking—no matter what about—you are expressing it as if you were in a conversation with God. For example, if you see a guy who looks as if he is about to pick a fight with a classmate, instead of just thinking to yourself, *What is* this guy *up to?* you might ask, as if talking to God, "What is this guy up to? Is something wrong with him today?" And you would be listening, tuned in to God, to see if you were prompted with an answer or a sense that you should do or say something.

Another way to expand your prayer life is to create more prayer habits. People often pray before meals to thank God for food. But there are other points during the day when you can pray. Why not pray every time you enter your house or your room, and thank God for a place to call home? Or every time you take a shower? Or you could pray every time you come home from being with friends or church, and thank God for the people in your life.

Find creative ways to turn your thoughts into prayers, and you'll sense God talking to you all day long.

Live it out: Try to turn your undirected thoughts into conversations with God.
Pray about it: Pray about everything and anything that comes to mind today. Pray continually.

Oh, Say, Can You See?

Ears that hear and eyes that see—the Lord has made them both. Proverbs 20:12.

Soon after my husband, Robert, and I got married, he started asking me, "Does this match?" when choosing his clothes for the day. Being a bit of a fashion lover, I never turn down the chance to talk about clothes, so I was always happy to assist. Plus, he did seem to need the help, as proven by the days he dressed himself solo and ended up with a neon-green shirt and army-green shorts battling for attention. ("They're the same color," he would explain. "How could they not match?")

As it turns out, neon green and army green really do look the same to Robert. After years of dressing himself in vibrant color combinations, he took a simple test that revealed he is color-blind. (Amusingly, he took the test at the elementary school where he teaches a class. Sitting in a child-sized chair as the optician quizzed him, he was surrounded by a gaggle of 5-year-olds taunting him, saying, "You can't see that color? How can you not see that? *Everybody* can see that!")

When I found out that Robert is color-blind, I felt sad that he isn't able to view the beautiful array of colors in nature. He, on the other hand, thinks it's no big deal (to which I can only say, "That's because you don't know what you're missing!"). Nevertheless, at times his limited color spectrum has come in handy for me, such as when my hair stylist drastically transformed me from a brunet to a redhead. (As I arrived home, prepared to explain myself, he gave me a peck on the cheek and casually said, "I like your hair. It looks as if you decided not to change it much after all.")

The Bible says that none of us can see things perfectly now. We will all have blurry, impaired vision until Jesus returns. "Now we see things imperfectly like puzzling reflections in a mirror, but then we will see everything with perfect clarity. All that I know now is partial and incomplete, but then I will know everything completely, just as God now knows me completely" (1 Corinthians 13:12, NLT). Only then will we see things as God does. I'm sure we'll be amazed by all the things we weren't able to perceive all these years.

Live it out: When looking at a situation, remember God has a better view of it than you do.
Pray about it: Tell God you will trust Him, even when you can't see the bigger picture.

AUG 6

Get Creative!

In the beginning God created. Genesis 1:1.

God is creative. Just look at what He did at Creation! Animals, birds, plants, oceans, stars. Using endless combinations of shapes, sizes, and colors, He is the ultimate source of creative power. Since we are made in His image, we also have God-given creative power. When we produce beautiful or magnificent things, we are using those creative forces.

For example, when artists paint gorgeous landscapes, God has given them the imagination and ability to do so. When a musician writes and performs a stirring song, God has given them the talent for the task. The same is true when an architect conceives a spectacular building or a writer composes an inspiring book.

Creativity comes from God. He wants us to use it to bless others and make the world a better place—the same way He employs His creative forces. Even if you think you aren't creative, you are. Everyone created in God's image (and that's everyone) has some creativity coursing through their veins. You just have to discover your own area of it. Maybe you are skilled with technical things and can build something from a pile of nuts, bolts, and wires. Perhaps you are talented in the kitchen and can make a yummy meal without a recipe. Or you may be skilled with words and can make any story funny and exciting when you tell it. Creativity comes in lots of forms. When you discover your special abilities and put them to use, you are honoring God.

Live it out: Let your creativity flow! Do something today to celebrate your God-given creativity. Bake bread, sketch the view from your window, repair your mom's laptop, build a model rocket with your little brother. The sky's the limit: just think of something creative and go for it!

Pray about it: Next time you begin a project or school assignment, ask God for creative power.

The Reward for Catching a Foul Ball

Remembering the words the Lord Jesus himself said: "It is more blessed to give than to receive." Acts 20:35.

Every boy attending a pro baseball game knows how cool it is to catch a foul ball. Twelve-year-old Ian McMillan is no exception. Ian, who plays catcher for a Little League team, attended an Arizona Diamondbacks game with his friends. In a perfect combination of luck and skill, Ian snagged a prized possession: a foul ball.

But he wasn't the only one gunning for it. A younger boy—a stranger to Ian—was also trying his luck. He was obviously heartbroken and almost in tears after he missed the ball. Seeing the boy's disappointment, Ian gave his well-earned souvenir to the sad child.

Ian's good deed didn't go unnoticed. His kind act was played—and replayed—on television, and ABC News even named him Person of the Week. The boy also had some other exciting rewards: he was called up to the announcer's booth at the game, given an autographed bat, and got to throw the ceremonial first pitch at a subsequent Diamondbacks game.

God promises that our kind deeds will always get a good reward. "And if anyone gives even a cup of cold water to one of these little ones who is my disciple, truly I tell you, that person will definitely not lose their reward" (Matthew 10:42). The reward might not be an autographed baseball bat, but God will be sure to honor your kindness.

Live it out: Watch for an opportunity today to do something nice for someone else.
Pray about it: Ask God to help you develop a generous, kind spirit.

Feeling the Love
for Your Brother or Sister

A friend loves at all times, and a brother is born for a difficult time.
Proverbs 17:17, HCSB.

I grew up in a full house—a family with six children. As you can imagine, there were some fights and jealousies. If you are part of a family with two kids, then double—no, triple—the amount of drama you've personally experienced, and it will be closer to what it's like to have six kids in one household.

We all loved each other (and survived to love each other still), but at times one of us would call another a name or throw someone into a wall (Unnamed Sibling, you know who you are). But there existed a funny pattern: we thought it was OK to pick a fight with a sibling, but if someone *outside of the family* tried to taunt that sibling, we would be furious and wouldn't stand for it. We would defend each other against all outsiders. No matter what.

The Bible says it this way: "A friend loves at all times, and a brother is born for a difficult time" (Proverbs 17:17, HCSB). In other words, one of the reasons that God gives us siblings is so that we'll have someone on our side on the rough days, such as when one of you is getting picked on. And even if you don't have a sibling, God can bring friends into your life who will love you and support you "at all times."

Since God has a special plan for siblings, why waste so much time and energy fighting with them. And as they always say, once you're older, you and your sibling(s) will probably be best friends—so why not start being friends now?

Live it out: Write down the name of everyone in your family. Beside each name, write a list of that person's good qualities. Don't write anything negative—only positive. Every time one of them starts to annoy you, think about their good qualities. Pull out that list when you need a reminder.

Pray about it: Thank God for each family member by name. Pray specifically for a blessing for each person.

Crazy, Different, Good

For my thoughts are not your thoughts, neither are your ways my ways. Isaiah 55:8.

Sometimes Jesus said things that sounded like crazy talk. "The last will be first, and the first will be last" (Matthew 20;16). "For whoever wants to save their life will lose it, but whoever loses their life for me and the gospel will save it" (Mark 8:35). Compared to what most people believed, it all sounded, well, downright foolish. And apparently that was God's plan. According to Paul, "God chose the foolish things of the world to shame the wise" (1 Corinthians 1:27). That doesn't mean His followers are stupid and shouldn't use their brains. It just that God's ways might seem a little crazy sometimes, because we don't understand them.

Isaiah 55:8, 9 records it this way: "'For my thoughts are not your thoughts, neither are your ways my ways,' declares the Lord. 'As the heavens are higher than the earth, so are my ways higher than your ways and my thoughts than your thoughts.'" In other words, God's ways may puzzle us sometimes, but they are always *better* than our own.

So what does all this crazy talk have to do with your life? A lot, actually. If you follow Jesus, you're going to end up doing some things that to other people just don't make sense. For example, suppose there is someone who is being cruel to you, calling you names or spreading rumors about you. Most people would say that you should be tough in response. Let that person know that you won't stand for it. But Jesus said, "I tell you, love your enemies and pray for those who persecute you" (Matthew 5:44). I know, it sounds like crazy talk, but Jesus tells us that we should literally pray for our nemeses—and be loving to them! Romans 12:14 advises the same thing: "Give blessing and not curses to those who are cruel to you" (BBE).

God's upside-down, crazy-different-good way of thinking will affect you in other manners. Maybe He'll ask you to speak up for Him, or turn down an opportunity that doesn't match His plans for you. Or perhaps He'll ask you to be friends with someone who isn't friendly. Whatever foolish thing He asks of you, do it! Because, as Paul said, "The foolishness of God is wiser than human wisdom" (1 Corinthians 1:25).

Live it out: Is God asking you to do something "foolish" for Him? Don't worry about what other people think. Just follow God with all you've got!

Pray about it: Pray, "God, teach me to see things as You do. Give me the courage to be a fool for You!"

Live It Out!

Depend on the Lord; trust him, and he will take care of you. Psalm 37:5, NCV.

An idea that stood out to me from this week's devotional readings:

_____

_____

_____

A verse from this week's devotions that was powerful to me:

_____

_____

_____

A "Live it out" challenge I tried this week:

_____

_____

_____

Something that happened this week that was a blessing:

_____

_____

_____

My prayer today (thanks, requests, praises):

_____

_____

_____

Hooked on Happiness

Happy is the man who is guided by you. Psalm 94:12, BBE.

Not everybody wants to be famous. Nor does everybody care about having a lot of money. But almost everybody would say they want to be happy. The only problem is this: the quest for happiness sometimes makes people miserable.

Especially for teens, the search for happiness can lead to addictions. It can be any kind of addiction: food, sex, cutting, drugs, alcohol, pornography. All of them release "feel good" chemicals in the body, giving a temporary sensation of happiness. Even if it's just for a moment, such additions seem to offer a temporary escape from sadness. Unfortunately the buzz doesn't last long, and the next buzz requires more of the addictive substance or behavior. It leaves the person trapped and desperate for the next hit (whether it's chocolate or sexual attention). And each time they turn to the addiction, it destroys them a little more.

Unfortunately, some Christians misrepresent Christ. They make it look as if following Christ will zap any happiness you do have. Although they may claim that there is joy in Christ, they frown, criticize, and complain all the time. But that's not what Christ is all about. In fact, the Bible says, "Happy is the worshipper of the Lord" (Psalm 128:1, BBE). The psalmist also said to God, "Happy is the man whose hope is in you" (Psalm 84:12, BBE).

If there is really true happiness in following God, why do so many of us search for happiness in other places? Because Satan has done a bang-up job of convincing us that following God will dash any chance for happiness. He wants us to think that chasing after our addictions will make us happy. Stop believing Satan's lies. Test God's promises by putting your hope in Him, and see if it brings you happiness.

And what about those addictions? If you're struggling with one, talk to your parent or a trustworthy adult from church. Explain to them that you're struggling and need help. Ask them not to judge you, but to help you. Also tell God you're sorry and that you want a fresh start. And step by step, you'll be on your way toward true, real-life, long-lasting happiness.

Live it out: If you're struggling with an addiction, don't do it alone. Ask for help today.

Pray about it: Ask God for forgiveness and a fresh start. Be completely honest about your struggles. Talk to Him as a friend and counselor.

Quick and Easy Health Tricks

Long life to you! Good health to you and your household! And good health to all that is yours! I Samuel 25:6.

Lose 30 pounds in two weeks!" "Get ripped and build muscle *fast*!" The health industry spews out a lot of hype. Most products or promises that guarantee quick results are really scams that aren't healthy at all. True health isn't just about being thin or ripped. It's about having a healthy mind, body, and spirit.

While you shouldn't fall for the promises that a pill can make you healthier overnight, there are, however, some quick and easy things you can do to make your body happier and healthier right now. Here are just a few simple suggestions:

- **Laugh until it's funny.** A good laugh can help relax your muscles, strengthen your immune system, and lower your blood pressure. So laughing at a funny joke actually helps you fight off colds and flu. Want to know something even crazier? Faking a laugh has the same health benefits! Even if you don't think something is hilarious, give it a little laugh anyway, and it will be good for your body. So when something strikes you as humorous, give it the biggest laugh you can. It will be good for you.
- **Straighten up.** Turns out, you really should listen when your mom tells you, "Sit up straight!" The right posture minimizes pains in your neck and back, prevents your spine from becoming fixed in an abnormal position, and en- sures that your joints don't wear abnormally.
- **Go nuts.** According to an extensive study, eating just a handful of nuts at least five times a week can add two years to your life. If almonds, walnuts, and pe- cans can offer you two more fun, energetic years, why not eat them?

Live it out: Don't fall for health hype. Instead, commit to truly being healthy, not just to *looking* healthy. Today, begin to incorporate one of the health tips listed above into your life.

Pray about it: Ask God to help you have a healthy perspective about health.

Curse-free Comedy

Do not let any unwholesome talk come out of your mouths, but only what is helpful for building others up according to their needs, that it may benefit those who listen. Ephesians 4:29.

Chris Rock is a comedian, actor, writer, and producer who has become rich and famous by being funny . . . and *vulgar*. His stand-up comedy is a land mine of swearwords. When he opens his mouth, adults know to make children leave the room.

Yet he is the first to admit he is foul-mouthed and crude. He seems so confident in his offensiveness that you'd expect him to be proud of his trademark cussing. In contrast, though, he actually encourages up-and-coming comics to take a different path and keep it clean.

"When I'm talkin' to young comics, I tell 'em don't curse," he said in an interview with CBS. "I swear, I tell them all the time." The real talent, he says, is in being entertaining without cussing.

It's also a more valuable talent, according to Chris. "'Cause the money's not in cursing, you know? I mean, I'm doin' fine, I got a big house, but [comic] Ray Romano would laugh at my house. Ray Romano would [say], like 'Are you kiddin'? You want me to live in *that*?'" In another interview Chris said that comedian Jerry Seinfeld makes exponentially more than he does, because he keeps his routines curse-free. Trying to explain what he means, Chris said that his own income in comparison to Seinfeld's is as drastically different as a homeless person's income is in comparison to Chris's.

Even someone famous for cursing advises against it. It takes true flair and restraint to make your point, be funny, or express your feelings *without* resorting to crude language. Chris Rock's advice agrees with the apostle Paul's: "Let there be no filthiness nor foolish talk nor crude joking, which are out of place, but instead let there be thanksgiving" (Ephesians 5:4, ESV).

Live it out: Are there some swearwords in your vocab? This week, take the effort to make your point, be funny, or express your feelings without using such words.

Pray about it: As Ephesians 5:4 advises, say words of thanksgiving. Today say a prayer of thanks for all God has done for you.

Bible Verses for Teens

For you have been my hope, Sovereign Lord, my confidence since my youth.
Psalm 71:5.

Some teenagers think the Bible is boring. If you're one of those who would rather leave Bible study to the adults, it's time to reconsider. The Bible has a lot of words of wisdom especially for young people. Take a look at some of the verses just for you:

- "Don't let anyone look down on you because you are young, but set an example for the believers in speech, in conduct, in love, in faith and in purity" (1 Timothy 4:12).
- "Listen to your father, who gave you life, and do not despise your mother when she is old" (Proverbs 23:22).
- "Remember your Creator in the days of your youth, before the days of trouble come and the years approach when you will say, 'I find no pleasure in them'" (Ecclesiastes 12:1).
- "My child, if sinners entice you, turn your back on them!" (Proverbs 1:10, NLT).
- "Listen, my son, to your father's instruction and do not forsake your mother's teaching. They are a garland to grace your head and a chain to adorn your neck" (Proverbs 1:8, 9).
- "Flee the evil desires of youth and pursue righteousness, faith, love and peace, along with those who call on the Lord out of a pure heart. Don't have anything to do with foolish and stupid arguments, because you know they produce quarrels" (2 Timothy 2:22, 23).
- "Honor your father and your mother, so that you may live long in the land the Lord your God is giving you" (Exodus 20:12).
- "Never speak harshly to an older man, but appeal to him respectfully as you would to your own father. Talk to younger men as you would to your own brothers. Treat older women as you would your mother, and treat younger women with all purity as you would your own sisters" (1 Timothy 5:1, 2, NLT).

Live it out: Do you have a Bible study plan? Set up a system to spend more time in the Bible, so that you can read more of what God has to say to you. For example, choose a book of the Bible and read a chapter from it each night. Or start a youth study group at your church or school.

Pray about it: Thank God for including verses for youth in the Bible. Thank Him for caring about you during this time in your life.

What Are You Looking for in a Relationship?

May he give you the desire of your heart and make all your plans succeed. Psalm 20:4.

I recently saw a talk show about women looking for their "Mr. Right." Each of the panelists told the same story: they just couldn't find a guy who was "good enough." One of the women had a list so long the host lost track of how many items were on it. It went a little something like this: "handsome, at least six feet tall, brown hair, blue eyes, tan, makes more than $250,000 a year, between the ages of 38-42, from the West Coast, goofy but serious, talkative but quiet, plays golf, good dresser, owns a nice home, has a nice car, surfer, has no pets, wants two children . . ." The list went on and on with *detailed* characteristics that the woman considered nonnegotiable. Finally the host interrupted the hard-to-please woman and said, "Sounds as if you want someone *perfect*. Are you looking for a husband or Jesus?"

After that story I'm a little ashamed to admit it, but years ago I too wrote a list of things I hoped to find in a mate. (In my defense, it didn't sound like the ones on that talk show.) I wrote it during college, but I completely forgot about it until I found it years after my wedding. When I rediscovered it, I realized my husband had every characteristic on there. He was an answer to a prayer I had forgotten that I had prayed.

I had only one absolutely absurd thing on the list. I knew I was pushing my luck with this one, but I asked God for a guy who didn't have ex-girlfriends. (I'd had a bad experience with someone who always compared me to other girls, and I didn't want to live the rest of my life that way.) Would you believe it, God gave me an attractive, funny, friendly, smart Christian guy who in his mid-20s had never had a girlfriend? I was even his first kiss! (Even now I can hear the "Hallelujah Chorus" just thinking about it!)

When it comes to lists, here's the breakdown. Don't make one like those on the talk show. Don't be shallow and restrict God. *But* don't be afraid to make a list of godly traits—and stick to it. When it comes to character traits, keep your standard high. No one is perfect, but they can be perfect for you. Don't settle for less than what God has in store for you.

Live it out: Make a list of the traits of a godly spouse and pray over it, asking God to lead you.

Pray about it: Ask for the patience to wait for the person whom God has prepared for you.

The Lost Ring

Rejoice with me; I have found my lost coin. Luke 15:9.

Somehow I have managed to lose my wedding band twice. Now, when I say lose, I don't mean lose as in leaving it on the bathroom counter and finding it a few days later. I mean *lose* as in *Where in this big, big world is that thing?*

The first time I was taking a break at work with coworkers, walking through a grassy field to get some fresh air and sunshine. Somewhere along our wanderings the ring slipped off my finger. By the time I realized it was gone, I was back at my desk, already having trouble imagining where it could be. For days my friends and I used our work breaks to retrace our steps, keeping our eyes fixed on the ground. Nevertheless, the grass was too tall, and the area too vast, so I eventually gave up hope. Amazingly, weeks later another colleague, who didn't even know my ring was lost, spotted it out in the field (his eagle eye can be attributed to years of hunting for treasures and relics with a metal detector).

A year later I lost that same ring again when walking through our neighborhood. Again I didn't realize it was missing until I was miles away from it. My husband and I spent hours walking up and down the streets, as I tried to remember which sidewalks I had taken. Neighbors came out and looked in their yards and cheered us on as we searched. And once again, to everyone's amazement, we found that ring.

After losing that little treasure—and spending hours and hours hunting it down—I was elated to recover it. The longer something has been lost—and the more impossible it seems to find—the more your joy is magnified at its return. In a small way, I understand the story in Luke 15 of the woman hunting for a valuable silver coin: "Doesn't she light a lamp, sweep the house and search carefully until she finds it? And when she finds it, she calls her friends and neighbors together and says, 'Rejoice with me; I have found my lost coin'" (Luke 15: 8, 9). Luke goes on to explain that God rejoices when He finds lost people: "In the same way, I tell you, there is rejoicing in the presence of the angels of God over one sinner who repents" (verse 10). God never stops looking for us, and when He finds us, He celebrates!

Live it out: Come out of hiding, so that God can rejoice over finding you.
Pray about it: Thank God for loving you enough to search for you anywhere and everywhere.

Live It Out!

If anyone belongs to Christ, there is a new creation. The old things have gone; everything is made new! 2 Corinthians 5:17, NCV.

An idea that stood out to me from this week's devotional readings:

_____

_____

_____

A verse from this week's devotions that was powerful to me:

_____

_____

_____

A "Live it out" challenge I tried this week:

_____

_____

_____

Something that happened this week that was a blessing:

_____

_____

_____

My prayer today (thanks, requests, praises):

_____

_____

_____

Your Ears Can't Smell

Each one of us has a body with many parts, and these parts all have different uses.
Romans 12:4, NCV.

Your ears can't smell. Your eyes can't hear. Your mouth can't walk. Nor can your elbows talk. But why would they need to? You have other body parts that do those particular functions.

Every part of the body has its own important role. It's OK that your elbow doesn't talk: your mouth can do that. And why would your ears need to smell if your nose has that taken care of anyway?

The Bible says that all of the people in the church together form a body. Some of us can sing. Others of us can preach. And still others of us can cook and host dinners. When we all come together, we're like a perfectly designed body.

Romans 12:4-8 describes how we fit together: "Each one of us has a body with many parts, and these parts all have different uses. In the same way, we are many, but in Christ we are all one body. Each one is a part of that body, and each part belongs to all the other parts. We all have different gifts, each of which came because of the grace God gave us. The person who has the gift of prophecy should use that gift in agreement with the faith. Anyone who has the gift of serving should serve. Anyone who has the gift of teaching should teach. Whoever has the gift of encouraging others should encourage. Whoever has the gift of giving to others should give freely. Anyone who has the gift of being a leader should try hard when he leads. Whoever has the gift of showing mercy to others should do so with joy" (NCV).

God has made you for a very special purpose. If you don't contribute your part, the entire body will miss out. Don't be jealous of someone who can do something you can't. They're just fulfilling their part. Instead, focus on what God has designed you to do.

Live it out: Volunteer at church to serve in your area of interest and skill. If you're not sure of your role in the body, ask people who know you what they think your strengths are, or ask a pastor or teacher about taking a spiritual gifts test.
Pray about it: Ask God to help you identify and develop your spiritual gifts and talents.

Waddling Like a Penguin

Let us walk in the light of the Lord. Isaiah 2:5.

Have you ever tried on a pair of shoes in a store, but they were connected with one of those plastic security loops? All you want to do is check if the shoes fit, but you're stuck waddling around, taking embarrassingly tiny steps because the shoes are tied together. (Yeah, I know, that's annoying, right?) Well, imagine always having to go about like that.

That awkward little waddle is exactly how penguins walk every day. They have a very short distance between their feet, which causes them to toddle and totter. No surprise, then, that they look a little gawky on land. (They do, however, make up for it in the water, where their torpedo shape and little feet help them move with ease.)

Luckily, we're not stuck waddling through life. Even though our stride is more graceful than a penguin's, the Bible still gives quite a bit of instruction on how we should walk. Look at these pointers on how to travel through life:

- **Walk with the right crowd.** "Walk with the wise and become wise" (Proverbs 13:20).
- **Walk in obedience.** "Blessed are all who fear the Lord, who walk in obedience to him" (Psalm 128:1).
- **Don't be scared when you walk.** "Even though I walk through the darkest valley, I will fear no evil, for you are with me; your rod and your staff, they comfort me" (Psalm 23:4).
- **Don't walk around with troublemakers.** "Blessed is the one who does not walk in step with the wicked or stand in the way that sinners take or sit in the company of mockers" (Psalm 1:1).

God promises to help you journey through life. If you lose your footing or start feeling clumsy, He will speak words of guidance and encouragement to you. "Whether you turn to the right or to the left, your ears will hear a voice behind you, saying, 'This is the way; walk in it'" (Isaiah 30:21).

Live it out: Think of today as a path you are walking. When you make decisions, ask yourself if you're headed in the right direction. If you're not sure which direction to go, ask God for guidance.

Pray about it: Ask God to walk through life with you.

239

AUG 20

Encouragement for Tough Days

Give your worries to the Lord, and he will take care of you. He will never let good people down. Psalm 55:22, NCV.

When you're facing a tough day, remember God's got your back! The perfect combination of strength and love, He can handle anything that comes your way. Take a look at some of these reminders:

- "God has said this, and I have heard it over and over: God is strong. The Lord is loving" (Psalm 62:11, 12, NCV).
- "God is our protection and our strength. He always helps in times of trouble" (Psalm 46:1, NCV).
- "The Lord gives me strength and makes me sing; he has saved me. He is my God, and I will praise him" (Exodus 15:2, NCV).
- "He has put his angels in charge of you to watch over you wherever you go" (Psalm 91:11, NCV).
- "What, then, shall we say in response to these things? If God is for us, who can be against us?" (Romans 8:31).
- "The Lord is good, giving protection in times of trouble. He knows who trusts in him" (Nahum 1:7, NCV).
- "You, Lord, are my lamp; the Lord turns my darkness into light. With your help I can advance against a troop, with my God I can scale a wall" (2 Samuel 22:29, 30).
- "Now to him who is able to do immeasurably more than all we ask or imagine, according to his power that is at work within us, to him be glory in the church and in Christ Jesus throughout all generations, for ever and ever! Amen" (Ephesians 3:20).

Live it out: Start a collection of encouraging verses that you can read when you're having a hard day. Keep the list in your Bible or on your computer or phone, so that you can reference it when you need it.

Pray about it: Turn one of the verses from today's reading into a prayer.

Who You *Really* Are

For we are God's masterpiece. Ephesians 2:10, NLT.

Sometimes we're our own worst enemies. We are hard on ourselves and don't forgive ourselves when we mess up. Sometimes we even insult ourselves. Sure, we usually don't say those insults out loud, but we often have a little voice inside that says, "I'm such a loser," "I'm an idiot—it's no wonder no one likes me," or "I could never do that."

Don't let those self-defeating negative thoughts kick around in your mind any longer. The Bible is clear about your true identity. You're not a loser or an idiot. Just look at what God says you really are:

- **The apple of God's eye.** "For whoever touches you touches the apple of his eye" (Zechariah 2:8).
- **God's masterpiece.** "For we are God's masterpiece. He has created us anew in Christ Jesus, so we can do the good things he planned for us long ago" (Ephesians 2:10, NLT).
- **Jesus' friend.** "I no longer call you servants, because a servant does not know his master's business. Instead, I have called you friends, for everything that I learned from my Father I have made known to you" (John 15:15).
- **God's child.** "Yet to all who did receive him, to those who believed in his name, he gave the right to become children of God" (John 1:12).
- **A citizen of heaven.** "But our citizenship is in heaven. And we eagerly await a Savior from there, the Lord Jesus Christ" (Philippians 3:20).
- **The temple of God.** "Don't you know that you are God's temple and that God's Spirit lives in you?" (1 Corinthians 3:16, NCV).

Live it out: Next time a cruel thought about yourself claws its way into your mind, fight back! Replace those negative thoughts with these verses, and start seeing yourself as God does.

Pray about it: Praise God for giving you a new identity. Thank Him for making you His child, His friend, and His masterpiece!

Try, Try Again

But as for you, be strong and do not give up. 2 Chronicles 15:7.

George Weiss is in his 80s, but he is just beginning to live his dream. For more than 50 years he has been creating new inventions. His tinkering has resulted in more than 80 unique devices, many now collecting dust in his basement. There was the car-key buckle, and the Christmas ornament that opened to form a cross. And then there was the "Do It Your Shelf" storage system. Not to mention the dozens and dozens of other ideas.

Despite all his hard work, none of the inventions ever took off—that is, until now.

Recently a company liked his idea for a word game so much that they invested in it. The game, called Dabble, is now in stores nationwide. Soon after its release it even won the Game of the Year award from *Creative Child Magazine*.

George never would have had that victory if he had given up after one rejection . . . or 10 rejections . . . or 79 rejections. He kept trying, even though people thought he was a failure.

When tempted to give up, hold on. Keep trying! A lot of things require time and practice. Don't be discouraged if you hear a no or two on your way to a yes. Cling to the visions God has given you. Check out these verses that will inspire you to keep trying and not give up:

- "Then Jesus told his disciples a parable to show them that they should always pray and not give up" (Luke 18:1).
- "But as for you, be strong and do not give up, for your work will be rewarded" (2 Chron. 15:7).
- "Let us not become weary in doing good, for at the proper time we will reap a harvest if we do not give up" (Galatians 6:9).
- "If he stumbles, he will not fall, because the Lord holds his hand" (Psalm 37:24, NCV).

Live it out: Is there something you are tempted to quit? Don't give up now—give it your all!

Pray about it: Ask God to help you have the guts and grit to keep trying even when you feel like calling it quits.

Ride the Wind Day

The wind blows wherever it pleases. You hear its sound, but you cannot tell where it comes from or where it is going. So it is with everyone born of the Spirit. John 3:7, 8.

August 23 is Ride the Wind Day, a little-known holiday that encourages people to catch a ride on the breeze. Traditional observance includes flying a kite, flying in an airplane, parachuting, hang-gliding, riding a motorcycle, or riding in a sailboat. Chances are you don't have any of those things penciled in on your schedule for the day. So here's a simpler way to celebrate Ride the Wind Day. Check out a fascinating Bible story about wind.

Here's one for you: A Pharisee named Nicodemus sneaked out to talk to Jesus at night so no one would see him. Jesus made their late-night conversation highly intriguing when He told Nicodemus that followers of God had to be born again. The Jewish leader thought Jesus' words were absurd. "'How can someone be born when they are old?' Nicodemus asked. 'Surely they cannot enter a second time into their mother's womb to be born!'" (John 3:4).

Jesus quickly clarified: "You should not be surprised at my saving, 'You must be born again.' The wind blows wherever it pleases. You hear its sound, but you cannot tell where it comes from or where it is going. So it is with everyone born of the Spirit" (verses 7, 8).

The wind, Jesus explained, is real, even though we can't see it. Likewise, being born again is real, even though we can't see that either. The invisible wind rustles the grass and whips the trees. Similarly, when we invite the Holy Spirit into our lives, it is an invisible act, but there will be visible consequences. Galatians 5:22, 23 says those visible results are "love, joy, peace, patience, kindness, goodness, faithfulness, gentleness, self-control" (NCV).

It won't happen overnight, but we will slowly be changed by the Spirit. Day by day our actions and words will show that the wind of the Spirit has been blowing through our lives.

Live it out: Invite the Holy Spirit into your life. Even though you can't see Him, trust that He is with you.

Pray about it: Pray that the wind of the Spirit will blow through your life.

Live It Out!

Jesus answered, "I am the way and the truth and the life. No one comes to the Father except through me." John 14:6.

An idea that stood out to me from this week's devotional readings:

_____

_____

_____

A verse from this week's devotions that was powerful to me:

_____

_____

_____

A "Live it out" challenge I tried this week:

_____

_____

_____

Something that happened this week that was a blessing:

_____

_____

_____

My prayer today (thanks, requests, praises):

_____

_____

_____

What Would It Take to Change Your Mind?

As he neared Damascus on his journey, suddenly a light from heaven flashed around him. He fell to the ground and heard a voice say to him, "Saul, Saul, why do you persecute me?" Acts 9:3, 4.

If you really believed something, what would it take to change your mind? Saul (later known as Paul) was a stubborn, hard-to-convince kind of fella. So it took *a lot* to change his mind. God was going to have to go to extreme measures to set Saul on a new course.

Just take a look at his story. Saul hated Jesus' followers. He wanted them imprisoned, punished, dead. While the believers were spreading the gospel, "Saul was still breathing out murderous threats against the Lord's disciples" (Acts 9:1).

One day, as Saul headed to Damascus to bully the believers, a light flashed from heaven. "He fell to the ground and heard a voice say to him, 'Saul, Saul, why do you persecute me?'" (verse 4).

Shocked and confused, Saul asked who was speaking to him. He heard the thunderous response: "I am Jesus, whom you are persecuting" (verse 5).

The Lord commanded Saul to go into Damascus, where he would get further instructions. As Saul got up off the ground, he opened his eyes and realized he couldn't see a thing. He remained blind for three days, until God, through Ananias, restored his sight.

To change Saul's mind, God indeed took extreme measures. He actually stopped Saul on the road to Damascus, spoke to him from heaven, and struck him blind. According to the Bible, once Saul's sight was restored, he saw everything differently: "Immediately, something like scales fell from Saul's eyes, and he could see again. He got up and was baptized" (verse 18).

Live it out: Don't be so stubborn that God has to take extreme measures to change your mind. If He is trying to convince you of something, listen to Him.
Pray about it: Thank God for patiently working with you, helping you to see the truth.

Bad Boy Turned Good

At once he began to preach in the synagogues that Jesus is the Son of God.
Acts 9:20.

God can take what seem to be bad traits and use them for good. Look at Saul, for example. The man was strong-willed, hard-driving, and persuasive. Unfortunately, he used all of that force and energy to persecute the Christians.

However, God knew that Saul's strong-willed determination could serve a good cause. That's why He wouldn't rest until Saul switched sides and fought for truth.

After Saul was struck blind on the way to Damascus, God asked Ananias to go to him and restore his sight. Ananias, however, was hesitant. He told God, "I have heard many reports about this man and all the harm he has done to your holy people in Jerusalem. And he has come here with authority from the chief priests to arrest all who call on your name" (Acts 9:13, 14).

Ananias didn't see Saul's potential for good—just his *past*. God, however, wanted to use all of Saul's strengths for a good cause. He explained to Ananias: "Go! This man is my chosen instrument to proclaim my name to the Gentiles and their kings and to the people of Israel" (verse 15).

Saul did change drastically, and he began to use his talents to help God's cause. As you can imagine, his sudden change delighted God, but confused everyone else. "At once he began to preach in the synagogues that Jesus is the Son of God. All those who heard him were astonished and asked, 'Isn't he the man who raised havoc in Jerusalem among those who call on this name? And hasn't he come here to take them as prisoners to the chief priests?' Yet Saul grew more and more powerful and baffled the Jews living in Damascus by proving that Jesus is the Messiah" (verses 20-22).

Saul (later known as Paul) became one of God's greatest spokespeople of all time. God just needed to help him channel all his energies and talents in the right direction.

Live it out: Make a list of your dominant characteristics. Note how you could use those traits for good. For example, are you talkative? stubborn? easily bored? How can God shape such tendencies to serve His cause?

Pray about it: Ask God to direct your abilities and traits, so that you can be a positive, godly influence.

Putting Yourself to the Test

Let us examine our ways and test them, and let us return to the Lord.
Lamentations 3:40.

I've never met anyone who lists "test taking" as one of their hobbies or interests. It just isn't something most people look forward to and enjoy. In reality, most students hate tests (who knows, maybe even teachers hate them too, but they just don't admit it!).

If you're one of those people who wishes you never had to see another pop quiz or test again, brace yourself. You might not like what you're about to read. Here it is: *God likes tests.* In fact, He says we should give ourselves an exam from time to time. Not a geometry test or a physics quiz, but a spiritual review.

The Lord says that we need to check ourselves to see if we are really living out what we say we believe: "Examine yourselves to see whether you are in the faith; test yourselves. Do you not realize that Christ Jesus is in you—unless, of course, you fail the test?" (2 Corinthians 13:5).

To give yourself a spiritual test, set aside some quiet time with God. Begin the exam by taking an honest look at your life. Galatians 6:4 says, "Each one should test their own actions." Are you doing things you feel guilty about? Do you have habits that are pulling you away from God instead of closer to Him? If so, don't give up hope. You won't flunk the test if you have problems in your life. The only way you'll blow this test is if you aren't honest. If you come clean with God about your troubles, He will not turn you away.

After you've tested yourself by asking the hard questions, the final part of the exam is to do something about it. For example, if it makes you realize that you aren't close to God, think of ways you can develop a better relationship with Him. Perhaps you can set aside a few minutes at the end of each day to talk to Him about what happened that day.

Don't be afraid to take this test. God is an awesome instructor and will help you get a passing score!

Live it out: Give yourself a spiritual test. Set aside time to ask yourself how your relationship with God is. After you think and pray about it, decide what you can do to grow closer to Him.

Pray about it: Ask God to reveal to you anything that is blocking you from following Him.

You Quirky Thing, You

Do not conform to the pattern of this world. Romans 12:2.

There's nothing wrong with being a little bit different. In fact, it's the funny quirks and oddities that make people so interesting and lovable. My sister, for example, can't bear the sound of someone clipping their fingernails. She has hypersensitive hearing and can somehow detect the use of fingernail clippers within a one-mile radius. When I hear her humorously singing at the top of her lungs while running water in the sink, I know she is attempting to drown out the sound of someone in the house clipping their nails.

My husband has a few quirks of his own too. Take, for example, the man's ability to turn every meal into something barbeque flavored. Give him mashed potatoes, and he'll put barbeque sauce on them. Give him macaroni and cheese, and he'll top it off with barbeque sauce. (To his credit, I have yet to see him put barbeque sauce on Chinese food, but that's mainly because we haven't yet found a Chinese restaurant that keeps BBQ sauce on hand.)

In such harmless ways, it's fun to see our uniqueness come out. However, at times it is difficult to be different. When I was in high school, for instance, I went to a public school, in which my religion, diet, and lifestyle were completely unlike those of my classmates. Sometimes I was uncomfortable with my differences. As I got older, I learned to celebrate and appreciate them, but it took a little time (and life experience) to make peace with being different because of my beliefs.

One day during those tricky high school years, I came across a calendar with a Bible verse on it that really spoke to me. It said: "But ye are a chosen generation, a royal priesthood, an holy nation, a peculiar people; that ye should shew forth the praises of him who hath called you out of darkness into his marvelous light" (1 Peter 2:9, KJV). That verse holds a life-changing message: you should feel special—not terrible—if you are different, because you are following God!

Live it out: In what ways are you different because of your beliefs? Are you ever ashamed of those differences? What can you do to make peace with the uniqueness that comes from following God?

Pray about it: Ask God for boldness and happiness as you follow His unique plan.

These Are a Few of My Favorite Things

I will delight in your decrees and not forget your word. Psalm 119:16, NLT.

What is your favorite food? Your favorite class at school? How about a favorite day of the week? Or a favorite vacation?

Your favorite things reveal a lot about you. That's why when people are getting to know each other, they ask about each other's favorite things. It's a great way to learn more about what is important and valuable to them.

Now what about your favorite *spiritual* things? Those things indicate a lot about you too. Take a minute to think about and jot down your favorite things in each of the following categories:

Favorite Bible verse: _Psalm 139:13-140_

Favorite book of the Bible: _Esther & Ruth_

Favorite person in the Bible: _Jesus, Esther, Ruth_

Favorite story about Jesus in the Bible: _Too many_

Favorite place to spend quiet time with God: _Living Room_

Favorite uplifting spiritual song: _Too many_

Favorite thing about church: _All of it_

Live it out: The more time you spend growing spiritually, the more favorite spiritual things you'll have. Pay attention to verses, songs, or Bible stories that speak to you. Let them become a part of your spiritual identity.

Pray about it: Thank God for the freedom to study the Bible and grow spiritually.

AUG 30

What's the Deal With Baptism?

Repent and be baptized, every one of you, in the name of Jesus Christ for the forgiveness of your sins. Acts 2:38.

One of my friends was baptized when she was 6. I was baptized when I was 22. Another one of my friends was extremely emotional on the day of her baptism. I didn't cry or have strong emotions—I just felt calm. Every year one of my other friends celebrates the anniversary of her baptism as her "New Birthday." I'm not quite sure what day of the year I got baptized, so I wouldn't even know which month to serve a New Birthday cake.

Everyone experiences their baptism in a different way. For some people, it is a very exciting day. For others, it is a very frightening one. However, we all have one thing in common: it is the day that we publicly announce we are going on a journey with God. It doesn't mean we have it all figured out or that we won't mess up anymore. Nor does it indicate that we are any better than people who aren't baptized. But it does demonstrate that we don't want to do life on our own. We want to start a new life with Jesus as our Savior. Killing and burying the old plan of living for ourselves, we are replacing it with a new plan to follow God. That's why we get "buried" in the water: we're deep-sixing the old way of life and rising up to a new one.

Baptism doesn't keep you from messing up or being tempted anymore. (In fact, Jesus faced some of His most powerful temptations right after His baptism.) But as we continue to trust and serve God, we'll keep getting spiritually stronger. Our sense of gratitude, joy, and faith will grow as we live with Christ.

Live it out: If you have not been baptized and feel called to take that step, talk to your pastor. But if you have been baptized, what did it mean to you? Share your spiritual story with a friend, and ask about theirs. Tell them about where you got baptized, what was going on in your life at the time, and how you felt toward God. Talking about it will be a great spiritual boost for you and your friend.

Pray about it: Thank God for giving you the opportunity to start a new life through baptism.

Live It Out!

For we live by faith, not by sight. 2 Corinthians 5:7.

An idea that stood out to me from this week's devotional readings:

_____

_____

_____

A verse from this week's devotions that was powerful to me:

_____

_____

_____

A "Live it out" challenge I tried this week:

_____

_____

_____

Something that happened this week that was a blessing:

_____

_____

_____

My prayer today (thanks, requests, praises):

_____

_____

_____

SEP 1

They Did the Crime: When Are They Going to Do the Time?

Do not say, "I'll pay you back for this wrong!" Wait for the Lord, and he will avenge you. Proverbs 20:22.

In 1955 four men in India were charged with a crime. The authorities accused them of defrauding a government-run transport company by buying bogus motor parts. Their trial began two years later, in 1957. Unbelievably, the hearings continued, off and on, for 33 long years. Finally in 1990 the judge concluded that there wasn't enough proof to find the men guilty. When the crime allegedly took place, the four men were 47, 36, 28, and 27 years old. By the time they got their not-guilty verdict, they were 82, 71, 63, and 62. They had spent most of their adult lives waiting for that verdict!

When people do us wrong, we want to make sure they get their verdict and punishment right away. And usually we would like to be the one to give it to them. If a friend betrays us, we intend to make sure they suffer. Should a guy make us look bad, we want him to look worse—and now! And if a girl talks trash about us, we want people talking trash about *her*, not us! We think, *They did the crime—when are they going to do the time?*

The Bible is clear about the best plan of action in such cases. When someone has wronged you, leave the revenge up to God. Don't try to create payback. God will set things right. Romans 12:19 puts it this way: "My friends, do not try to punish others when they wrong you, but wait for God to punish them with his anger. It is written, 'I will punish those who do wrong; I will repay them,' says the Lord" (NCV).

It's not up to us to be someone's judge and jury. God will set things right. Hopefully it won't take as long as India's legal system, but even if it does, it will be in God's perfect timing.

Live it out: If you are holding a grudge against someone and want payback, it's time to let it go. Every time it comes to mind, pray about it. Keep asking God to release you from the negative feelings.

Pray about it: Pray openly and honestly about any grudges you are holding. Ask God to free you from the desire to dish out revenge.

The Cool Kids, the Jocks, and the Nerds

In humility value others above yourselves. Philippians 2:3.

Right now, if I asked you to name a jock, a nerd, a cool kid, a rich kid, and a geek, you probably could do so. That's because high schoolers have the bad habit of giving people labels. It's nothing new. Probably it happened when your parents—and even your grandparents—were in high school too.

We tend to define people by the clique or group they belong to, and then we even stereotype those groups. The jocks get all the dates. Everyone admires the cool kids. The geeks write computer programs in their basements. And the nerds wear thick glasses and always know the answer in chemistry class.

However, labels like that aren't fair. We are all so much more than a term someone slapped on us behind our back. Instead, we are complex and constantly evolving. The guy you think is the ultimate cool kid now may not be so cool in a few years.

When I was in high school, one group of cool kids seemed absolutely untouchable. They were cheerleaders and athletes who dressed cool, had cool cars, and had cool confidence. Now a lot of those cool kids are struggling, still driving those same cars and wearing those same clothes. Quite a few of them dropped out of college, started drinking, and took jobs at the local grocery store or fast-food place. Many of those cool kids now envy the nerds who left town and went to college, got married, had kids, got good jobs, and bought new houses and cars. The nerds don't seem so nerdy anymore, and the cool kids don't seem so cool.

Here's the thing with labels: they don't really work. If you've gotten a bad label, don't let it get you down. Let God—not others—define you. And if you've given someone a label, erase it. When you take a closer look, you'll realize people are much more than just a little label.

Live it out: Refuse to label people. Think of everyone as equals loved by God. He has placed immeasurable value on every single person—no matter what label they've received.

Pray about it: Ask God to help you define your worth by what He thinks of you, not by how others regard you.

Do Something

Do what God's teaching says; when you only listen and do nothing, you are fooling yourselves. James 1: 22, NCV.

There's a simple solution to most problems: *Do something.*

Well, it's a simple idea, but it's not always so easy to accomplish. When something isn't going well, the temptation is to complain. But if you want a real game changer, refuse to gripe—and do something instead.

Say, for instance, you are bored. Get up and create some nonboring thing to do. Rally your friends together for a volleyball game. Read a book. Call your cousin. *Do something!*

If your church's youth group is putting you to sleep, don't complain. Do something instead. Get the most interesting, energetic people in your group, and go talk to your youth leader. Have a list of suggestions of things that you'd like to do. Volunteer to help organize an outing. Offer to do a skit, sing a song, or help plan a weekend activity. *Do something!*

The rule applies in relationships, too. If one of your classmates seems upset at you, don't ignore them or talk about them behind their back. *Do something!* Go to them with a friendly attitude and ask if there's anything wrong. Or invite them to study with you after school.

When you catch yourself worrying about anything, ask yourself if there's something you need to do about it. If so, get to work doing it. For example, if you're concerned about a test tomorrow, review and study the material. Once you've done your part, you'll feel better. It's amazing how doing something can turn a situation around.

Live it out: Have a "do something" attitude. Next time you're tempted to complain, stop and think of something you can do to improve the situation instead.

Pray about it: Ask God to help you have the courage and wisdom to do something to make situations better.

A Name You'll Never Forget

See, I have written your name on the palms of my hands. Isaiah 49:16, NLT.

I come from a family of people with out-of-the-ordinary names. My sisters are named Cinnamon and Ginger, so people often say, "No, really, what are your *real* names?" or "Yeah, right, and I bet you have brothers named Paprika and Oregano." My dad and his siblings also have interesting names. His family had 11 children in it, and all of their names begin with the letter O: Otis, Orlene, Oma, Oliver, Orville, Oletha, Opal, Ola, Ora, Oren, and Olen. His mom used to say that if she had ended up having a twelfth child, she would have named it Oops.

Having a unique name makes a person memorable. One of the most unusual names in the Bible is Mephibosheth. (Go ahead and say it aloud five times fast. It's a total tongue twister!) However, he is memorable not just because of his distinctive name, but also because of his interesting story.

Mephibosheth was the son of Jonathan, who had been a loyal friend to David. After Jonathan died in battle, David missed his best friend terribly. Years after Jonathan's death David thought to ask around to see if any of Jonathan's family was still alive. He discovered that indeed Jonathan had a son. Mephibosheth had been very young when his father died, and he became crippled because of being dropped soon after.

King David sent for him, which must have scared him terribly. When the disabled Mephibosheth approached the king, David's heart was full of compassion and sympathy for him. He remembered Jonathan's kindness, and he wanted to pay back that kindness by doing everything he could for Jonathan's son. He invited Mephibosheth from then on to eat with him at the king's table. Also he gave him all of the land and possessions that had once belonged to Mephibosheth's grandfather, King Saul. David even made arrangements for someone to farm the land for him.

Mephibosheth's story proves that strange names aren't the only thing people remember. Kindness will never be forgotten either.

Live it out: Think of someone who has been kind to you, and do something special for them.
Pray about it: Thank God for His kindness to you—and for never forgetting you.

SEP 5

A Two-Step Plan for Surviving Bad Days

Therefore put on the full armor of God, so that when the day of evil comes, you may be able to stand your ground, and after you have done everything, to stand.
Ephesians 6:13.

Some days you just don't have much fight in you. The goal is simply to survive and make it through the day.

On days like that, it's good to know that God understands. In fact, He even advises us about what to do on those down days. In Ephesians 6 He gives us a two-step plan for surviving them. Step one: "Put on the full armor of God, so that you can take your stand against the devil's schemes" (verse 11). That armor includes a belt of truth, a breastplate of righteousness, a shield of faith, a helmet of salvation, and the sword of the Spirit (the Word of God). It sounds like a fantastic plan, but on rough days it's hard to rally a sense of faith, truth, and righteousness. That is where step two comes in.

Step two: Stand. After you put on the full armor of God, you don't have to fight the foes all by yourself. God just wants you to stand there holding on to truth, faith, righteousness, and the Word of God. He'll wage the battle for you. Ephesians 6:13 summarizes the two steps: "Therefore put on the full armor of God [step 1], so that when the day of evil comes, you may be able to stand your ground, and after you have done everything, to stand [step 2]."

Once you've done those two steps, wait and see what God does to help you. "Now then, stand still and see this great thing the Lord is about to do before your eyes!" (1 Samuel 12:16). Armor up and stand tall. Then God will show up to help you face anything the day holds!

Live it out: Think of specific ways you can put on the armor of God (truth, righteousness, faith, salvation, the Word of God). Choose one of those things you can do today—and armor up!

Pray about it: On tough days, double up on prayer. Ask God to show up and help you fight through the day.

A Worry-free Life

Do not be anxious about anything, but in every situation, by prayer and petition, with thanksgiving, present your requests to God. Philippians 4:6.

Worry is sneaky. It just creeps into your mind, and before you know it, you're fretting and don't even realize it. Maybe you're concerned whether you'll do well on a difficult test, if you looked stupid when the teacher called on you during class and you didn't know the answer, if you'll get an invitation to the big party, or if your parents will ever stop fighting. You might say, "Oh, I don't worry. I just *think* about stuff." But if you're thinking about it with a sense of anxiety, that is worry.

I once heard someone say that worry is prayer to Satan. It is dwelling on fears and potential negative outcomes. Jesus taught us that instead of worrying, we should have faith and trust that God can take care of our lives. Read these words of Jesus whenever you're tempted to worry:

"Therefore I tell you, do not worry about your life, what you will eat or drink; or about your body, what you will wear. Is not life more than food, and the body more than clothes? Look at the birds of the air; they do not sow or reap or store away in barns, and yet your heavenly Father feeds them. Are you not much more valuable than they? Can any one of you by worrying add a single hour to your life?

"And why do you worry about clothes? See how the flowers of the field grow. They do not labor or spin. Yet I tell you that not even Solomon in all his splendor was dressed like one of these. If that is how God clothes the grass of the field, which is here today and tomorrow is thrown into the fire, will He not much more clothe you—you of little faith? So do not worry, saying, 'What shall we eat?' or 'What shall we drink?' or 'What shall we wear?' For the pagans run after all these things, and your heavenly Father knows that you need them. But seek first his kingdom and his righteousness, and all these things will be given to you as well. Therefore do not worry about tomorrow, for tomorrow will worry about itself. Each day has enough trouble of its own" (Matthew 6:25-34).

Live it out: It's time to stop worrying. Trust God to help you to face whatever comes your way.
Pray about it: Whenever you catch yourself worrying about something, immediately start praying about it instead.

Live It Out!

The Lord is my light and my salvation—whom shall I fear? The Lord is the stronghold of my life—of whom shall I be afraid? Psalm 27:1.

An idea that stood out to me from this week's devotional readings:

_____

_____

_____

A verse from this week's devotions that was powerful to me:

_____

_____

_____

A "Live it out" challenge I tried this week:

_____

_____

_____

Something that happened this week that was a blessing:

_____

_____

_____

My prayer today (thanks, requests, praises):

_____

_____

_____

Writing a Bucket List

Teach us to number our days, that we may gain a heart of wisdom. Psalm 90:12.

Fifteen-year-old Alice Pyne has been fighting cancer since she was 11. As the cancer became more aggressive, she realized she didn't have much longer to live. Knowing this, the British teen decided to make the most of the time she had left. So Alice created a "bucket list," a list of all the things she wants to do before, well, she kicks the bucket.

In 2011 Alice turned her simple list into a blog, "Alice's Bucket List," that quickly went viral. Each time she checks something off her list, thousands of cyber-supporters from around the world cheer her on. So far, she has already marked a number of things off her list, including swimming with sharks, having a photo shoot with her friends, and entering her dog in a Labrador show. Other things she hopes to do from her list include traveling to Kenya, going whale watching, and visit "Cadbury World and eat loads of chocolate."

Alice is making the most of her days, because she knows she probably won't have many more. The psalmist says even healthy people should learn to count their days like this: "Teach us to number our days, that we may gain a heart of wisdom" (Psalm 90:12). In other words, we all need to realize that we have only a limited time on earth, because that will motivate us to make the most of every single day. Even if you live to be 80 or 90, you'll look back, and it will seem the days just flew by.

Each day is a gift from God, so try to make it special. Don't let fears or tears hold you back. Live the abundant life that God has planned for you.

Live it out: Make a bucket list, a list of things you'd like to do before you die. Don't stack the list only with selfish pursuits. Add some things that will improve your community, show love to others, and glorify God.

Pray about it: Thank God for your life! Thank Him for another day—and ask Him to help you make the most of it.

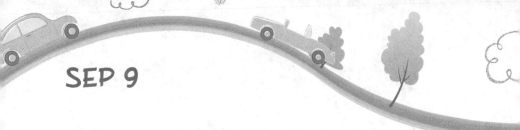

SEP 9

The Bad Reputation of Christians

Therefore, we are Christ's representatives. 2 Corinthians 5:20, GW.

What do non-Christian teens and young adults think of Christians? According to research, it's a mixed review. Extensive studies among non-Christians, ages 16-29, reveal that they have a predominantly unfavorable impression of Christians.

Take a look at some of the most common negative descriptions non-Christians used to describe Christians: judgmental, old-fashioned, out of touch with reality, hypocritical, and insensitive to others. If you met someone who was all of those things, you probably wouldn't like them, would you? No wonder so many non-Christians don't want to get to know Christians! That description sounds nothing like Christ, so it's disturbing that His followers have gotten that kind of reputation.

Fortunately, the research also found that some non-Christians have favorable impressions of Christians. The good things that non-Christians noticed about Christianity include faith, friendliness, good values, and hope for the future.

If someone asked you to describe Christ, what kind of words would you use? I would say He was loving, accepting, compassionate, wise, patient, bold, and kind.

As His representatives, we should strive to have those same characteristics. Sure, we aren't perfect, but we can do our part not to damage His reputation and misrepresent Him. When we are judgmental, insensitive, and hypocritical, non-Christians get a bad impression of not only us, but Christ Himself as well.

It takes time and effort, but we can become more like Christ. As we serve others, show compassion, and make an effort to connect with people, we'll become His representatives. Jesus Christ has been loving and patient with us, so He wants us to be loving and patient with others.

Live it out: Pay attention to how you treat others. Look for an opportunity to be Christlike to someone today.

Pray about it: Ask God to continue to transform you to be more like Him.

The Old Man With the Long White Beard

I am in the Father and the Father is in me. John 14:11.

When you picture God the Father, what does He look like? For many people, the mental image is of a serious man with white hair and a long white beard who sits on His throne day and night. Probably He doesn't smile much, and He is a strict disciplinarian. Because He is all about business, not pleasure, He wouldn't be the type to hug, and He definitely wouldn't hang out with teenagers.

Now, when you picture God the Son—Jesus, that is—what is He like? For many people, Jesus seems to be much nicer and more approachable than God the Father. Jesus, after all, hung out with sinners, went to parties, and chose 12 regular-old-Joes to be His followers. Probably He laughed and cried a lot. He kissed children and looked people in the eye when they talked. And He healed people and cheered them up.

If you can relate to any of those mental images, you're not alone. A lot of people think of God and Jesus as having completely different attitudes and traits. Even the disciples who spent time with Jesus weren't quite sure what God the Father was like. Philip asked Jesus, "Lord, show us the Father" (John 14:8). In other words, he was asking Jesus to tell them what the Father is like.

Jesus responded by making it clear that the Father was just like Him. "Jesus answered: 'Don't you know me, Philip, even after I have been among you such a long time? Anyone who has seen me has seen the Father. . . . Believe me when I say that I am in the Father and the Father is in me'" (verses 9-11). Jesus wanted them to understand that if they loved Him, they would love the Father just the same. The Father is just as tender and accepting as the Son. He isn't some mean, distant deity always ready to punish and destroy. The Father and the Son both love people.

Next time you picture God the Father, remember what Jesus said: "If you really know me, you will know my Father as well" (verse 7). According to that, we're a part of one big loving family. Our Father is kind, tender, and simply crazy about us.

Live it out: Have you ever thought of God the Father as distant and cold? How do Jesus' words change your understanding of God the Father?

Pray about it: Thank God the Father for being such a loving heavenly parent to you.

Is That Any of Your Business?

Jesus answered, "If I want him to remain alive until I return, what is that to you? You must follow me." John 21:22.

Early one morning after Jesus' death and resurrection, when seven of the disciples were out fishing, Jesus appeared on the shore to meet them. After miraculously helping them catch fish, the Savior built a fire on the shore and invited them to have breakfast with Him.

Once finished with breakfast, Jesus pulled Peter aside for a private conversation. Remember that the disciple had publicly denied Jesus three times before His crucifixion. Now Jesus wanted to reconcile and set Peter on the right path. He asked the man if he truly loved Him, and He gave Peter the mission to feed His sheep. One last thing Jesus mentioned was Peter's future: He predicted how Peter would die. When Peter heard it, he pointed back to where John was walking, and said, "What about him? What will happen to him?"

Jesus answered, "If I want him to remain alive until I return, what is that to you? You must follow me" (John 21:22). In other words: "It's none of your business what happens to him. I'm asking you to follow Me. That's your business."

There are three kinds of business: my business, your business, and God's business. When Peter started asking Jesus what was going to happen to John, that wasn't his affair. It was both John's and God's business. Jesus wanted Peter to focus on his own responsibilities: loving God and feeding His sheep.

Whenever you start focusing on or gossiping about other people's lives, stop and remember that that is *their* business. Instead, get busy doing your own. What does God want you to do? What is He speaking to your heart? In what areas of life is He trying to grow and teach you? How can you cooperate with Him? Focus on that. That is your business.

God is good enough, kind enough, and powerful enough to handle all the big stuff outside of your control. Trust Him to take care of His business while you handle yours.

Live it out: When tempted to worry about or talk about something, ask yourself, *Is this God's business, my business, or someone else's business?*

Pray about it: Ask for God's blessing and power as you take on your business. In your prayer, surrender to Him all the things that aren't yours.

Alive and Well in the Land of the Living

I remain confident of this: I will see the goodness of the Lord in the land of the living. Psalm 27:13.

My friend Brandon told me the other day that he feels dead inside. He has been hurt and disappointed so many times that his heart feels as if it has just shut down.

In the book *Walden* writer Henry David Thoreau noted, "The mass of men lead lives of quiet desperation." In other words, a lot of people out there also feel dead inside, just like my friend Brandon.

God wants us all to be fully alive. Jesus Himself announced on earth, "I have come that they may have life, and have it to the full" (John 10:10). He doesn't want us just to survive, but to thrive. Jesus didn't give us life so that we could barely get by, all miserable and weak. Rather, He intends that we should live it to the fullest!

There is a phrase I love that appears several times in the Bible. It is "the land of the living." Take a look at a couple of the verses that include it:

- "I remain confident of this: I will see the goodness of the Lord in *the land of the living*" (Psalm 27:13).
- "For you, Lord, have delivered me from death, my eyes from tears, my feet from stumbling, that I may walk before the Lord in *the land of the living*" (Psalm 116:8, 9).

I like that phrase because it paints a great picture in my mind. In "the land of the living," I imagine people fully alive—just as Jesus described in John 10:10. People in the land of the living are happy and confident. They are not emotionally or spiritually dead, but see God's goodness all around them. Walking tall, they not only look forward to the future but make the most of every single day.

Each morning God invites us to join Him in the land of the living. Why just stand by and watch others live to the fullest? Join in! Live to the fullest!

Live it out: Find a way to become more fully alive today. Start a conversation, give a present, smile often, laugh more, learn something. Whenever you make the most of an opportunity, you become a part of the land of the living.

Pray about it: Ask God to help you to become fully alive—a citizen of the land of the living.

SEP 13

What It Really Means to Meditate

His delight is in the law of the Lord, and in His law he meditates day and night.
Psalm 1:1, 2, NKJV.

I don't like eating or drinking after people, so whenever someone asks to take a sip of my drink or a bite of my food, I just say, "Sure, I'm finished with it. You can just have it." That's my polite way of saying, "I don't want to drink or eat after you, so there's no need to give it back to me after you've had some."

Unfortunately, as Christians we have sometimes taken this same "You can just have it" attitude with things far more important than food. Let me explain. Take the idea of meditation, for example. Throughout the Bible we read of the importance of meditation. However, we rarely hear the idea discussed in church now. Many Christians consider it as New Age or something done only in Eastern religions. Although some other religions use meditation, that doesn't mean we should give up the idea of *biblical* meditation. If we do that, it would be like saying, "Sure, I'm finished with it. You can just have it."

Meditation, *as described in the Bible*, means taking quiet time to reflect on the things God wants us to consider. Some topics He says we should meditate on:

- **God's promises.** David said, "My eyes stay open through the watches of the night, that I may *meditate* on your promises" (Psalm 119:148). If you are feeling upset or unsettled, mediate or think about one of God's promises to give peace (John 14:27, for example).
- **God's unfailing love.** "Within your temple, O God, we *meditate* on your unfailing love" (Psalm 48:9). Think about the cross and other ways that God has shown love to you.
- **God's law.** "Keep this Book of the Law always on your lips; *meditate* on it day and night" (Joshua 1:8). Think about the things God has commanded. He wouldn't ask you to do them unless they would make your life better.
- **Creation.** David wrote, "I *meditate* on all your works and consider what your hands have done" (Psalm 143:5). Think about the stars, the planets, the ocean—everything God has created—and let all of those works and wonders remind you how awesome He is.

Live it out: Choose one of these areas of biblical meditation, and spend quiet time reflecting.
Pray about it: Thank God for His promises, unfailing love, law, and creation.

Live It Out!

It is better to trust the Lord than to trust people. Psalm 118:8, NCV.

An idea that stood out to me from this week's devotional readings:

_____

_____

_____

A verse from this week's devotions that was powerful to me:

_____

_____

_____

A "Live it out" challenge I tried this week:

_____

_____

_____

Something that happened this week that was a blessing:

_____

_____

_____

My prayer today (thanks, requests, praises):

_____

_____

_____

Sticks and Stones May Break My Bones

Do not seek revenge or bear a grudge against anyone among your people, but love your neighbor as yourself. Leviticus 19:18.

Seventeen-year-old Eric Mohat dreaded going to school every day. His classmates harassed him constantly and mercilessly called him names. Some of Eric's classmates say it got so bad that the teachers didn't even step in to stop the bullying.

One day during class one of the bullies turned to Eric and said loud enough for everyone to hear, "Why don't you go home and shoot yourself? No one will miss you." And Eric did. He went home and committed suicide. Unable to imagine enduring another day of torment, he ended his life.

What's even more heartbreaking is that three of his classmates who were also bullied did the same thing that year. Each of them had lost hope that the future would be better.

The old childhood chant says, "Sticks and stones may break my bones, but words will never hurt me." But it is wrong. Sometimes words hurt even more than sticks and stones. In fact, every day approximately 160,000 kids nationwide stay home from school because they fear being bullied. They know how much it hurts, and they want to avoid it!

If you are a bully, knock it off! Even if you think your behavior is all in fun, it's not. Bullying can do serious damage. And remember, Jesus always stood up for the weak.

And if you are being bullied, keep in mind the bigger picture. Talk to God about it, and go to a trusted adult—even if you fear that it will make things worse. Remember too that people who are bullied often end up going on to be extremely successful adults. And, as they say, let the bullies call you whatever they want now: one day they'll call you "Boss."

Live it out: Stand up for the bullied, and refuse to be a bully!
Pray about it: Pray, by name, for your classmates who are both bullies and bullied.

Collecting Rocks

Samuel took a stone and set it up. . . . He named it Ebenezer, saying, "Thus far the Lord has helped us."
1 Samuel 7:12.

It's not *written in stone* anywhere, but according to the Internet, today is Collect Rocks Day. Not everything you read on the Internet is *rock-solid*, though, so I suppose this could be bad information. Nevertheless, Collect Rocks Day is worth noting for a couple reasons. First, a day honoring rock collecting is just bizarre enough to be interesting. Second, the idea of collecting rocks does appear in the Bible, so it must be a good one.

Several times in the Old Testament, followers of God collect or set up rocks to honor a special event. For example, after God gave the Israelites a victory over the Philistines, "Samuel took a stone and set it up between Mizpah and Shen. He named it Ebenzer, saying, 'Thus far the Lord has helped us'" (1 Samuel 7:12). The stone was a memorial, a reminder of God's aid.

Jacob was another rock collector in the Bible. One night while traveling he slept alone, with a stone as his pillow. He dreamed of a stairway to heaven filled with angels. In that dream the Lord spoke hope-filled, encouraging words to him. When he awoke, He was thrilled, saying, "How awesome is this place! This is none other than the house of God; this is the gate of heaven" (Genesis 28:17). To honor the amazing encounter with God, "Jacob took the stone he had placed under his head and set it up as a pillar and poured oil on top of it. He called that place Bethel, though the city used to be called Luz" (verses 18, 19). Then Jacob went on to make a special vow and commitment to God.

So in the Old Testament God's followers set up rocks as memorials to His goodness. Now, most of us won't collect large stones as reminders about God, but we can look back and remember the victories He has given us. Think about the times He has helped you or given you happy experiences. Remembering those victories will give you confidence to face whatever comes your way next.

Live it out: Collect "rocks" by making a list of all the times God has helped you in the past. Look back on it when you need a reminder of His goodness to you.
Pray about it: Thank God for the things He has done for you—and be specific.

The Teacher Becomes the Student

Now go; I will help you speak and will teach you what to say. Exodus 4:12.

I've been a student and I've been a teacher, and I think being a student is easier. I know, I know, some of you are protesting, "But students have to do all the homework!" It's true, but teachers have to figure out what homework to assign, explain it, grade it, calculate your overall grade, keep all the rowdies under control while actually trying to teach something in the meantime, and then give you the dreaded news that there's more homework.

Now, whether it's easy or hard, being a teacher is definitely the best way to learn. That may sound random, since you'd think being a *student* would be best. Nevertheless, there's an old adage that says the best way to learn something is to teach it. (You would probably agree with that if you've ever tried to help someone do a math problem or write a paper.) When you have to explain something to someone else, it really forces you to study and understand it.

One of my first jobs was teaching writing and composition at a community college. Most of the students were adults who were going back to school after spending 10 or 20 years raising kids or working as a mechanic. And, now, here they were at the local community college, with me, some girl their kids' age, trying to teach them to write a paper.

I have to admit that until I found myself forced to explain the writing process, I didn't really think much about what it included. I just wrote without considering what steps it involved. When I had to put the process into words and teach it, I had to break it down in my mind. I began to understand it better the more I thought about and discussed it.

A lot of Christians don't talk to others about God, because they feel that they don't understand their own beliefs well enough to explain them. Many Christians also assume they don't know enough to teach a class at church or lead a youth group meeting. But here's the deal: if you want to learn, teach. Volunteer to help your youth leader. Get the material for the next lesson, study it during the week, and then give it a go as a teacher's assistant. You will learn tons that way. Or try telling a friend what you believe about God: it will force you to really think, grow, and learn.

Live it out: Teach or explain something this week. You will learn something too!
Pray about it: Pray for wisdom and the desire always to keep learning.

Be a Force for Good

Walk with the wise and become wise, for a companion of fools suffers harm.
Proverbs 13:20.

You don't have to be a victim of negative peer pressure. In fact, you are strong enough to rise above it. One way to do that is to become a force for *positive* peer pressure. Peer pressure works two ways: for good or for evil. For example, when you are around peers who are up to no good, you may feel forced to join them in order to fit in. On the other hand, when you are with people who think it's cool to be nice, inclusive, or service-oriented, you may find yourself motivated to join them.

The way to become a force of positive peer pressure is by creating a new culture, one that makes people feel accepted when they do good things. For example, you can work with a teacher or pastor to plan a short-term mission trip. Ask your peers to get involved. Together you and your friends can raise funds, plan, and eventually serve on the trip. Then in those times you are around people pressuring you to do negative things, the memories from these positive experiences will remind you that not all of your peers are buying in to negative influences.

Another way to beat down negative peer pressure is to choose to surround yourself with positive peers. There are really cool teens who stay out of trouble and create a positive culture. Find those teens and be friends with them!

Finally, when facing negative peer pressure, keep in mind who you really want to please. Ask yourself this question from the Bible: "Am I now trying to win the approval of human beings, or of God?" (Galatians 1:10). If you're seeking human favor, you will only be let down in the end. Ask yourself what God would want you to do in the situation, and choose to seek His approval instead of that of your peers.

Live it out: Don't let negative peer pressure victimize you. When tempted by it, stand up and be a leader instead of a follower. Be a force for good.

Pray about it: Ask God for the courage and confidence to resist negative pressure.

SEP 19

Why Everyone Needs a Mentor

Listen to advice and accept correction, and in the end you will be wise.
Proverbs 19:20, NCV.

Jesus picked some pretty rowdy guys to be His 12 disciples. If they were around today, they probably wouldn't be the straight-A students who sit quietly on the front row in class, raising their hand whenever the teacher asks a question. In fact, a few of them would probably be the guys who throw spit wads, wear camouflage jackets, and land themselves in the principal's office for talking back to the teacher.

Nevertheless, most of Jesus' disciples experienced a major turnaround. In the end they turned out to be admirable, stand-up men. What brought about the change? A relationship with the Savior. After spending time with Him, these rough and rowdy guys became gentlemen, passionate about God and the gospel.

Jesus saw their potential. He patiently brought out the good in them, encouraged them, and taught them about God. Besides being their Savior, He was also their teacher and mentor.

A mentor is a wise and trusted person who is a counselor, teacher, and guide. Just as Jesus did for His disciples, a mentor offers advice and guidance to help someone grow into the person that God wants them to become. Everyone—no matter how young or old—can benefit from having a mentor. I've had mentors in all stages of my life who have helped me in my career, relationships, and spiritual life.

If you don't have a mentor, seek one out. Think of an adult in your church, school, or community who is wise and Christlike. Ask them to be your mentor. Most adults will feel honored and privileged to be asked, and they will gladly help you. When you need advice about relationships, God, school, your parents, or the future, set up a time to talk to your mentor. It doesn't have to be awkward or uncomfortable: just think of it as building a friendship with a wise person who has life experience.

Live it out: Ask a Christian adult to be your mentor. Tell them you would like to be able to turn to them with questions or concerns.

Pray about it: Ask God to lead you to a mentor who can share Christ's love and wisdom with you.

Out-of-This-World Variety

For in him all things were created: things in heaven and on earth, visible and invisible. Colossians 1:16.

The sky's the limit—that is, if you have the money to reach the sky. Space tourism offers recreational space travel for those of us who aren't trained astronauts. Anyone can go—as long as you are able to pay the price, which can begin anywhere from $20 million to $35 million.

Since only a handful of people have been able to afford that experience, most of us have to get our out-of-this-world thrills another way. A cheaper and more attainable plan is to enter the other world all around us: the ocean. For much less than the price of a seat on a spacecraft, we can visit the undersea domain by snorkeling or scuba diving. Below the water's surface is a sphere entirely different from our dry existence. The creatures there move, breathe, eat, play, sleep, and work differently than we do.

The first time I went snorkeling, I was immediately delighted by all the creatures of vivid colors and varying sizes darting around me. Thousands—no, millions—of unique creatures zipped everywhere!

God must have had so much fun at creation. He could have just made 10 or 12 kinds of fish, and we still would have been impressed. Or He could have produced just 10 or 20 kinds of birds. Again, we wouldn't have known any better. The Lord also could have made just one kind of person, but He didn't. Instead, He has designed people of all colors, shapes, and sizes. Thus we have different personalities, laughs, voices, walks, likes, and dislikes.

God values the diversity and uniqueness of His creations, and He wants us to appreciate that diversity too. His kingdom is made up of a gorgeous assortment of people. In Revelation 7:9 John describes the beautiful, vast array of people who will make up the community of God: "There before me was a great multitude that no one could count, from every nation, tribe, people and language, standing before the throne and before the Lamb."

Live it out: Is there someone whose different culture or appearance has kept you from knowing them? Get to know them, and celebrate their differences.
Pray about it: Thank God for making each of us unique. If He hadn't, life would be boring!

SEP 21

Live It Out!

God began doing a good work in you, and I am sure he will continue it until it is finished when Jesus Christ comes again. Philippians 1:6, NCV.

An idea that stood out to me from this week's devotional readings:

_____

_____

_____

A verse from this week's devotions that was powerful to me:

_____

_____

_____

A "Live it out" challenge I tried this week:

_____

_____

_____

Something that happened this week that was a blessing:

_____

_____

_____

My prayer today (thanks, requests, praises):

_____

_____

_____

Put All You've Got Into Life

Hard work brings rewards. Proverbs 12:14, NLT.

Hard work pays off. The Bible promises you'll be rewarded if you put all you've got into school, work, or any other activity. Check out some biblical passages that encourage you to do your very best. Let the following verses motivate you to give your very best effort to whatever you're facing today:

- "Whatever your hand finds to do, do it with all your might" (Ecclesiastes 9:10).

- "Do you see someone skilled in their work? They will serve before kings; they will not serve before officials of low rank" (Proverbs 22:29).

- "Lazy people want much but get little, but those who work hard will prosper" (Proverbs 13:4, NLT).

- "Wise words bring many benefits, and hard work brings rewards" (Proverbs 12:14, NLT).

- "All hard work brings a profit, but mere talk leads only to poverty" (Proverbs 14:23).

Live it out: In what area of your life could you use a little hard work? Is there a subject in school you are struggling with? Are you starting a new hobby or sport? Try approaching whatever the situation is with a boost of hard work! Don't lose motivation. Give it all you've got, and see what a difference hard work can make in your life.

Pray about it: When you're tempted to give up or be lazy, pray about it. Ask God to help you have the desire and energy to keep working.

A Complete Life Transplant

We too may live a new life. Romans 6:4.

After years of helping save lives, Dr. Dmitry Nikitin was killed—by one of his patients.

Dr. Nikitin was a transplant surgeon in Orlando, Florida. A married father of four, he was well-liked, intelligent, and quiet. In May 2011, after what seemed to be just another day on the job, the doctor headed to his car in the hospital's parking garage. There one of his former patients, Nelson Flecha, gunned him down.

Just a year before, Dr. Nikitin had saved Nelson's life when he performed a liver and kidney transplant on him. Now, in a sad turn of events, Nelson took the doctor's life. Because Nelson was paranoid that the transplant would fail, he wanted to punish the doctor. After shooting the doctor several times, Nelson killed himself.

It sounds absurd: why would someone kill the very person who saved their life? Who could do such a thing? Sadly, according to the Bible, any of us could be tempted to do that very thing. Hebrews 6:6 says that when we turn away from the truth about Jesus, we "are crucifying the Son of God all over again." Jesus saved our lives, but when we reject Him, it's as if we are putting Him back onto the cross.

Nelson got a liver and kidney transplant, so we would expect him to be appreciative. But we've gotten a complete life transplant. God has given us an entirely new life. Why shouldn't we be appreciative too? Honor the new existence God has given you by living a life of worship, joy, and gratitude.

Live it out: Take a few moments to think about how God has saved your life. In response, what can you do today to show your gratitude for the gift of life? Whether it is showing love to others, spending time with God, or singing praise songs, find a way to live out your appreciation today.

Pray about it: Thank God for dying so that you can live. Ask forgiveness for the times you have taken Him for granted.

Appearance Revolution

I praise you because you made me in an amazing and wonderful way. What you have done is wonderful. Psalm 139:14, NCV.

If you look too long at picture-perfect actors, airbrushed models, or super-buff pro athletes, you'll end up feeling totally inadequate. We noncelebrity, regular people start to think we can't measure up. Girls consider themselves too fat. Guys feel too scrawny. Girls think their nose is too big, or guys regard their abs as too flabby.

According to research, the more time teenagers watch movies and music videos, the more likely they will be dissatisfied with their own bodies. It's not just teenagers who feel this way, though. The same goes for younger kids, too. In a study of fifth graders, 10-year-old boys and girls reported dissatisfaction with their own bodies after watching a music video by Britney Spears or a clip from a popular sitcom.

Overexposure to Hollywood images leaves us feeling worse about ourselves every time. We watch videos, movies, and TV shows to feel as if we're a part of pop culture, but we end up convinced that we don't measure up.

It's time for Christians to lead a revolution when it comes to image and appearance, one that starts when you appreciate the way that God created you. If He wanted you to be taller or blonder, He would have made you that way. Instead of obsessing over appearances, focus on being healthy. Choose nutritious foods, be active, and be thankful for the body God gave you.

Don't let media make you feel inadequate. And, while you're at it, don't let *you* make yourself feel inadequate. One study found that people regard themselves as 20 percent less attractive than others perceive them. That just goes to show: you are your hardest critic. God designed you to be a one-and-only. Thank Him for lovingly creating each aspect of your appearance.

Live it out: Make a list of 10 things you like about your appearance. Especially if you are self-critical, force yourself to come up with no less than 10. Do it as an act of adoration for God, not as an act of self-adoration.

Pray about it: Thank God for creating you to be the one-and-only you.

SEP 25

Starting the Appearance Revolution

My dear friend, I know your soul is doing fine, and I pray that you are doing well in every way and that your health is good. 3 John 2, NCV.

By the age of 17, 78 percent of teen girls are unhappy with their appearance. That means the majority of the girls in your high school think they are unattractive. Girls aren't the only ones struggling with feelings of inadequacy, though. A lot of guys feel as if they don't measure up either.

If you ever feel ugly or unattractive, it's time to look at things from God's perspective. Here are a few things you can do to start a revolution in the way you see yourself.

- **Be active.** Exercise not only helps you lose weight and be fit—it also helps decrease stress and combat depression. The good feelings that come with exercise will even increase your sense of self-worth and attractiveness.
- **Eat healthy.** If you want to lose weight, don't starve yourself. Instead, cut back on junky foods and eat more fruits, vegetables, nuts, and whole grains.
- **Look for beauty everywhere.** Start to appreciate things that are beautiful. Whether it is a car or a birthday cake, take the time to appreciate color, texture, and design. As you train your eye to see beauty all around you, you'll be more likely to see it in people—including yourself.
- **Go to bed early.** Everybody needs their "beauty sleep." A good night's rest will help you feel happier and more energetic—which makes you more attractive. Sufficient sleep will also help you avoid weight gain, because you're more likely to snack and overeat if you're tired.
- **Work with what you've got.** If possible, try to wear clothes that fit you well, rather than ones that are too tight or too loose. Pay attention to the colors that look best on you, and wear them often. Get a haircut if you need one. Make the most of what you've got.

Live it out: Choose one of the things from today's list and put it into action this week.

Pray about it: Ask God to help you not be so hard on yourself and for Him to help you see yourself the way that He does.

Lessons Learned From Housework

I am teaching you today—yes, you—so you will trust in the Lord.
Proverbs 22:19, NLT.

My mother is a supermom, the type who cooks, washes dishes, does laundry, sweeps, vacuums, takes out the trash, irons clothes, washes the windows, cleans the toilets. *What,* you might ask, *is left for the kids in the family to do as chores?* Well, honestly, not much. She takes care of everything, which was lucky for me when I was young—but led to a jolting wake-up call when I was older.

There I was, 18 years old and headed off for college—life on my own. My childhood bedroom was packed with the boxes of things that would accompany me. There in the piles were an array of necessities, including clothes, food, even an iron and laundry detergent. But as I looked at it all, a feeling of anxiety slowly crept over me. I didn't exactly know how to do laundry or cook or iron. Umm, Mom had always taken care of that.

So it was that my first college class was Getting Ready for Real Life 101. Mom was the instructor, and she taught it crash-course-style in our laundry room and kitchen. No bonus points or essay questions—just real-life, hands-on instruction.

To my credit (and my mom's), I turned out just fine. I can now confidently handle any household task that comes my way. Remove a stain? I'm your girl. Bake a pie? Not a problem. Prepare a last-minute healthy meal? I'm on it.

I've learned a lot from doing household chores, but one lesson in particular stands out: *The sooner you take care of something, the better.* This, of course, applies to learning to do household chores, but also to a lot of the household chores themselves. It's much easier to scrub a dish clean if you do it right away, before the food hardens on there. It's a lot better to fold clothes right out of the dryer, before any wrinkles attack. And it's a lot simpler to remove a stain from the sofa quickly before the stain digs its claws in and won't come out.

Many other things in life follow this same rule: the sooner, the better. The sooner you say an apology, the better. The sooner you show respect or volunteer to help, the better. The sooner you say "Thank you," the better.

Live it out: Think of a nice thing you've wanted to do but keep putting off. Do it today.
Pray about it: Thank God for being with you as you tackle the things you've been avoiding.

The Two Versions of Me

Teach me your way, Lord, that I may rely on your faithfulness; give me an undivided heart, that I may fear your name. Psalm 86:11.

Some people seem to have two totally different personalities: they act one way sometimes, and the complete opposite other times! They may be syrupy sweet one moment, but when they think no one is watching they can become, well, a bit of a monster.

That must have been the case with Barbara Ricci, a contestant in the Mrs. New York State pageant. At the beauty pageant Barbara won the title "Mrs. Congeniality" by a landslide. The judges and contestants thought she was the friendliest, gentlest, kindest woman—they even gave her a sash and flowers to prove it. Little did they know that Barbara wasn't always so pleasant. Just six months before the contest, Barbara had gone to trial on charges for running down in her car the 11-year-old daughter of a neighbor with whom Barbara had been fighting. That's not very congenial. In addition, two years before that, Barbara had lost her cool and punched and kicked a police officer at a school board meeting. The court found her guilty of harassment. That's not very congenial either.

We all have good days and bad days, and it's normal to have a little rise and fall in our moods. But if you are living a double life—trying to be one thing sometimes but being something totally different at others—then you're not living the life that God intended for you. In fact, He longs to help us get rid of the extremes of phony niceness and genuine meanness. Ezekiel 11:19 records God's promise: "I will give them an undivided heart and put a new spirit in them; I will remove from them their heart of stone and give them a heart of flesh."

In response to your genuine prayer of surrender, God will set to work repairing your divided heart.

Live it out: Be honest with yourself: do you have a streak of anger or meanness that you try to hide but that keeps showing up? Talk openly to God about it, and ask Him to help change your heart.

Pray about it: Take God up on His offer to give you an undivided, pure heart. Ask Him for it, and believe that He can do it!

Live It Out!

Take delight in the Lord, and he will give you the desires of your heart. Psalm 37:4.

An idea that stood out to me from this week's devotional readings:

_____

_____

_____

A verse from this week's devotions that was powerful to me:

_____

_____

_____

A "Live it out" challenge I tried this week:

_____

_____

_____

Something that happened this week that was a blessing:

_____

_____

_____

My prayer today (thanks, requests, praises):

_____

_____

_____

SEP 29

The Book of Mental Health

Finally, brothers and sisters, whatever is true, whatever is noble, whatever is right, whatever is pure, whatever is lovely, whatever is admirable—if anything is excellent or praiseworthy—think about such things. Philippians 4:8.

If I had known when I was in school that I would end up marrying a man whose first language is Spanish, I really would have paid more attention in Spanish class. Even though I don't remember all those Spanish vocabulary words now, a few pieces of advice my Spanish teacher gave us still stick in my mind. In between conjugating Spanish verbs, she often inserted random thoughts on life and God.

One day she told us that the book of Philippians is the book of mental health. At first we thought she meant it was for people who were psychotic or schizophrenic. But she went on to explain that it is the perfect read for anyone who wants a mental or emotional boost. If you are discouraged, depressed, a little down in the dumps, suicidal, hopeless—or even if you're already happy but want to be happier—then open up the book of Philippians!

Take a look at some of these mood-boosting pick-me-ups from the book of mental health:

- "My God will meet all your needs according to the riches of his glory in Christ Jesus" (Philippians 4:19).
- "I can do all things through Him who strengthens me" (verse 13, NASB).
- "Being confident of this, that he who began a good work in you will carry it on to completion until the day of Christ Jesus" (Philippians 1:6).
- "Rejoice in the Lord always. I will say it again: Rejoice! . . . Do not be anxious about anything, but in every situation, by prayer and petition, with thanksgiving, present your requests to God. And the peace of God, which transcends all understanding, will guard your hearts and your minds in Christ Jesus" (Philippians 4:4-7).

Live it out: Read the entire book of Philippians this week (it's only four chapters). Underline all the verses that speak to you, so that you can go back and find them easily when you need a boost.

Pray about it: Incorporate one of the verses from Philippians into your prayer today.

Cutting Away the Pain

Surely he took up our pain and bore our suffering. Isaiah 53:4.

Although she is only 16 years old, Katie has had a hard life. For as long as she can remember, she has been abused. She's never felt safe, even in her own home. Her stepfather is one of her abusers, and her mother—the person she expected to protect her—pretends nothing is wrong.

Katie began cutting herself, not to get attention, but to release some of the pain trapped inside of her. Her emotional pain was strong and deep, and she didn't know a better way to get it out. When she first started cutting, it was small incisions on her arms, but in time that led to deeper, larger ones on her arms and legs. Like all addictions, it took more the next time to get the same feeling as the time before. Eventually Katie was making dangerous slashes in her flesh.

Her counselor, a friend of mine, struggled to help Katie find a healthier way to release the emotional pain. As a counselor, she knew there wasn't going to be a simple substitute. In fact, the counselor realized that stopping it would mean that Katie would have to face her emotional pain. She would have to let herself feel it— and only then would she be able to heal it. It might hurt more emotionally in the short term, but it would bring wholeness and happiness in the long term.

Sometimes we do things to try to numb the pain, such as cutting, drinking, overeating, or drowning out reality with constant music, video games, movies, or Internet. We do whatever we can to avoid emotional pain that comes from abuse, rejection, fear, self-hatred, anger, or feelings of inadequacy. But sometimes God is asking us to face the pain. It won't hurt forever, but in order to heal it, we have to acknowledge it and bring it to God. He promises to take our pain and replace it with something good. The Bible says that God will give "a crown of beauty instead of ashes, the oil of joy instead of mourning, and a garment of praise instead of a spirit of despair" (Isaiah 61:3). When you take all your horrible feelings and experiences to Him, He will turn them into something beautiful.

Live it out: If you or someone you know is a cutter, go to an adult for help *today*. Admit the emotional pain behind the cutting, and see how God can turn that pain into something good.

Pray about it: Thank God for taking bad experiences and transforming them.

The Bible Then and Now

Your word, Lord, is eternal. Psalm 119:89.

Times change. What's hot today won't be tomorrow. Have you ever listened to music on an eight-track or a cassette tape? I didn't think so. Ever arrived at school in a horse and buggy? I'm pretty sure that's a no too. Do you currently have a MySpace page? . . . I rest my case.

Some trends last for a few years, while others vanish after just a few months. No matter what, things are always changing. That's what makes the words of the Bible so amazing. They have stuck around for *thousands* of years and are just as meaningful today as when first written. Talk about standing the test of time!

If you think the Bible is outdated, think again. The prophet Isaiah said this about God's Word: "The grass withers and the flowers fall, but the word of our God endures forever" (Isaiah 40:8). Considering he wrote that around 681 B.C., I'd say he was on to something.

David also declared the timelessness of God's Word: "Your word, Lord, is eternal; it stands firm in the heavens" (Psalm 119:89). And he, like Isaiah, wrote these words thousands of years ago.

The promises and encouragement in the Bible haven't gone out of style or lost their value. Amazingly, the Bible is still relevant even though it is ancient.

Live it out: Choose one of your favorite verses in the Bible. Using a study Bible or an Internet search, do a little research and find out the approximate date of the writing of that book of the Bible. Next, find multiple versions of the verse to see how people have reworded that same passage throughout the years.

Pray about it: Thank God for preserving the Bible for thousands of years so that you and other believers could read it.

An Imaginary Person and an Invisible God

For we live by faith, not by sight. 2 Corinthians 5:7.

Before the days of the Food Network and celebrity chefs (such as Rachel Ray and Jamie Oliver), cooking was a little less glamorous. The closest thing to a celebrity chef was Betty Crocker . . . but it turns out she wasn't even a real person.

For decades many considered Betty Crocker the standard of excellence for cooking, baking, and housekeeping. She had numerous cookbooks and even her own radio show. The only problem? Betty Crocker was completely made up.

In the early 1900s the Washburn Crosby Company received hundreds of letters each week from women who wanted baking advice. To make the responses more personal, the company decided to create a person—Betty Crocker—to sign the letters. As the years passed, people wanted to know more about this cooking whiz, so the company had a contest to find someone to provide Betty's signature. Then they hired an actor to be her voice on the radio. And finally they hired an artist to produce a painting of the imaginary Betty.

As long as people saw pictures of Betty Crocker and heard her voice on the radio, they assumed that she was real. People thought, *Of course she is real: we have seen her and heard her!* If you can see and hear someone, it's pretty easy to believe in them. The real challenge comes when you are asked to believe in someone you can't see, hear, or touch.

Jesus Himself knew that faith would be harder for those of us who don't have the chance to see and touch Him. He even explained this to His disciple Thomas: "Then Jesus told him, 'Because you have seen me, you have believed; blessed are those who have not seen and yet have believed'" (John 20:29).

Jesus calls us to have outrageous faith in Him, even though we can't see Him. As Paul declares: "We live by faith, not by sight" (2 Corinthians 5:7). That is, after all, what faith is all about.

Live it out: Even though you can't see God fully, think of ways you can perceive Him at work around you. Let those things help build your faith. Every day, make it your mission to look for evidence of God. Try to consider living by faith instead of sight as an adventure instead of a crisis.
Pray about it: Pray for the courage to live by faith, not sight.

Timing Is Everything

There is a time for everything. Ecclesiastes 3:1.

Talk to any comedian, and they'll tell you timing is everything. A funny comment at the wrong time isn't humorous anymore. But a zinger produced at just the right time will have the crowd roaring with laughter.

Jokesters aren't the only ones who realize the power of timing. Anyone good at what they do—whether they are a preacher or a pro athlete—knows that timing matters.

Wise King Solomon poetically explained that there is a good—and bad—time for everything:

"There is a time for everything,
   and a season for every activity under the heavens:
a time to be born and a time to die,
   a time to plant and a time to uproot,
a time to kill and a time to heal,
   a time to tear down and a time to build,
a time to weep and a time to laugh,
   a time to mourn and a time to dance,
a time to scatter stones and a time to gather them,
   a time to embrace and a time to refrain from embracing,
a time to search and a time to give up,
   a time to keep and a time to throw away,
a time to tear and a time to mend,
   a time to be silent and a time to speak,
a time to love and a time to hate,
   a time for war and a time for peace" (Ecclesiastes 3:1-8).

Solomon sums it up with this: "He has made everything beautiful in its time" (verse 11). The right action or word at the right moment will be beautiful. Don't rush or delay—aim for God's timing.

Live it out: Pay attention to your timing. Are you doing a good thing at a bad time?

Pray about it: Ask God to help you run on His clock instead of your own.

A Work in Progress

For we are God's masterpiece. Ephesians 2:10, NLT.

My husband and I love vacations in Europe. We go sightseeing. (Be thankful that we're not your parents, because we would totally embarrass you by taking cheesy photos in front of everything. You know the type—like when people position themselves so it looks as if they're holding up the Leaning Tower of Pisa with their bare hands. Yeah, photos like that.) We eat lots of good food. (Way to go, Italy! Who *wouldn't* want to eat pizza and pasta every day?) And we pack our days full of fun adventures, including trips to museums.

It is incredible to see museums filled with masterpieces by great artists such as Vincent van Gogh, Leonardo da Vinci, Michelangelo, Rembrandt, and Monet. When you look at their finished artwork, you realize why people travel from all around the world to see it.

You might be surprised, however, to discover many unfinished works in Europe's art museums. You will find canvasses with only half a painting on it, the beginning of portraits abandoned for other projects, and sketches left undone because the artists died before they could complete the work. Even though such pieces are not finished, they are treasured and hung on the walls of the museum. People consider them significant simply because of who started them.

Some days it may not feel like it, but *you* are God's masterpiece. Those days you might regard yourself more like a work in progress than a masterpiece. That's OK, because unlike the artists who left behind unfinished work, God promised He will complete His masterpiece. Philippians 1:6 is a promise you can claim: "Being confident of this, that he who began a good work in you will carry it on to completion until the day of Christ Jesus." He takes His time and doesn't rush. Day by day He will work with you to turn your life into a simply stunning masterpiece.

Live it out: When you feel worthless or hopeless, read Ephesians 2:10 and Philippians 1:6 to remind yourself that God is at work in your life.

Pray about it: Thank God for seeing you as a masterpiece and for promising not to give up on you.

Live It Out!

Rejoice in the Lord always. I will say it again: Rejoice! Philippians 4:4.

An idea that stood out to me from this week's devotional readings:

_____

_____

_____

A verse from this week's devotions that was powerful to me:

_____

_____

_____

A "Live it out" challenge I tried this week:

_____

_____

_____

Something that happened this week that was a blessing:

_____

_____

_____

My prayer today (thanks, requests, praises):

_____

_____

_____

The Perfect Song and the Perfect Prayer at the Perfect Time

But you, Lord, are a compassionate and gracious God, slow to anger, abounding in love and faithfulness. Psalm 86:15.

What can you do during tough times to make things better? You can't always get the circumstances to calm down, but you can get your *spirit* to become more relaxed. When you're not sure what else to do, put into practice the tried-and-true techniques of praying and listening to uplifting music. That's what the book of Psalms is all about. It's filled with songs and prayers, many written during tough times.

Here is part of a song prayer by David that you too can pray during difficult days:

"Hear me, Lord, and answer me,
> for I am poor and needy. . . .
You are my God; have mercy on me, Lord,
> for I call to you all day long.
Bring joy to your servant, Lord,
> for I put my trust in you.
You, Lord, are forgiving and good,
> abounding in love to all who call to you.
Hear my prayer, Lord;
> listen to my cry for mercy.
When I am in distress, I call to you,
> because you answer me. . . .
I will praise you, Lord my God, with all my heart;
> I will glorify your name forever.
For great is your love toward me" (Psalm 86:1-13).

Live it out: The next time you're having a bad day, turn off the Top 40 tunes and listen to Christian music instead. Let it soak into your spirit, and you'll begin to feel your mood change.

Pray about it: Choose one of the psalms as your prayer. Include the verses in your prayer, stopping to interject your own thoughts and feelings.

Skeleton in the Closet

And as I was prophesying, there was a noise, a rattling sound, and the bones came together, bone to bone. Ezekiel 37:7.

Have you ever seen a skeleton? Even one harmlessly hanging in a science classroom, just minding its own business, can be a little creepy (especially if you stare at it for very long). Imagine, then, how strange and eerie it would be to see an entire valley of skeletons come to life—like something straight out of a horror movie! That is exactly what happened to Ezekiel.

In Ezekiel 37 the prophet describes how God swept him away into the middle of a valley piled high with bones. God asked Ezekiel, "Son of man, can these bones live?" (Ezekiel 37:3). Dazed and uncertain, Ezekiel replied, "Sovereign Lord, you alone know" (verse 3).

God then commanded him to prophesy to the bones. How crazy—to preach to bones! But I suppose it didn't seem any crazier to Ezekiel then standing in a valley of bones, so he went ahead and started prophesying. As he spoke, the words of God awakened the Spirit of God in that valley. The bones began to rattle, then began to attach to other bones to form bodies, and finally tendons, flesh, and skin covered those bodies.

That would have been amazing enough, but God didn't stop there. He breathed life into them. But He didn't bring them back to life to sit around that valley and chitchat. Instead, He revived them to do incredible things! Ezekiel describes how "they came to life and stood up on their feet—a vast army" (verse 10). God put those scattered bones together to create a powerful troop of people to get to work for Him.

Do you ever feel like a pile of bones? As if the pieces are all there, but you aren't fully alive? God can bring you back to life. Ask Him to breathe life into you—and you'll be amazed. When He brings you to life, He won't do it halfway. He will fully awaken you to be a part of His army—just like that valley of dry bones.

Live it out: Are there areas of your life in which you don't feel fully alive? What can you do this week to begin to come to life in that area?

Pray about it: Prayerfully read Ezekiel 37:1-14. Ask God what He wants to teach you from that story.

Now, That's a Comeback Story

So then, it was not you who sent me here, but God. Genesis 45:8.

Everybody likes a great comeback story—one in which the underdog manages to score a happy, prizewinning ending. Such feel-good stories give us hope that anything could happen: we could go from rags to riches, geek to chic, wimpy to wonderful.

If you want a remarkable comeback story, look no further than the book of Genesis. There you'll find the truly unbelievable tale of Joseph.

Joseph was his father's favorite son. (You can tell already that this isn't going to go well, because no one likes Mom or Dad showing favoritism.) As you might imagine, Joseph's brothers struggled with a very serious case of sibling rivalry. Genesis 37:4 says, "When his brothers saw that their father loved him more than any of them, they hated him and could not speak a kind word to him." They detested him so much that they sold him into slavery and told their father that Joseph had died. (Makes you feel better about the fact that you screamed at your little brother, doesn't it? At least you didn't peddle him to slavers.)

The experience could have broken a lesser man, but Joseph relied wholly on God and became stronger and wiser as time passed. After years of hard work—and even undeserved time in prison—Joseph went from a despicable slave to the ruler of Egypt. God had blessed him beyond anything he or his brothers could have ever imagined.

When you read the story of Joseph (go ahead, read it in Genesis 37-50—it's unbelievable), you'll see what a spiritual hero he was. One of his finest moments was his meeting up with his brothers years after they mistreated him. Instead of holding a grudge, he completely forgave them and assured them that God had used their cruelty to accomplish great things. He told them: "And now, do not be distressed and do not be angry with yourselves for selling me here, because it was to save lives that God sent me ahead of you. . . . So then, it was not you who sent me here, but God" (Genesis 45:5-8).

The greatest comeback stories end just like that: with an underdog giving God the glory for great things. Remember, the Lord wants to redeem your story, just as He did for Joseph.

Live it out: Read the story of Joseph, and be reminded that God can work everything for good.
Pray about it: Ask God to be the Lord of your life and to lead you through the good and bad.

OCT 9

Passing Judgment on Yourself

Do not judge, or you too will be judged. Matthew 7:1.

It's a tricky thing, how much easier it is to see other people's flaws than our own. We can just look at someone else and tell whether they are phony, self-centered, shallow, or rude. Of course, we don't always notice that we too might be a little phony, self-centered, shallow, or rude.

You know that old saying "It takes one to know one"? When it comes to judging, that sometimes applies. For example, people who are phony are the best at spotting other phonies. (Now, they may not think they *themselves* are a phony, but they nevertheless might be.) We recognize what we are familiar with. Shallowness can spot shallowness. Selfishness can detect selfishness.

Sometimes we criticize things or attitudes we envy or secretly have. For example, maybe you mutter about a guy who has been with a lot of girls. That doesn't mean you also have, but perhaps you envy his popularity and ability to attract them—or maybe you are a girl who wishes you alone had his attention.

Before you judge anyone, think about what it reveals about you. Do you have the same problem? Are you jealous or bitter? When you are tempted to judge others, Jesus advised that you first look at yourself to see if it applies to you, too: "Do not judge, or you too will be judged. For in the same way you judge others, you will be judged, and with the measure you use, it will be measured to you. Why do you look at the speck of sawdust in your brother's eye and pay no attention to the plank in your own eye? How can you say to your brother, 'Let me take the speck out of your eye,' when all the time there is a plank in your own eye? You hypocrite, first take the plank out of your own eye, and then you will see clearly to remove the speck from your brother's eye" (Matthew 7:1-5).

Live it out: When you are tempted to judge someone, stop yourself and do a self-evaluation. Does that judgment apply to you? If so, work on fixing yourself, not someone else.

Pray about it: Ask God to help you see yourself clearly, so that you can grow and learn.

Did You Hear About That?

Gossip separates close friends. Proverbs 16:28.

I recently heard a joke about three longtime friends who were sitting around bored. With nothing better to do, one of them suggested they confess their worst sins to each other. Out of boredom—and curiosity—everyone agreed.

The first friend admitted he was cheating on his girlfriend. "I have a real problem with lust," he confessed. "I just can't control myself!"

The second friend disclosed that he had a problem with stealing. "I've shoplifted from stores, stolen things out of other kids' lockers, and taken money from my parents' wallets. I just can't control myself!"

The third friend was quiet for a second and then said, "Well, my problem is the sin of gossip. Not only can't I control myself, I can't wait to tell someone about this!"

While that story is funny, the impact of gossip isn't. Gossip is tricky, because it creates a false sense of friendship when you're doing it. You and someone else are sharing secret, spicy information, so you experience a rush of connection with each other. However, just like a lot of other bad ideas, gossip feels good for a second but bad in the end.

When it's happening, gossip seems harmless. You think, *What damage can it do?* I'm just telling one person. But gossip doesn't stay put—it keeps spreading. If that one person tells just one other, and that individual shares it with just one more . . . well, you see how this can get messy fast. When that juicy piece of news gets around to the person you were talking about (and don't be surprised if it does), it can do serious damage to your relationship.

Live it out: To be a good friend, follow this gossip-crushing rule: don't say anything behind someone's back that you wouldn't say to their face.

Pray about it: Ask God to help you have the self-control to keep your lips zipped.

OCT 11

I'd Rather Be a Doorkeeper

Better is one day in your courts than a thousand elsewhere. Psalm 84:10.

Would you rather live in a tent that you own, or in a mansion in which you are a servant? Would you rather dwell in a nice house with a lot of rowdies who are always in trouble with the law, or a tiny, modest home with no one around?

Psalm 84 is a song that poses a related question: would you rather be a doorkeeper in the house of God or share the tents of the wicked? The song's message is unquestionable: the best option is to live with God, even as a servant. Here is part of the song:

"How lovely is your dwelling place,
    Lord Almighty!
My soul yearns, even faints,
    for the courts of the Lord;
my heart and my flesh cry out
    for the living God.
Even the sparrow has found a home,
    and the swallow a nest for herself,
where she may have her young—
    a place near your altar,
Lord Almighty, my King and my God.
    Blessed are those who dwell in your house;
they are ever praising you. . . .
    Better is one day in your courts
than a thousand elsewhere;
    I would rather be a doorkeeper in the house of my God
than dwell in the tents of the wicked" (verses 1-10).

Live it out: Volunteer to be a greeter at church for a week. Meet people with enthusiasm, as if you were welcoming them into the very house of God.
Pray about it: Praise God for the opportunity to live with Him.

Live It Out!

"I am the Alpha and the Omega," says the Lord God, "who is, and who was, and who is to come, the Almighty." Revelation 1:8.

An idea that stood out to me from this week's devotional readings:

_____

_____

_____

A verse from this week's devotions that was powerful to me:

_____

_____

_____

A "Live it out" challenge I tried this week:

_____

_____

_____

Something that happened this week that was a blessing:

_____

_____

_____

My prayer today (thanks, requests, praises):

_____

_____

_____

OCT 13

Without a Doubt

Stop doubting and believe. John 20:27.

Left unchecked, I can be a bit of a skeptic. I hear someone tell a grandiose story, and part of me doubts that it's true. Or someone talks about a miracle product that can make you thinner and healthier, and I'm the first to shoot it down. I hate to admit it, but I suppose today, International Skeptics Day, is for people just like me.

This little-known holiday, celebrated on October 13, honors all the doubters out there. So today how could we not remember the most famous doubter of all time: Thomas?

After His resurrection Jesus appeared to a group of His disciples. You can only imagine how thrilled and overjoyed they must have been! Now, because of some really bad timing or a little providential intervention, Thomas wasn't there. Of course, he found out about it soon enough, though. The moment the other disciples saw him, they were jumping up and down, excitedly telling him they had seen Jesus.

Thomas must have thought all of them were either lying or confused, because he didn't believe them. "But he said to them, 'Unless I see the nail marks in his hands and put my finger where the nails were, and put my hand into his side, I will not believe'" (John 20:25). According to the Bible, it looks as if Thomas moped around doubting for quite a while, because it was an entire week later before Jesus showed up in his presence.

When He saw Thomas, Jesus said to him, "Put your finger here; see my hands. Reach out your hand and put it into my side. Stop doubting and believe" (verse 27). Only then did Thomas accept the reality of Jesus' resurrection.

Jesus responded, "Because you have seen me, you have believed; blessed are those who have not seen and yet have believed" (verse 29). When he said that, Christ must have been thinking ahead to all the doubters and skeptics who would come after Thomas. He promised that if we believe and have faith we won't be disappointed. So today on International Skeptics Day, take Jesus' words to heart: "Stop doubting and believe!"

Live it out: Are you a bit of a skeptic? What can you do to build your faith and decrease your doubt? Read Matthew 21:21 and Mark 11:23. What is God's message to you in those verses?

Pray about it: Ask God to help you to believe and not doubt what the Bible says about Him.

Learning to Learn

I will instruct you and teach you in the way you should go. Psalm 32:8.

I have a friend who dropped out of school because he wanted to be a "student of life." For a few years he waited on tables, but when the tips weren't worth it anymore, he tried to land a better job. He quickly realized, however, that listing "life" as his alma mater on his résumé wasn't really working. So after a few years in the school of hard knocks, he signed up to go back to regular school.

We don't have to drop out of school to learn about life. In reality, we are all students of life. Even during the years we're learning facts and figures in a classroom, we're also acquiring life lessons—lessons about God, relationships, priorities, and ourselves.

Almost everything is a learning process. A guy doesn't just wake up one morning and know how to do trigonometry. He has to learn. Nor does a baby come into the world with the ability to walk and talk. She has to learn. Once you accept that everything is a learning process, it gives you the freedom to experiment, to ask questions, and even to fail if need be.

As Christians, there are a lot of things we *assume* that we all should just know. How to pray, for example. If you follow God, you should know how to pray, right? While prayer is talking to God (that sounds basic enough), there are things you can learn about how to pray more effectively. Thus even prayer is a learning process.

Jesus' disciples knew this, so they asked Him to help them *learn* to pray: "One day Jesus was praying in a certain place. When he finished, one of his disciples said to him, 'Lord, teach us to pray, just as John taught his disciples'" (Luke 11:1). Since prayer (like lots of other things) is a learning process, it's OK if we mess up sometimes, if we fall asleep while we're praying, or if we get stumped and run out of things to say. It's OK, because we're still learning.

Life is full of opportunities to discover new things. As a student of life, you will make mistakes and will need to ask questions. It's all a part of the learning process.

Live it out: Is there something you would like to know about? Whatever it is—whether it is how to pray or how to speak Spanish—do one thing this week to help you learn more about it.

Pray about it: As you go through the day, ask God to help you gain the lessons He is trying to teach you.

Now, That's Epic

No eye has seen, no ear has heard, and no mind has imagined what God has prepared for those who love him. I Corinthians 2:9, NLT.

The epic film *Ben-Hur* tells of a prominent Hebrew man, Judah Ben-Hur, who lived during the time of Jesus. As the story develops, Ben-Hur's friend Messala becomes a Roman official and asks Ben-Hur to help crush Jewish uprisings. When Messala goes so far as to pressure Ben-Hur to turn in his own friends, Ben-Hur refuses. Infuriated, Messala makes a public example of Ben-Hur by throwing him and his family into jail. Ben-Hur is then separated from his family and sold as a slave. The remainder of the movie tells the story of Ben-Hur seeking to find redemption from the injustice done to him.

The story has many themes: love, revenge, Christ, forgiveness, friendship, perseverance. It cannot be explained in one simple word. Like *Ben-Hur*, most epic stories are complex. Great stories involve ups and downs, victory and defeat.

Without a doubt, the greatest story of all time is that of Jesus Christ. It is beautifully complex and involves mercy and justice, building up and tearing down, peace and pain, life and death.

Often we desire our lives to be easygoing, fun, and happy all the time. We don't want any difficulties, challenges, or disappointments. But if you would like your life to be extraordinary, you have to accept that it will involve shadow and light, wins and losses. Amazing, heroic lives are full of risks, challenges, courage, and faith. If you trust God, you won't want a safe, small life. You'll want the epic story He has planned just for you.

Whether you're facing good or bad times right now, remember that God has extraordinary plans for you. Stick with Him, and you'll be thrilled as He guides you through all the twists and turns of a wonderful life.

Live it out: When you sense God asking you to do something difficult, don't hesitate or worry about failure. Live the large, exciting life that God has for you.

Pray about it: Say a prayer of surrender to God. Tell Him you are willing to face whatever He brings your way, because you trust Him.

If You Don't Have Anything Nice to Say . . .

The words of the reckless pierce like swords, but the tongue of the wise brings healing. Proverbs 12:18.

Recently a friend invited me to be part of a challenge to go without talking negatively about anyone for 24 hours. *Not a problem,* I thought. *Game on.*

I was certain that it would be kid stuff, so simple. That was until 20 minutes after I started the no-negativity experiment, when I called someone a moron. Uh, yeah, 20 minutes in. And yes, I actually used the word "moron."

Here's how it went. A friend of mine had just finished reading a book in which the author had divulged a lot of private information, personal details that we the public didn't really need to know. My friend asked what I thought, and I sent a text saying, "You're right. The author is a moron for having written this."

I hit "send" and then looked up from my phone with the sudden realization that I had already flunked the no-negativity test. I had called someone a moron. After only 20 minutes.

Now that I was on guard, the next 23 hours and 40 minutes of the experiment were better but not perfect. When a comment seemed too close to call, I tried to remain silent and err on the side of caution.

The no-negativity challenge taught me how easy it is to be careless with words. It takes practice and self-discipline, but it feels good to stop the negativity from flowing out of your mouth. Paul said it this way, "Do not let any unwholesome talk come out of your mouths, but only what is helpful for building others up according to their needs, that it may benefit those who listen" (Ephesians 4:29). According to that verse, here's a good way to filter yourself: before you say something questionable, ask yourself, *Is it necessary? Is it helpful? Is it beneficial?* Better to ask yourself those three questions first than to groan later, *Why did I say that?*

Live it out: Try not to say anything negative today. And then do the same again tomorrow. Keep working on it until it becomes a part of your life.
Pray about it: Ask God to help you learn day by day what needs to be said—and what doesn't deserve the airtime.

The Danger
of Following Your Heart

Search me, God, and know my heart; test me and know my anxious thoughts.
Psalm 139:23.

"Follow your heart!" It's a common piece of advice and inspiration floating all around us. If you're not sure what to do, "follow your heart." When deciding between homework or a movie, "follow your heart." And should you fall madly in love with that bad boy down the street, "follow your heart."

Following your heart sounds passionate and fun, but the Bible actually warns against trusting your own heart as a guide. Jeremiah 17:9 declares, "The heart is deceitful above all things and beyond cure. Who can understand it?" In other words, when your heart is involved, you're not always honest with yourself. You don't see things clearly, and it's hard to grasp the truth about situations. That's why the psalmist David asked God to look into every dark corner of his heart so that he could be honest with himself: "Search me, God, and know my heart; test me and know my anxious thoughts. See if there is any offensive way in me, and lead me in the way everlasting" (Psalm 139:23, 24).

When you're tempted to follow your heart, stop and pray the same prayer that David did. Ask God to examine your heart and make sure there aren't any lies or sins in there. Try to follow God, not just your own impulses. Ask Him for guidance. With big decisions, talk to Christians you respect and ask for their advice. You know how you can look at someone else's life and see things they can't? The same is true when others view your life. Allow those trusted people to help guide you, so that you don't have to rely solely on your heart. Your heart, after all, doesn't always see things clearly.

Live it out: When tempted to make a decision based on your feelings, stop and pray about it first. Ask yourself, *Does what my heart says match what the Bible tells me?* If they don't agree, follow the Bible instead.

Pray about it: Ask God to search your heart and purify it from deceitfulness.

The Upside-down Kingdom

Jesus called the Twelve and said, "Anyone who wants to be first must be the very last, and the servant of all." Mark 9:35.

The 12 guys who became Jesus' closest followers surely thought they were headed for fame and fortune. I can just see it now, the gang of them sitting around imagining the nice homes, expensive robes, and teams of servants they would have one day. After all, they believed Jesus would be king in the future. And if He was going to be king, then as His closest friends, they would end up powerful and influential too.

The desire for greatness always seemed to be kicking around in their minds. At one point the 12 rowdies even broke out into a fight about it: "An argument started among the disciples as to which of them would be the greatest" (Luke 9:46). When Jesus saw this, He knew His disciples still didn't understand what kind of kingdom He was building. In response, He tried to explain that everything was upside-down in His kingdom: "For it is the one who is least among you all who is the greatest" (verse 48).

Another time, Jesus attempted to explain it again: "Jesus called the Twelve and said, 'Anyone who wants to be first must be the very last, and the servant of all'" (Mark 9:35). The Twelve probably didn't like the sounds of that at all. They wanted to *have* servants, not *be* them.

Jesus didn't just talk the talk about being a servant—He acted like one as He served people all day every day. Before His death He even got down on His knees and washed the dirt off the disciples' feet, setting yet another example of how to be a true servant.

In God's upside-down kingdom the heroes are not the ones who become rich and famous. Instead, they are the people who meet the needs of others. In fact, God will personally applaud those servants one day. He will call them from the back of the line to the front and say: "Well done, good and faithful servant! . . . Come and share your master's happiness!" (Matthew 25:23).

Live it out: Find a way to serve someone today. Don't do it to make yourself look good or to draw attention to yourself, but as a loving act.
Pray about it: Pray, "Lord reveal to me today how You want me to serve You and others."

Live It Out!

The righteous person may have many troubles, but the Lord delivers him from them all. Psalm 34:19.

An idea that stood out to me from this week's devotional readings:

_____

_____

_____

A verse from this week's devotions that was powerful to me:

_____

_____

_____

A "Live it out" challenge I tried this week:

_____

_____

_____

Something that happened this week that was a blessing:

_____

_____

_____

My prayer today (thanks, requests, praises):

_____

_____

_____

Don't Crush My Heart

Above all else, guard your heart, for everything you do flows from it.
Proverbs 4:23.

You can't get them off your mind. You think about them all day, every day. You replay what they said to you again and again. Every time they come around, your palms get a little sweaty and your stomach a little jumpy. If any of this sounds familiar, you, my friend, might have yourself a crush.

At some point it happens to us all. You don't know why, but that one special person is your undoing. You are crushing hard. If you feel as if your emotions are pouring out at full blast, take a second to slow down, so that your heart doesn't end up crushed to pieces. Here are a few things to keep in mind:

- **Become friends.** The best way to get to know others is to be their friend. Try to calmly and prayerfully dial down your emotions so that you can speak to the person without getting completely flustered.
- **Take a hint.** If that special someone tells you they aren't interested in you in the same way, believe them. Don't try to pressure or convince them otherwise. Instead—and this is the most important part—just continue to be nice and friendly. Give yourselves the chance to be friends without any pressure.
- **Don't exaggerate the situation.** If you get rejected by a crush, don't think that means it will happen the rest of your life with every person you might like. When it's the right person and the right time, there will be no rejection involved.
- **Let God define your value.** Don't let your sense of worth rest completely on what this one person thinks of you. Be confident, knowing that God has already said you are valuable.

Live it out: If you are crushing on someone, discuss it with an older person whom you respect. Talk it through so that you can understand your feelings and what you should do about them.

Pray about it: Ask God to give you calmness and confidence about the relationships He has planned for you. Pray that He—not your emotions—will guide your decisions.

OCT 21

Getting More Than You Deserve

Blessed is the nation whose God is the Lord, the people he chose
for his inheritance. Psalm 33:12.

Billionaire businesswoman Leona Helmsley was nicknamed the Queen of Mean because she was heartless and tormenting to everyone who crossed her path. When she died in 2007, she had a lot of money—but not a lot of friends. Some people said that she didn't like anyone enough to leave her fortune to them, so at her death she left $12 million to . . . *wait for it* . . . her dog. Yes, in her last will and testament, she actually arranged that her tiny Maltese, Trouble, would receive a hefty fortune.

Turns out that money wasn't the only thing Trouble inherited. Trouble also ended up inheriting a little trouble of his own. Once word got out that the tiny pup was richer than most people, the creature became the target of dozens of death and kidnapping threats. His keeper received menacing calls declaring, "I will kill that dog! I need that money!"

While most of us would like to inherit a cool 12 mill, none of us wants trouble. Unfortunately, however, we have all received an inheritance that brought with it some problems. Everyone on earth has inherited a sinful nature from earth's first parents, Adam and Eve.

Fortunately, though, there is great news worth more than millions of dollars. God never intended to leave us alone to deal with a cursed, messed-up inheritance. Through the life and death of Jesus He made a way for us to overcome it. Because of His amazing love for us, we are set to inherit eternal life and all the riches and rewards of knowing God. He is constantly at work, inviting us into a never-ending, loving relationship.

Some people would say that a dog doesn't deserve $12 million. They're probably right. But we don't deserve all the love God lavishes on us either. Luckily for us, when God is involved, things always turn out so much better than we deserve.

Live it out: Treat people better than you think they merit. In this way, you will be dealing with them as Christ has with you.

Pray about it: Thank God for the cross and His plan that made a way for us to trade our sinful inheritance for a fantastic, blessed one.

Is This Going to Be on the Test?

For the word of God is alive and active. Hebrews 4:12.

When adults tell you education is valuable, they're right. Nevertheless, on days a substitute teacher hands you a stack of seemingly pointless worksheets (that you're pretty sure will never even be graded), you start to doubt the worth of the classroom.

Then other days you feel bombarded with data. Fortunately, as your eyes glaze over with information overload, some brave soul raises his or her hand and asks what everyone else is wondering: "Is this going to be on the test?"

Some of the things you learn in school may seem useless at the time (but trust me, it turns out you actually *will* use the principles of algebra in real life). And some facts are crammed so tightly and quickly into your brain that they stick around only long enough to make it through the quiz.

However, there is some information that is guaranteed to be worthwhile and useful as long as you live. Anything (yes, *anything*) you learn from Scripture will be valuable for you for the rest of your life. God promises that the Bible is not dead, useless facts. It will actually come alive and spark something inside of you: "For the word of God is alive and active. Sharper than any double-edged sword, it penetrates even to dividing soul and spirit, joints and marrow; it judges the thoughts and attitudes of the heart" (Hebrews 4:12).

Proverbs 2 lists a number of great things that will happen if you store the Bible in your mind: you'll have success; God will protect you; you will know what to do in tricky situations; you will be wise; you will be saved from wicked people. Proverbs 3:1, 2 goes on to guarantee that when you store the Bible in your mind and heart, you will live a long, prosperous, peaceful life: "My son, do not forget my teaching, but keep my commands in your heart, for they will prolong your life many years and bring you peace and prosperity."

If you fill your mind and heart with Scripture, it will stay there long after any pop quiz: "The grass withers and the flowers fall, but the word of our God endures forever" (Isaiah 40:8).

Live it out: Today choose a Bible verse to memorize and plant it in your heart and mind.

Pray about it: Ask God to help you remember the Scriptures you have read or studied.

A Judge-free Zone

The Lord is gracious and compassionate, slow to anger and rich in love.
Psalm 145:8.

Nerd alert: I recently sat on a jury and took more notes than I did my entire seventh-grade year. People usually regard jury duty as dreadful and boring, but mine turned out to be fascinating. I sat on a trial that played out like a prime-time drama—gang stabbings, bloody shanks, heroine packets, prison fights, marked money, and undercover drug deals.

Before the court allowed any of us to serve as jurors, it asked a series of questions to make sure we would be impartial and competent. It included such questions as "Do you know, or have any connection, with the defendant?"

Another was "Does your religion forbid you from sitting in judgment of a fellow human being?" My answer, not spoken aloud, came to mind quickly: *No, in my religion we're actually pretty good at it.* I laughed to myself at the thought, but I knew in my heart that judgment in the church is no laughing matter. Many people have been devastated when they felt judged by their church community.

A lot of Christians would deny they judge people: instead we say we're "calling it as I see it," "sizing people up," or "using the gift of discernment." But just because we label it something other than judging doesn't make it any less judgmental.

I had a breakthrough about judgment when I was on jury duty. It was this: I judged someone guilty and at the same time I felt incredible compassion for him. Compassion that made me want to cry, to speak words of hope to the guilty. I saw evidence (and video footage!) of the cruelty he had inflicted, and I just felt really sad for him. I wondered about his life, his family, why he had chosen a gang as his chance for a future. The experience made me incredibly grateful that the judge of my life is compassionate. If I—a selfish, judgmental person—can have compassion for the guilty, what greater compassion our loving God must have for all of us.

Live it out: Make an effort this week to be especially kind to a person you have previously judged harshly.
Pray about it: Thank God for showing you enormous amounts of love and compassion even though you are flawed and sinful.

The Promises of Romans 8

What, then, shall we say in response to these things? If God is for us, who can be against us? Romans 8:31.

Today, take a look at some of the amazing promises in Romans 8. When you claim them, it will change your world! Here are just a few that will help you during difficult times:

- **When it looks as if things are falling apart all around you, claim this promise:** "And we know that in all things God works for the good of those who love him, who have been called according to his purpose" (Romans 8:28).
- **When you feel bullied or left out, claim this promise:** "What, then, shall we say in response to these things? If God is for us, who can be against us? He who did not spare his own Son, but gave him up for us all—how will he not also, along with him, graciously give us all things?" (verses 31, 32).
- **When you feel unlovable or defeated, claim this promise:** "In all these things we are more than conquerors through him who loved us. For I am convinced that neither death nor life, neither angels nor demons, neither the present nor the future, nor any powers, neither height nor depth, nor anything else in all creation, will be able to separate us from the love of God that is in Christ Jesus our Lord" (verses 37-39).
- **When you feel that you need to pray but don't know what to say, claim this promise:** "In the same way, the Spirit helps us in our weakness. We do not know what we ought to pray for, but the Spirit himself intercedes for us through wordless groans. And he who searches our hearts knows the mind of the Spirit, because the Spirit intercedes for God's people in accordance with the will of God" (verses 26, 27).

Live it out: Read the entire chapter of Romans 8. Underline the verses that mean the most to you.

Pray about it: Turn one of the promises of Romans 8 into a prayer. Pray those words, and tell God that you believe Him and are taking Him at His word.

OCT 25

Speeding Into Trouble

Unfailing love and truth have met together. Righteousness and peace have kissed!
Psalm 85:10, NLT.

If you are a driver, you *hate* it when a police officer pulls you over for speeding (yikes!). But if you do get pulled over, you *love* it when the officer goes easy and just gives you a verbal warning instead of a ticket (yea!). Anyone who has ever had that experience knows the sinking feeling of dread that comes with the flashing lights—and the happiness that floods you when those lights are turned off and you head for home without a ticket.

I've heard quite a few preachers tell stories about getting pulled over by a nice officer who lets them off the hook. Such ministers even use their stories to teach the grace of God. They explain it this way: as a driver, they were guilty of breaking the speeding law, but the officer showed them grace and said they didn't have to pay. Then they go on to explain that like those speeding incidents, we have all broken God's law, but God extends His grace so that we don't have to pay the penalty.

But the speeding-ticket comparison has a problem. With the car-and-cop story, *no one* paid the penalty even though the law was broken.

Imagine this more accurate scenario: you are before a judge because you are guilty of speeding. The judge says, "You are free to go. You do not have to pay the penalty for breaking the law. I will not ask you to pay this speeding ticket." As you turn to leave, you see the judge reach into his or her back pocket and pull out a wallet. He or she counts out $215, the cost of the ticket, and pays the full amount. Now, *that* is what Jesus did. *He* paid our penalty. God did not ignore the law or say that it didn't matter. Instead, Jesus died on the cross and displayed both grace and justice. We did the crime, but He did the time.

Live it out: How does it make you feel to know that Jesus paid for your penalty on the cross?

Pray about it: Thank God for the fact that Jesus died on the cross to pay for your crime.

Live It Out!

You make known to me the path of life; you will fill me with joy in your presence, with eternal pleasures at your right hand. Psalm 16:11.

An idea that stood out to me from this week's devotional readings:

_____
_____
_____

A verse from this week's devotions that was powerful to me:

_____
_____
_____

A "Live it out" challenge I tried this week:

_____
_____
_____

Something that happened this week that was a blessing:

_____
_____
_____

My prayer today (thanks, requests, praises):

_____
_____
_____

Excuses, Excuses

This is what you are to say to the Israelites: "I AM has sent me to you." Exodus 3:14.

When God chooses you for a special assignment, it's a good idea not to try to talk Him out of it. That's exactly what Moses did, though, when God called him to lead the Israelites out of slavery.

You would think that the voice of God coming from a burning bush would have been enough to convince Moses to go along with the divine plan, but he still resisted. Picture this: it had been just another ho-hum day for Moses. He was out watching sheep in the desert (yawn) when the angel of the Lord appeared to him in flames of fire in a bush that did not get consumed.

The Lord told Moses, "I have indeed seen the misery of my people in Egypt. I have heard them crying out because of their slave drivers, and I am concerned about their suffering. So I have come down to rescue them. . . . So now, go. I am sending you to Pharaoh to bring my people the Israelites out of Egypt" (Exodus 3:7-10).

To make a long story short, allow me to give you a paraphrased list of some of the excuses Moses used to try to get out of his assignment:

"Me? I'm a nobody! Find somebody who is important, famous, or on payroll to do this kind of thing" (see verse 11).

"What if they don't believe me and think I made the whole thing up?" (see Exodus 4:1).

"I stutter! Plus, I am terrified of public speaking!" (see verse 10).

When God wouldn't accept any of these excuses, Moses finally just broke down and begged: "Please send someone else" (verse 13). Fortunately, the Lord wasn't a pushover, and a little tantrum didn't worry Him. He told Moses that He would provide everything necessary to accomplish the task. Finally Moses agreed, and it was the best thing that ever happened to him. He became a part of a thrilling, epic story that changed the course of history.

When God calls you to do something, don't try to talk Him out of it. Instead, thank Him for the privilege—and trust Him to give you everything you need to accomplish the job.

Live it out: Is God asking you to do something? Don't hesitate or make excuses. Start today.

Pray about it: Pray for the courage to move past your fears and excuses.

That's the Way the Cookie Grumbles

Do everything without grumbling. Philippians 2:14.

When things aren't going well, what do you do? Some people get to work to improve the situation, while others just start complaining. Complaining is exactly what the Israelites did. God had just freed them from a miserable life as slaves, and Moses was leading them through the desert to a better life. You would think they would be happy to be moving on, but after long days trekking through the sand they were simply tired, ungrateful, and cranky.

They even started having selective memory. Looking back on it, they began to think life in Egypt maybe hadn't been so bad after all. As they became increasingly hungry and hopeless, they began to whine that they would rather have remained as slaves for the rest of their lives. They complained day and night: "It would have been better for us to serve the Egyptians than to die in the desert!" (Exodus 14:12). "If only we had died by the Lord's hand in Egypt! There we sat around pots of meat and ate all the food we wanted, but you have brought us out into this desert to starve this entire assembly to death" (Exodus 16:3).

The Israelites just kept saying the same thing again and again. Blaming Moses for everything, as if the whole thing had been his stupid idea, they forgot that it was all *God's* idea. Exhausted by the constant complaining, Moses and his brother Aaron reminded the Israelites: "You are not grumbling against us, but against the Lord." (In other words: "You cranky kids might want to tone it down a little, because you're going to have to take this up with God, not just little ol' me.") The brother leaders went on to give this message from God to the Israelites: "Come before the Lord, for he has heard your grumbling" (verse 9).

The Lord was patient with the people, but their trip would have been a lot shorter and sweeter if they had zipped their lips and stopped griping.

Even though we're not in a desert, we are all on a journey. If you're tempted to grumble, remember you are complaining against God, not just people or circumstances. As you go through life, take this travel advice from Philippians 2:14: "Do everything without grumbling."

Live it out: Try not to complain about anything today. Instead, find something to compliment.

Pray about it: Thank God for all the blessings He has given you along life's journey.

The Long, Winding, Watery Road

Do not be afraid. Stand firm and you will see the deliverance the Lord will bring you today. Exodus 14:13.

When God leads us, He doesn't always pick the shortest route. In fact, the Bible says that He deliberately chose *not* to take the Israelites on the shortest path. "When Pharaoh let the people go, God did not lead them on the road through the Philistine country, though that was shorter. . . . So God led the people around by the desert road toward the Red Sea" (Exodus 13:17, 18). God had His reasons, of course. He knew the Israelites wouldn't be prepared to face possible war if they went through Philistine country. Nevertheless, no one knew what God was thinking by leading them straight toward the Red Sea! How would they ever get past that?

To make matters worse, as the Israelites neared the Red Sea, Pharaoh decided he didn't want to let his slaves go after all. He had gathered his troops to pursue the Israelites and return them to captivity.

As Pharaoh approached, the Israelites were terrified. Moses, however, did not lose faith. He encouraged them to trust God: "Moses answered the people, 'Do not be afraid. Stand firm and you will see the deliverance the Lord will bring you today. The Egyptians you see today you will never see again. The Lord will fight for you; you need only to be still'" (Exodus 14:13, 14).

God did indeed deliver His followers. He parted the Red Sea so that the Israelites could walk through on dry land. As their enemies rushed toward them, the Lord swept the waters back together, burying the Egyptians in a watery grave.

It may feel as if you are standing in front of a Red Sea. God has led you on a long path that has put you right at the water's edge. You have no idea how you're going to get across. Whether you are facing a sea or a mountain, if God wants you on the other side, He will get you there. Do exactly what Moses commanded: don't be afraid, stand firm, and watch carefully—because the Lord is about to deliver you.

Live it out: If you are facing a difficult area in life, step out in faith and trust God's leading.

Pray about it: Pray for the courage to keep walking on the path that God has called you to, even when you don't know what's coming next.

How About a Little Positivity?

We should go up and take possession of the land, for we can certainly do it.
Numbers 13:30.

There they were. The Israelites were on the very edge of that sweet, sweet Promised Land of Canaan. Rumor had it that milk and honey flowed in the Promised Land . . . and the Israelites could almost taste it. Oh, and when the wind picked up just right, they were certain they could even smell it.

But alas, now that they were actually near the Promised Land they were scared. Scared to death. Ten of the spies who had scoped out Canaan came back saying that it would be *impossible* to take the land from the tough guys who lived there. And those spies really worked the Israelites into a frenzy with their terrifying stories. I can just hear them talking to the crowd in an exaggerated, eerie voice: "The land we explored devours those living in it. All the people we saw there are of great size. . . . We seemed like grasshoppers in our own eyes" (Numbers 13:32, 33).

But despite all the fear and despair, Joshua and Caleb still tried to persuade the crowd: "Let's go for it! God is on our side!" The crowd, however, couldn't be rallied. Well, not in a good way, that is. They did end up rallying together, but it was to complain, cry, and start a campaign to stone Joshua and Caleb. (Yes, the Bible says they actually did all of those things.)

God didn't remain silent. He said to Moses, "How long will they refuse to believe in me, in spite of all the signs I have performed among them?" (Numbers 14:11). "Not one of you will enter the land I swore with uplifted hand to make your home, except Caleb son of Jephunneh and Joshua son of Nun" (verse 30). So there it was: because they didn't believe God was powerful enough to help them, He retracted the offer. None of those doubters were going to get the chance to live in the Promised Land. That is, except Caleb and Joshua, the voices of positivity.

If God leads you to a situation that you dismiss as impossible, you will miss out on an amazing opportunity. But if you, like Joshua and Caleb, have God-sized faith, you will end up a part of something absolutely incredible.

Live it out: If you are tempted to complain or doubt today, try out a positive attitude instead.
Pray about it: Ask God to help you see the possibilities in a situation, not just the problems.

OCT 31

A Snake in the Grass . . . and in the Tent . . . and in the Food

Whoever believes in him shall not perish but have eternal life. John 3:16.

The Israelites were in a ratty mood. But really, what was new? They had been that way for nearly 40 years. The trip from Egypt (where they had been slaves) to Canaan (their new home of absolute awesomeness) should have taken only 11 days. But because they were so nasty and coldhearted, God gave them time to sort things out by taking them the long way home. And when I say *the long way home,* I mean the *very* long way home. When it was all said and done, God had them weaving through the desert for 40 years instead of 11 days.

For 40 long years those cranky Israelites kept asking their leader Moses, "Are we there yet?" (And you know there must have been times Moses would just slump his shoulders and say, "No, we're not there yet! And if you don't stop whining, I'm going to give you something to whine about!")

And then, as if they didn't have enough to complain about already, poisonous serpents started slithering throughout their camp. The snakes were everywhere: in their tents, in their beds, and in their food. Indeed, now those whiners really did have something to whine about! All around them loved ones were dying from snakebites.

The Israelites went to Moses and admitted that their attitude was out of line. They also asked him to pray for God to take away the snakes. And the Lord responded, but not how they expected. Instead of removing the snakes, He gave a cure for those who had been bitten. He asked Moses to put up a tall pole with a brass serpent on the very top of it. When someone who had been bitten glanced at the serpent on the pole, they were healed.

The serpent on the pole symbolized Jesus, who years later would hang on a cross. When people look at Him on the cross and believe that He can save them, He does just that.

Live it out: Spend a few minutes thinking about Jesus hanging on the cross to save you.

Pray about it: Say a prayer of thanks that Jesus hung on the cross to be the cure for your healing.

God's Long-term Plan

In the hope of eternal life, which God, who does not lie, promised before the beginning of time. Titus 1:2.

Would you date a person you knew would cheat on you? Would you plan a beach vacation to a place that you knew a hurricane would ravage while you were there? Would you invest every penny you have in a stock you knew would fail? Or would you move all your belongings into a new house you knew was going to burn down?

If we knew bad things were coming our way, most of us would choose a path that would allow us to avoid the pain and problems. God, however, is altogether more complex than we are. Before Creation, He knew that people could sin, yet He created us anyway. He might have chosen to avoid the pain and problems, but instead He made a plan to redeem us.

The Bible describes Jesus as "the Lamb who was slain from the creation of the world" (Revelation 13:8). That means the cross was part of the plan as soon as Creation was part of the plan. When God created people, He established a way to save them.

From the very beginning, God knew things would all work out in the end, but He was also aware that there would be lots of pain in the meantime.

Some people say that the cross was the price of sin. You could put it another way, too: the cross was the price of Creation. The plan of salvation existed from the beginning of time. Jesus ran through the worst-case scenario in His mind. He knew that if He created us and we sinned, He would have to die—and He chose to create us anyway.

Live it out: How does it make you feel to realize that God knew Jesus would have to die so that you could be born and live eternally? How can you express your gratitude for God's timeless and enormous love?

Pray about it: Thank God for loving you so much that He made a plan to save you before you were even born.

Live It Out!

Depend on the Lord in whatever you do, and your plans will succeed.
Proverbs 16:3, NCV.

An idea that stood out to me from this week's devotional readings:

_____

_____

_____

A verse from this week's devotions that was powerful to me:

_____

_____

_____

A "Live it out" challenge I tried this week:

_____

_____

_____

Something that happened this week that was a blessing:

_____

_____

_____

My prayer today (thanks, requests, praises):

_____

_____

_____

A Reality Check and a Swimming Pool

For the Son of Man came to seek and to save the lost. Luke 19:10.

Imagine a grown man sitting in a kiddie pool, a small plastic pool two feet wide. He is splashing, laughing, playing with a rubber duckie and a plastic battleship. From out of nowhere a distressed lifeguard swoops in and drags him from the pool onto dry land. The panting lifeguard, struggling to catch his breath, announces, "I've saved you!" The maddened "swimmer" responds, "Saved me from what, buddy? I was having a great time!"

A lot of us are like the man in the kiddie pool. Life seems safe enough. We have a few toys and distractions, so that we don't feel the need for anyone to pull us out of the pool.

However, God views our condition differently. Life on earth isn't like life in a kiddie pool. He sees us as though we are in a bottomless ocean surrounded not by rubber duckies, but by sharks. No longer able to tread water, because our muscles are exhausted, we face certain death. It is then that the lifeguard swoops in to save us from the deadly sea. When the lifeguard declares, "I have saved you!" we do not wonder, "Saved me from what?" Instead, we are fully aware of our need and our gratitude.

Here's the difference between life in the kiddie pool and that in the ocean. Sometimes sin just doesn't look all that bad to us. We don't realize the magnitude of sin and salvation. God, however, recognizes that we would be lost (drowning!) unless a Savior came to swoop us up and carry us to safety.

Do you see the beauty and power of Jesus' death on the cross? If you do, you have realized your need of God. But if you don't, it is possible you haven't yet grasped the depth of your sin and need. These two beliefs always go together:

1. We are sinners who desperately need a Savior.
2. God is gracious, loving, and eager to save.

Live it out: Read the Crucifixion story in Mark 15:1-39, and then take a few moments to quietly reflect on how much God loves you and wants to save you.
Pray about it: Thank God for saving you.

NOV 4

Fishing Without a License

"Come, follow me," Jesus said, "and I will send you out to fish for people."
Matthew 4:19.

Here's a story that sounds a little fishy to me.

In May 2011 Martin Reid, a farmer from Montreal, Quebec, applied for a fishing license. Not because he wanted to go fishing with a rod and reel in a nearby lake. No, it was because he wanted to remove the fish from his flooded *land*. After massive flooding, Martin's cornfields had been submerged in three feet of water. The desperate farmer needed to get rid of the carp swimming through his rows of corn. Martin had learned the hard way that he would need a license. You see, Martin's farm had also flooded back in 1993. Thinking nothing of it, he and his father had removed all of the fish swarming the flooded fields. But once the water and the fish were gone, Martin was flooded with another problem. He was fined $1,000 for having taken fish without a fishing license. The second offense, he was warned, would cost him a whopping $100,000.

So it was that Martin went and applied for a fishing license in May 2011, so that he could legally scoop the carp off his field without having to pay a $100,000 fine.

When Jesus chose His ministry helpers, the first people he selected were fishermen: "As Jesus was walking beside the Sea of Galilee, he saw two brothers, Simon called Peter and his brother Andrew. They were casting a net into the lake, for they were fishermen. 'Come, follow me,' Jesus said, 'and I will send you out to *fish for people.*' At once they left their nets and followed him" (Matthew 4:18-20).

The fishermen disciples didn't have any license or formal training in fishing for *people*. But Jesus called them to do that anyway. Jesus summons you to fish for people too. You may feel unqualified for the work, but Jesus doesn't require any special training or fishing license. He just wants you to talk to others about Him. If you cast the line, He'll take care of reeling in the catch. No license required.

Live it out: What does it mean to you to "fish for people"? Think of some practical, loving ways you can do that.

Pray about it: Ask God to help you reach out to others and help them come to Him.

How to Read the Bible

For the word of God is alive and active. Hebrews 4:12.

If someone asked you how to know God better, what would you say? If you're like the majority of Christians, you would suggest two things: prayer and Bible study. But while it seems we all realize that they are critical components of getting to know God, few of us know how to really incorporate them into our lives.

One of the most common things I hear from young believers (and older ones too!) is "I know I need to read the Bible, but I don't know where to start." Cracking open the Bible can seem overwhelming if you're not sure where to begin, so here are some tried and true ways to embark on your journey in the Word of God.

- **Start with Jesus.** The life of Jesus as recorded by Matthew, Mark, Luke, and John is a great place to commence. The Gospels are interesting and inspiring, because they are filled with amazing stories. Most important, they reveal how loving, accepting, and powerful Jesus is. The more you know about Him, the more you'll love Him.
- **Follow your heart.** If you sense the Holy Spirit has been trying to teach you about a certain topic, look it up in the Bible. For example, if you have an interest in learning more about faith or joy or love, find the key words in the concordance of your Bible. Then do a topical study, going from verse to verse.
- **Try what's popular.** Psalms and Proverbs are popular books for a reason: they speak straight to the heart. Psalms is filled with heartfelt words spoken to God. Proverbs is packed with some of the most practical information in the Bible. If you want to know how to live your best life, read Proverbs.
- **Mark it up.** Some may disagree, but I think it is important to mark up your Bible. Highlight the verses that are special to you, and you'll be more likely to read them again, because they're easy to find. You can even draw a star or an exclamation point by them to remind you that God spoke to you through that verse.

Live it out: Don't wait any longer. Try one of the Bible-reading pointers today.
Pray about it: Every single time you open the Word of God, pray for God's guidance.

NOV 6

The Story of the Scarlet Cord

By faith the prostitute Rahab, because she welcomed the spies, was not killed with those who were disobedient. Hebrews 11:31.

If you think Bible stories are boring, you haven't heard the story of the scarlet cord yet. It's like something straight out of a movie: danger, deceit, violence, and espionage.

It all started when Joshua, who was leading the Israelites, secretly sent two spies to find out how to seize Jericho. Once they snuck into the bustling city, they needed a place to stay; and somehow they ended up at the home of a prostitute, Rahab.

When the king heard about the spies (and kings always seem to learn about such things), he sent a message to Rahab to turn the spies over to the authorities immediately. But pretty little Rahab wouldn't be bullied. She told the king's messengers that the spies had already left, even though they were really hiding under stalks of grain on her rooftop.

Rahab rushed to the roof and told the spies she had just covered for them—big-time. She explained that she had done it because she believed God was going to give Jericho to them. Even more than that, she even declared that the Deity they followed was one true God. In return for protecting them, Rahab asked that they save her and her family when they returned to take the city. The spies agreed, telling her to put a scarlet cord in her window so that the soldiers would know not to harm them.

When the Israelites captured Jericho, they looked for that scarlet cord, and they kept their word. Rahab and her family were the only ones in all of Jericho to survive.

Thousands of years later James wrote that we can learn a lot from Rahab. He said she had a great combination of faith and action. She believed something, and she did something about it. "You see that a person is considered righteous by what they do and not by faith alone. In the same way, was not even Rahab the prostitute considered righteous for what she did when she gave lodging to the spies and sent them off in a different direction? As the body without the spirit is dead, so faith without deeds is dead" (James 2:24-26).

Live it out: Find a way this week to act on your faith in God. Don't just believe it—act on it!

Pray about it: Pray for the courage to be bold in your beliefs *and* in your actions.

Three-Minute Health Boosters

Dear friend, I pray that you may enjoy good health and that all may go well with you. 3 John 2.

Don't wait until you feel sick and tired (and old) before you start caring about your health. The sooner you develop healthy habits, the better. Making healthy choices might sound intimidating, but there are actually a lot of quick and easy things you can do. Here are a few health boosters you can do in three minutes or less. How easy is that?

- **Count your blessings.** When you acknowledge the good things in your life, you tap into positive emotions. Research has linked that type of positivity with better health, longer life, and greater well-being. Counting your blessings also helps eliminate negative feelings, such as chronic anger, worry, and hostility, which can contribute to poor health and disease. At the end of every day, think back or journal at least five things for which you were grateful.

- **Just breathe.** Have you ever been upset and someone told you, "Just calm down. Take a deep breath"? Come to find out, that is really good advice. Deep breathing refreshes your body, relaxes your muscles, and even lowers blood pressure. When you are tackling a big homework project, facing an athletic challenge, or doing something scary, be sure to take deep breaths.

- **Be more flexible.** Cardio and weight training aren't the only kinds of exercise. Flexibility is also an important component of fitness. Here's how it works: stretching increases your flexibility. And flexibility improves your health in a number of ways. It aids your circulation, posture, coordination, balance, and physical performance. Also it reduces pain and helps with injury prevention and stress relief. Take just a minute or two to stretch throughout the day. Reach up for the sky, or bend down and touch your toes. While sitting in your desk, twist from your hips. These tiny stretches can help keep you flexible. Who knows, maybe you'll even be able to do the splits if you keep up with the stretches!

Live it out: Try at least one of these two-minute health boosters today.
Pray about it: Thank God for your health!

At Least You Have Legs

Do everything without complaining or arguing. Philippians 2:14, NCV.

Throughout my teen years whenever I complained about anything, my dad would always say, "At least you have legs." The expression came from a story about a man who grumbled that he didn't have shoes—until he met a man who didn't have legs.

The other day my husband, my sister, and I were eating dinner at a restaurant. My sister asked how I was, and I started telling her about some problems I had been experiencing. Now, my sister grew up in the same household as I did, so I'm pretty sure her response was about to be "At least you have legs." But before she could get the words out, the TV screens in the restaurant started playing the story of a man without legs—or arms.

The news piece showed the man tackling all kinds of daily tasks, including making a sandwich by using his mouth, chin, and torso. As a dramatic finale, they depicted him participating in a triathlon, swimming with a fin attached to the end of his body, thrusting himself forward inch by inch. Throughout the segment my husband stared at the TV, shouting, "Are you watching this? This is *unbelievable*. Are you watching this?"

When it finished, I said, "Yeah, what I was complaining about earlier, just never mind that."

I have to admit my dad was right: our complaints seem less significant once we get a little perspective. Today instead of focusing on what you don't have, concentrate on what you do have. You'll be amazed how a little shift in viewpoint will make a big change in your attitude toward life.

Live it out: Instead of dwelling on your own complaints, think of someone who is going through a hard time and then do something to help that individual today.
Pray about it: Say a prayer consisting only of thanks. Tell God all the things—big and small—for which you are thankful.

Live It Out!

The Lord wants to show his mercy to you. He wants to rise and comfort you.
The Lord is a fair God, and everyone who waits for his help will be happy.
Isaiah 30:18, NCV.

An idea that stood out to me from this week's devotional readings:

_____
_____
_____

A verse from this week's devotions that was powerful to me:

_____
_____
_____

A "Live it out" challenge I tried this week:

_____
_____
_____

Something that happened this week that was a blessing:

_____
_____
_____

My prayer today (thanks, requests, praises):

_____
_____
_____

Which Will It Be:
Option A or Option B?

But if serving the Lord seems undesirable to you, then choose for yourselves this day whom you will serve.... But as for me and my household, we will serve the Lord. Joshua 24:15.

If someone offered (a) to buy you dinner at your favorite restaurant, or (b) to let you eat the crumbs off their kitchen floor, which would you choose?

Or what if someone said that they would (a) purchase you an entirely new wardrobe, or (b) let you sew your own clothes out of the dirty rags they use to change the oil on their car—which would you select?

How about this one? Would you rather accept (a) a check for $1 billion, or (b) a shiny nickel from the year you were born? Again, which would you take?

Now, if Someone offered you (a) a fascinating life full of adventure, or (b) a mediocre life full of ordinariness, which one would you opt for?

Chances are you'll never get those first three offers, although it doesn't hurt to have an answer ready just in case. However, that last one—the proposal of a fascinating life full of adventure—*that* one has already been extended to you. Jesus said He wants us to live to the fullest, to fill our lives all the way to the edges: "I have come that they may have life, and have it to the full" (John 10:10).

Don't settle for less than what God wants for you. And don't avoid risks because you're afraid to fail. Failure is a part of success—and life. Never let intimidation or insecurity keep you from getting to know other people. And don't live scared and defeated. Live to the full.

Live it out: The next time God gives you an opportunity to learn something, to explore a new activity, or to get to know someone—take a chance and try.
Pray about it: Thank God for the chance to live to the fullest. Pray for the courage and faith to live the life He has prepared for you.

Looking for Your Other Half

This is how love is made complete among us . . . : In this world we are like Jesus.
1 John 4:17.

In the 1990s romantic comedy *Jerry Maguire* Jerry (played by Tom Cruise) flies to California (after many twists and turns in the plot) to win back the heart of the girl he loves. In a scene so sappy it almost makes you sick, he tearfully declares, "I love you. You complete me."

In movie theaters around the world, women cried along with him when they heard that sentimental line: "You complete me." It expressed what a lot of people—guys and girls—wanted to hear. Quickly it became the mantra for those looking for love, for someone to complete them, to be their other half.

OK, so the line made a lot of women fall in love with Tom Cruise, and it led them to fantasize about a man saying it to them. But it doesn't represent what God has in mind for us. He wants us each to be complete in Him. Sure, we can love and marry someone who complements us and helps us to be better. But no human can complete us. If you are looking for someone to fill all the voids and fix all the problems in your life, then you will be disappointed. No person can do that.

All too often we make the mistake of putting all our trust in someone we're dating. Then we put almost no trust in God. The person becomes like a savior to us, and God gets ignored. But the only way truly to be complete is to love God first and foremost. When we are complete in God, we become confident. Then we won't be super-needy, looking for someone else to fulfill us.

Instead of searching for someone with a schmaltzy pickup line, focus on allowing God's love to become complete in you. As 1 John 4:12 says: "No one has ever seen God; but if we love one another, God lives in us and his love is made complete in us."

Live it out: Take a serious look at your expectations of a dating relationship. Are you searching for your other half, or for someone to be another whole? What practical things can you do to become complete in Christ, instead of looking for someone else to fulfill you?
Pray about it: Ask God to fill you with His love and to help you be complete and whole in Him.

There's a Verse for That

All Scripture is God-breathed and is useful for teaching, rebuking, correcting, and training in righteousness, so that the servant of God may be thoroughly equipped for every good work. 2 Timothy 3:16, 17.

When Apple promises, "There's an app for that," they mean it. Literally *hundreds of thousands* of apps exist for the iPhone and other iOS devices. If you want to pop virtual bubble wrap, there's an app for that. Should you crave to play a song on a virtual kazoo because you don't have a real kazoo handy, they have an app for you. And if you want an app about nothing, you guessed it. The nothing app costs only $.99, and is everything the title implies: nothing.

In almost any situation, you can find an app to help you, entertain you, or inform you. The Bible is the same way: it has a verse for every situation. Just one problem: most of us don't know how to find the verses that apply.

But just like finding the right app, it is possible to find the right verse. Here are a couple of tips for locating just the verse you need:

- **Scan the store.** Just as you would scan through the app store to see what's in there, you can read through the Bible without looking for something in particular. Make time for regular Bible study—just a few minutes each day—and the things you read will come back to mind on the days you need them.
- **Do a search.** When you're hunting for a specific app, you enter a key word, right? Do the same thing with the Bible. When facing a scary situation, do a search in the Bible for key words such as "fear" or "courage." Use the concordance in the back of your Bible, or a Bible search Web site.

As you become more familiar with the Bible, you'll realize it is packed with helpful, encouraging information. No matter what situation you encounter, there's a verse for that.

Live it out: Do a Bible search for a topic or word that is meaningful for you, such as "peace," "love," or "courage." Mark those verses in your Bible.

Pray about it: Every time you open your Bible, ask God to speak to you through His Word.

The Day of the Belt

My son, do not despise the Lord's discipline, and do not resent his rebuke, because the Lord disciplines those he loves, as a father the son he delights in.
Proverbs 3:11, 12.

Childhood is full of memorable moments, but that doesn't mean you will actually remember all of them once you get older. For instance, if your parents threw you a party when you were very young, you might not have any memory of it now. If they took you on a picnic, you might not recollect that, either. *But* if they spanked you, I have a funny feeling—if you're anything like I am—you probably do remember that.

Most of my childhood memories are definitely great, but one that made the top 10 list is, well, not so great. It's what I'll simply refer to as the day of the belt.

The day of the belt started like any other. My two sisters and I were playing loudly. I'm sure we sounded very happy. Actually, maybe we were fighting and seemed completely unhappy. Those details are a little fuzzy, so we won't worry about that. Nevertheless, at some point during the day of the belt, we disobeyed our father. You probably see where this is headed. But if you can't, I'll tell you: it's hurtling toward a father whipping his belt out of his pant loops and charging toward three disobedient girls.

As he hurtled toward us, we scattered. Divide and conquer, right? Wrong. I ran toward my sister's room, with a masterful plan to hide under her bed. But it unraveled when I got there and realized her wooden bed frame went all the way to the floor. There was no *under* her bed. And I didn't have a plan B. *Uh-oh.*

You can imagine the rest of the day of the belt. Let's just say we learned a lesson then—and we remembered it. Discipline just never feels good. It seems like a terrible thing, but the Bible says discipline is a form of love. In fact, it even declares the person who gets disciplined is fortunate and blessed. Psalm 94:12 proclaims, "Blessed is the one you discipline, Lord." When you sense the Lord is disciplining you, remember He is doing it because He loves you, not because He wants to hurt you.

Live it out: Are there things God or your parents are trying to teach you right now? If so, what do you need to do to cooperate with them?
Pray about it: Thank God for loving you enough to discipline and correct you.

If Someone Gave You a Million Dollars . . .

Remembering the words the Lord Jesus Himself said: "It is more blessed to give than to receive." Acts 20:35.

When Jesus was on earth, one of the things He spoke about most was money. In fact, two thirds of His parables involved it. Consider too that He was talking about money in a society that was very simple compared to ours. Just think how much more He would have to say about it in our materialistic, money-oriented society!

Money was one of Jesus' hot topics, because He wanted people to take time to evaluate their own relationship to their cash. It's a good idea for us to think about it too. Spend a few minutes answering the questions below. For maximum impact, write your answers on a piece of paper so that you can look back over them. Your answers will help you realize your own areas of strength and weakness when it comes to money.

- If someone gave you $1 million today, what percentage of it do you think you would keep for yourself? What percentage would you give to others?
- What percentage of your current possessions/money do you hold on to for yourself? What percentage do you give or share?
- Consider your answers to the previous two questions. Realistically, do you think the percentage of money you share would increase if you had more money? Why, or why not?
- If someone gave you $1 million and said you had to give all of it away—none of it could be spent on yourself—how would you use it?

Our culture urges us to gain, collect, and accrue, yet God's kingdom encourages us to give, share, and simplify. No matter what people around you are doing, make it your goal to live generously, not selfishly.

Live it out: Try out God's principle of generosity this week. Give to someone in need. If you don't have money to give, donate of your time or belongings.

Pray about it: Thank God specifically for some of the blessings He has generously given you.

The Top 10 Most Read Bible Verses

All Scripture is God-breathed and is useful for teaching, rebuking, correcting, and training in righteousness, so that the servant of God may be thoroughly equipped for every good work. 2 Timothy 3:16, 17.

Need a spiritual boost? Read or (if you're feeling ambitious) memorize the top 10 most read verses in the Bible:

1. "For God so loved the world that he gave his one and only Son, that whoever believes in him shall not perish but have eternal life" (John 3:16).
2. "'For I know the plans I have for you,' declares the Lord, 'plans to prosper you and not to harm you, plans to give you hope and a future'" (Jeremiah 29:11).
3. "And we know that in all things God works for the good of those who love him, who have been called according to his purpose" (Romans 8:28).
4. "I can do all this through him who gives me strength" (Philippians 4:13).
5. "In the beginning God created the heavens and the earth" (Genesis 1:1).
6. "Trust in the Lord with all your heart and lean not on your own understanding" (Proverbs 3:5).
7. "In all your ways submit to him, and he will make your paths straight" (verse 6).
8. "Do not conform to the pattern of this world, but be transformed by the renewing of your mind. Then you will be able to test and approve what God's will is—his good, pleasing and perfect will" (Romans 12:2).
9. "Do not be anxious about anything, but in every situation, by prayer and petition, with thanksgiving, present your requests to God" (Philippians 4:6).
10. "Therefore go and make disciples of all nations, baptizing them in the name of the Father and of the Son and of the Holy Spirit" (Matthew 28:19).

Live it out: Choose one of the verses from this list and write it somewhere you will see if often. Memorize it, and treasure it as a special message from God to you.
Pray about it: Thank God for giving you the hope-filled promises and guidance of the Bible.

NOV 16

Live It Out!

With God's power working in us, God can do much, much more than anything we can ask or imagine. Ephesians 3:20, NCV.

An idea that stood out to me from this week's devotional readings:

_____

_____

_____

A verse from this week's devotions that was powerful to me:

_____

_____

_____

A "Live it out" challenge I tried this week:

_____

_____

_____

Something that happened this week that was a blessing:

_____

_____

_____

My prayer today (thanks, requests, praises):

_____

_____

_____

A Spiritual Health Checkup

Jesus said to them, "It is not the healthy who need a doctor, but the sick. I have not come to call the righteous, but sinners." Mark 2:17.

A trip to the doctor's office is great motivation to stay well. As soon as you enter the waiting area, you find yourself surrounded by people coughing and sneezing, making you wonder if you'll leave sicker than you came. After realizing that they don't call it the *waiting* room for nothing ("What's taking so long?"), you finally make it back to the exam room, where you're placed on top of a table covered by stiff, crinkly paper . . . and you wait some more.

After you get poked and prodded and questioned, the doctor will likely give you the same diagnosis your mother made yesterday when you insisted that you didn't need to go to the doctor.

Since nobody enjoys such medical excursions, it's no surprise that people avoid the doctor as much as possible. (Dare I say that they avoid it like the plague? *Ouch.*) However, it is sometimes necessary to head to the doctor's office to check up on our physical health. Likewise, we sometimes need to examine our *spiritual* health. Just as we need physical exams sometimes, we need spiritual ones, too. Second Corinthians 13:5 says it this way: "Examine yourselves to see whether you are in the faith; test yourselves."

A spiritual checkup simply includes asking yourself some questions to see if there are any spiritual health problems. For example, take some time to consider, *Do I feel close to God? Do I sense His love and leading in my life?* If you end up with a sickly diagnosis, that just means it's time for more "medicine"—such as prayer, service, and Bible study. Don't get discouraged: God can heal any spiritual sickness.

Live it out: Set aside 10 minutes today to give yourself a spiritual health checkup. To diagnose problems, ask yourself such questions as *Would I like to feel closer to God? Am I treating people with love? Do I sense God's love and leading in my life?*
Pray about it: If your spiritual checkup makes you think it's time to boost your spiritual health, double up on your prayer time. Journal your prayers: your desires, struggles, fears, and requests.

Spiritual Red Flags

Be still, and know that I am God. Psalm 46:10.

Sometimes life just feels a little bit *off*, as if things aren't quite right. It doesn't happen overnight but just creeps up on you, and before you know it you're on edge, unsettled and restless inside. When this happens, it's a signal that it's time to slow down and be quiet with God. As God Himself said: "Be still, and know that I am God" (Psalm 46:10). When you slow down and remind yourself that God is in control, life won't feel as if it is spinning out of control.

When your spirit needs some quiet time with God, you will see some red flags in your life—reminders to slow down and make space for Him. Read through these common red flags, and check the ones that apply to your life:

_____ I am easily irritated or agitated. Little things annoy me.

_____ I often make negative or sarcastic comments.

_____ I pretend to be something I am not.

_____ If I died today, I don't know if I would be saved.

_____ There always seems to be a void in my life that needs to be filled.

_____ I am angry or disappointed with my church.

_____ I have one or more forms of media going most of the day. I fill potential quiet time with music, TV, Internet, talking, or texting.

_____ I feel that I should read the Bible, but I don't know where to begin.

_____ I am uncomfortable praying or talking about God in front of others.

_____ I think and daydream about things I would never tell God or my parents about.

Live it out: If you checked one or more of these red flags, it's time to "be still, and know that I am God." Set aside at least 10 minutes of quiet time every day this week to pray and read from the book of Psalms.

Pray about it: Talk to God about any of the red flags you checked on the list. Explain to Him your frustrations, and ask for His help and peace. Try journaling these prayers—in a journal or on your computer. It can help you feel a sense of relief as you write out everything to God.

In Pursuit of Physical Perfection

From Zion, perfect in beauty, God shines forth. Psalm 50:2.

Steve Erhardt is a Hollywood hairdresser addicted to cosmetic surgery. He has had more than 43 plastic surgeries. While he acknowledges spending "well over a quarter of a million dollars" on the procedures, he declines to give the exact amount. He also refuses to tell his age. Oh, and he also will not cease having cosmetic surgeries. In fact, he has no intentions of ever stopping, because he is admittedly obsessed with constant improvement. (Plus, he thinks it would be cool, albeit risky, to break the world record for having the most plastic surgeries.)

On a TV documentary about his obsession, Steve explained his need to constantly alter his appearance. "God just didn't have the mold for me, so I've made it better," he said.

Steve isn't the only one obsessed with trying to look perfect. In 2007 people underwent nearly 12 million cosmetic procedures and surgeries. If you do the math, that comes to 23 nose jobs, tummy tucks, or other appearance-enhancing procedures every single minute of the year.

Back in the day (as we over-30 adults like to say), a makeover included a trendy outfit and an updated hairstyle. Now, influenced by airbrushed magazine photos and over-the-top shows such as *Extreme Makeover, Dr. 90210,* and *Nip/Tuck,* our culture has become obsessed with the pursuit of physical perfection.

No amount of cosmetic surgery is going to make us perfect, though. Our only hope is in the ultimate makeover God has in our future. That will make us perfect—inside and out. As Revelation 21:5 says: "He who was seated on the throne said, 'I am making everything new!'" Until that ultimate makeover, don't obsess about having perfect looks. Instead, spend time getting to know God, who truly does have perfect beauty: "From Zion, perfect in beauty, God shines forth" (Psalm 50:2).

Live it out: What matters more to you: outer beauty or inner beauty? What can you do to begin to place more worth on inner beauty?

Pray about it: Ask God to help you look beyond appearances and see the true beauty in people.

Unchristian Christians

We are therefore Christ's ambassadors, as though God were making his appeal through us. 2 Corinthians 5:20.

Sometimes Christians are unchristian. They misrepresent Christ by being heartless, judgmental, and unloving. As a result, many nonbelievers don't want to have anything to do with Christ. They think, *If He's anything like Christians, then Jesus must be terrible.*

It isn't a new problem. People who profess to be God's representatives have been distorting what He is like for thousands of years. In fact, it was a problem when Jesus arrived on earth. The religious leaders created the impression of God as a harsh ruler who didn't have much of a heart. Into that scene Jesus arrived. God in flesh and bones, He was the true image of what God is like. He was here to clear up any misunderstandings or misrepresentations about God.

If you want to know what God is like, look at Jesus. What kind of people did Jesus hang out with? How did He respond to sinners? How did He deal with hypocrites? How did He treat sick people? How did He respond to brokenness and neediness? The answers to all of these questions reveal what God the Father is like too.

If you have friends or family members who are skeptical of Christ because of unchristian Christians, then it's time to show them what Christ is really about. Start by lavishing them with love. That's what Jesus would do. Be nice to them, listen to them, help them, show genuine concern for them. And if they ever mention their skepticism about Christians, discuss it with them. It's not a betrayal to admit that Christians aren't always like Christ. Speak openly about how Christians are still learning about God too. Most important, point them to Jesus, and show them love—no matter what.

Live it out: Don't just talk about what Jesus is like—live it out with your actions. Christ was compassionate and welcoming to sinners, so follow His example. Show Jesus' love to someone today.

Pray about it: Ask God to help you grow spiritually so that you can be a faithful representative of God.

Prayer Buddies

They all joined together constantly in prayer. Acts 1:14.

When you think of people involved in prayer ministry, what type of person do you imagine? Maybe you picture prayer warriors as little old ladies with white hair and hunched-over backs. Sweet little widows who wear floral dresses and thick, knee-high hose. Quiet little women who have been making Special K Loaf every Friday afternoon for 45 years.

There may indeed be a few prayer warriors out there who fit that description. But praying isn't just for the meek and mild. It is one of the most powerful, action-packed things you can do. Don't let the little old ladies have all the excitement. Start praying big, faith-filled prayers, and see God at work! Join the ranks of those prayer warriors, and it will forever change how you view God and life.

You're never too young to have a prayer partner. Think of someone—a friend or a person from church—with whom you feel comfortable talking, and ask if they would like to pray together regularly. You can set a day or time (for example, every Monday after school) and get together to talk and pray about what is happening in your lives. It will probably feel uncomfortable at first, but the more you do it, the more comfortable you'll become, and the more you'll realize that God is hearing and responding to your prayers.

The Bible says there is healing power when we share our struggles with someone and pray about it together: "Therefore confess your sins to each other and pray for each other so that you may be healed. The prayer of a righteous person is powerful and effective" (James 5:16). Did you catch that? God promises that when you pray with others, it will be powerful! Jesus made a similar promise: He said, "Where two or three come together in my name, there am I with them" (Matthew 18:20). Don't miss the opportunity to see God do mind-blowing, amazing things in your life. Find a buddy to pray with, and discover the life-changing power of prayer.

Live it out: Ask a friend to be your prayer partner, and set up a time (even if it's just once a month) to share about your lives and pray for each other. Even if you're not comfortable with the idea yet, you don't want to miss this opportunity!

Pray about it: Ask God to lead you to a trustworthy person who could be your prayer partner.

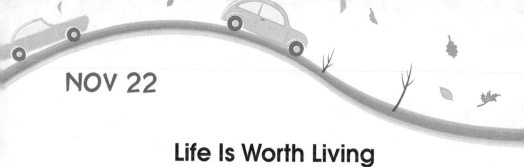

Life Is Worth Living

The Lord will keep you from all harm—he will watch over your life. Psalm 121:7.

Tiffany is a 16-year-old friend of mine who is cute, clever, bubbly, and stylish. Just looking at her, you would think her life was perfect. But you can't always judge by appearances.

Recently she sat with me, sobbing uncontrollably. Her parents were divorcing, and her mom was already dating someone new—someone who gave Tiffany and her sister the creeps. Tiffany had also just lost one of her best friends, Justin, who had died in a car accident. Plus, she was struggling at school. All the turmoil at home made it hard for her to concentrate in class, and her teachers were getting impatient with her.

Through her tears Tiffany said, "God doesn't care. If He cared, why would all this be happening? It's just not worth living anymore. If I just ended my life, all of this pain would finally come to an end."

Things seemed so bad to her that suicide was beginning to look like the only way to find relief. As she and I talked and prayed, she slowly became more calm and peaceful, and during the next few months she began to sense God's love and guidance. The process was slow, and she still felt sadness, but she began trusting God more.

When things seem hopeless and out of control, it can be hard to imagine that life will ever get better. Just like Tiffany, we can start to believe Satan's lie that life isn't worth living. But we have to remember that God is still running our world. And He is still good. We are in the middle of a massive cosmic fight between good and evil, so sad things will unfortunately still happen. But God has promised to set things right once again, to restore perfection and harmony. However, He operates on His own timetable. We want Him to hurry and fix things now, but He is slowly working behind the scenes, not rushing, because He wants to give all of us time to accept and trust Him. Second Peter 3:9 says, "The Lord is not slow in keeping his promise, as some understand slowness. Instead he is patient with you, not wanting anyone to perish, but everyone to come to repentance." In the meantime, we have to trust that He is loving and watching over us—even if He isn't acting as quickly as we would like.

Live it out: If you feel discouraged or depressed, go to an adult whom you trust and ask for help.

Pray about it: Thank God for working behind the scenes, even when you don't see Him.

Live It Out!

Fight the good fight of faith, grabbing hold of the life that continues forever.
I Timothy 6:12, NCV.

An idea that stood out to me from this week's devotional readings:

_____
_____
_____

A verse from this week's devotions that was powerful to me:

_____
_____
_____

A "Live it out" challenge I tried this week:

_____
_____
_____

Something that happened this week that was a blessing:

_____
_____
_____

My prayer today (thanks, requests, praises):

_____
_____
_____

Cheer Up, Things Are Worse Than You Thought!

Cheer up, friend! Your sins are forgiven. Matthew 9:2, GW.

In the song "Cheer Up" Christian musicians Ten Shekel Shirt popularized an interesting but confusing phrase. The song begins with the puzzling line: "Cheer up, you are worse off than you figure/But you are loved anyway."

If things are so bad—even worse than we thought—why should we cheer up? This riddle is actually the heart of the gospel. When we realize how bad things are—how sinful we are, how impossible it is for us to ever be good enough to be *good enough*—then we see how amazing God's love for us is. Even though we are bad (worse off than we realized), God loves us extravagantly. The worse our situation, the greater that God's love looks in comparison. The Bible says it this way: "Where sin abounded, grace did much more abound" (Romans 5:20, KJV). The worse things are, the more reason to be cheerful and happy about God's grace and love!

When Jesus came across sad or sick people, He reminded them to cheer up. He told a paralyzed man, "Cheer up, friend! Your sins are forgiven" (Matthew 9:2, GW). When He met a woman who had been sick and struggling for years, He told her, "Cheer up, daughter! Your faith has made you well" (verse 22, GW).

Jesus has given us the same message: "In the world you'll have trouble. But cheer up! I have overcome the world" (John 16:33, GW). If anyone on earth should be cheerful, it should be Christians! We follow a God who loves us extravagantly and has plans for us to live a perfect, eternal life. Even if things are worse off than you figured, you are loved anyway.

Live it out: Cheer up! Don't let bad news or difficult situations steal your happiness. The next time you're feeling discouraged or down, read John 16:33.

Pray about it: Ask God to help you have a cheerful perspective on life today.

The Hall of Faith

Now faith is the confidence that what we hope for will actually happen; it gives us assurance about things we cannot see. Hebrews 11:1, NLT.

One of the highest honors in certain fields or endeavors is to make it into its Hall of Fame. Imagine you were a clown (literally) who traveled with a circus your entire life, and then you made it into the Circus Hall of Fame. (Yes, that actually exists.) You'd be cheering and handing out animal-shaped balloons to everyone you know! Or let's say that every day after school you practiced polka music on your accordion for hours and hours; and before you know it, you're inducted into the real-life Polka Hall of Fame. You would play a lively tune to celebrate for sure! Or what if you lived in Toronto and liked to sketch superheroes, and then one day you're invited into the Canadian Cartoonist Hall of Fame. That would be very big news, eh?

Even though those Halls of Fame might not mean much to you, they mean a lot to clowns, polka players, and Canadian cartoonists. We are naturally interested in the heroes within our own groups. Since Christianity isn't a competition, you might assume it doesn't have a Hall of Fame, but in fact it does. The Bible actually lists the superstars of the faith—the noteworthy God followers who can inspire us to greater faith. Flip to Hebrews 11, and you'll discover the most fascinating Hall of Fame of all time—also known as the Hall of *Faith*.

Just check out these Hall of Famers: Noah, who built an ark even though he'd never seen rain before. Abraham, who was willing to sacrifice his own son. Moses, who refused to be known as Pharaoh's son, but lived a humble life instead. Gideon, Barak, Samson, David, Samuel. The book of Hebrews says that the list includes many others, those who have conquered kingdoms, shut the mouths of lions, quenched fires, escaped the edge of the sword, witnessed the resurrection of the dead, and endured prison and chains and torture.

If you want to feel you are a part of something spectacular, read the Hall of Faith in Hebrews 11. You'll see how exciting it is to be in a long line of Christians and how breathtaking a life of faith is. And you'll want to be a part of that Hall of Fame too!

Live it out: Next time you sense God urging you to do something, step out in faith.

Pray about it: Pray the prayer of the apostles in Luke 17:5: "Increase our faith!"

What's Wrong With Being a Nerd?

But the Lord said to Samuel, "Do not consider his appearance or his height, for I have rejected him. The Lord does not look at the things people look at. People look at the outward appearance, but the Lord looks at the heart." I Samuel 16:7.

At the high school I attended it was a *very big deal* if a girl was voted to be football homecoming royalty. Those few girls chosen to be the homecoming attendants wore formal gowns and were escorted out onto the field with the football players at the big homecoming game.

Now, the next thing I'm going to tell you needs to stay between you and me. Usually I don't admit this, but here goes. I was a nerd in high school. A shy, straight-A student, I didn't have nice clothes, a car, or very good social skills. I kept my nose down studying every night, and the only time guys called me was for help with geometry.

Now that you have the back story, picture this: one day during my senior year I was sitting in trigonometry class when the principal came on the intercom system to announce the homecoming royalty for the year. The football team had voted, and everyone in the school stopped what they were doing to hear the big news. Everyone, that is, except me. I just kept on with my trig. The popular cheerleaders in class became visibly nervous, hoping to hear their names. Suddenly my name was announced over the intercom. Everyone was confused, but started saying, "Heather, they said your name!" Quietly I looked up and turned to the other girl in our class named Heather, and said, "Oh, I'm sure they meant you." She was, after all, a stylish, wealthy, athletic, and popular cheerleader. But, it turns out, just like something out of a geek-to-chic Disney movie, they didn't mean her. They actually had chosen *me*.

One of the football players told me later they had all voted for me, because I was "real" and wasn't fake or phony. They liked that I was just me.

Don't buy in to the idea that you have to be something you aren't. God designed you to be unique and special. And just like those football players, God loves when you are just what you were created to be, quirks and all.

Live it out: Read 1 Samuel 16:7, and try to see people through God's eyes today.
Pray about it: Ask God to help you look at people's heart, not just their appearance.

I So Hate Consequences

Whatever you plant is what you'll harvest. Galatians 6:7, GW.

In the song "I So Hate Consequences," Christian musicians Reliant K address the dread of having to own up to what you've done wrong. The lyrics include the sincere cry: "God, don't make me face up to this/And I so hate consequences." The song ends well, however, with the realization that when we come to God, He doesn't just tell us "I told you so." Instead, he forgives us and helps us start over.

Nevertheless, life is full of consequences. Even though God is kind and forgiving, our actions still have those dreaded outcomes. The writer Robert Louis Stevenson said, "Sooner or later everyone sits down to a banquet of consequences." You might as well get your fork and knife ready, because there's going to be a feast of them for dinner.

The Bible says it another way: "Make no mistake about this: You can never make a fool out of God. Whatever you plant is what you'll harvest" (Galatians 6:7, GW). If you don't study for your test (that's what you plant), then you'll do poorly on the test (and that's what you harvest). Should you betray a friend (what you plant), then you'll do damage to your friendship (what you harvest). The lesson is simple: what you do will have results. Whether it is a small or large decision, your choice will have its effect.

This all can sound pretty dreadful, I suppose, and might make you agree with the song that declares "I so hate consequences." But there's great news about consequences, too. There is such a thing as *good* consequences. Good choices have good results. Galatians 6:8 explains: "Whoever sows to please their flesh, from the flesh will reap destruction; whoever sows to please the Spirit, from the Spirit will reap eternal life." You have the power to select what kind of consequences you will face. For example, if you are friendly, you will make friends. That's a great outcome.

For those times you're facing dreadful consequences, remember that God will forgive and give you a fresh start. Let those bad results inspire you to make better choices next time.

Live it out: Think back over the past few days. How did your choices result in consequences? Trace a result back to the decision that triggered it.

Pray about it: Ask God to help you think about the consequences before you make decisions.

Two Words That Can Change Your Life

Give thanks in all circumstances; for this is God's will for you in Christ Jesus.
I Thessalonians 5:18.

A few years ago John Kralik felt as if his life had hit rock bottom. His marriage had ended, his children weren't on speaking terms with him, his business was failing, and he had serious money problems. Everything seemed to be crumbling around him. It appeared as if he had absolutely nothing for which to be thankful.

Feeling hopeless, he took a hike one day in the mountains near Los Angeles. As he walked, he sensed a voice telling him, "Until you learn to be grateful for the things you have, you will not receive the things you want."

That one simple thought was a turning point for John. That day he decided he would begin to be grateful for the good things in his life. He set a yearlong goal: every day for 365 days he would write a thank-you note to someone. Kralik wanted to retrain his mind to focus on the positive instead of the negative.

John wrote thank-you notes to anyone and everyone he could think of: his son, the server at his favorite restaurant, old friends, coworkers. Some days it took a little effort to come up with of someone new to thank, but he always managed to find an individual.

By the end of his yearlong experiment, he felt like a new man. His thank-you notes had helped repair his relationships, and he began to feel more hopeful about the future.

If it worked for him, it can for you, too. The more people you thank, the more thankful you will become. When you look for people who deserve a thank-you, you'll find them. Those two little words can completely change your outlook on life.

Live it out: Take the thank-you challenge. Pick a length of time (a week, a month, or even a year) and send a thank-you to someone every day during it. You can use a handwritten note, an instant message, a text, or an e-mail.

Pray about it: Thank God every day for a special person or thing He has brought into your life.

You're Welcome Day

Let us be thankful. Hebrews 12:28.

Since Thanksgiving is a day to say "Thank You," it's only appropriate the day *after* Thanksgiving to reply "You're welcome." That's why some clever person officially made the Friday after Thanksgiving You're Welcome Day.

Saying "You're welcome" isn't so common anymore. Today the response to "Thank you" is more likely to be "No problem," "Sure thing," or a mumble that sounds like "Um-hum." Saying "You're welcome," however, is a gracious way to accept the thanks being given to you.

The Bible talks a lot about offering thanks to God; and most of us thank Him regularly in our prayers. But have you ever stopped to think about how God responds when you thank Him? I imagine Him flashing a huge smile and saying, "My pleasure. You are very welcome." I picture our gratitude thrilling Him. He is always doing good things for us, so I think it means a lot to Him when we stop, look up, and say thanks. When we send up a sincere "Thank You," He doesn't just keep His head down, skimming through the book of life while He mumbles, "Yeah, sure. Whatever. It was nothing. It just worked out that way." Nope, I'm pretty positive that He soaks it in. God loves and appreciates it when we love and appreciate Him.

In honor of You're Welcome Day, remember the power of "Thank you" and "You're welcome." Those kind words make relationships stronger and people happier. Use them in abundance when you're talking to your family, friends, and God.

One final thing. Thanks for reading this.

Live it out: When someone thanks you for something, look them in the eye and say, "You're welcome." Give out as many thank-yous and you're-welcomes as you can today.
Pray about it: Spend time in a prayer of sincere thanks. After your prayer, take a moment of silence to allow God to respond.

Live It Out!

Let us look only to Jesus, the One who began our faith and who makes it perfect. He suffered death on the cross. But he accepted the shame as if it were nothing because of the joy that God put before him. And now he is sitting at the right side of God's throne. Hebrews 12:2, NCV.

An idea that stood out to me from this week's devotional readings:

_____

_____

_____

A verse from this week's devotions that was powerful to me:

_____

_____

_____

A "Live it out" challenge I tried this week:

_____

_____

_____

Something that happened this week that was a blessing:

_____

_____

_____

My prayer today (thanks, requests, praises):

_____

_____

_____

Are We Saints, or Are We Sinners?

But the Pharisees and the teachers of the law muttered, "This man welcomes sinners and eats with them." Luke 15:2.

The church is a community of saints, right? You know, Brother So-and-so and Sister Such-and-such—all righteous children of God. Well, that's true in a way, because we are made holy through Christ. But there's more to the story. The church is also a community of sinful people. We're all messed-up individuals trying to make our way through life on a messed-up planet. Once sin showed up in our world, it dropped a bomb and devastated God's perfect creation. Things began falling apart, and everybody started wrestling with sin.

Fortunately, God has designed a beautiful master plan that redeems us and guarantees that we will live a perfect, better-than-you-can-imagine life for all of eternity. In the meantime, people still struggle—even Christians who are a part of the church. If we realize that, it will help us live more happily as a part of a church family.

Consider this. Since most think of the church simply as a community of saints, they hesitate to admit their problems and struggles. For example, if someone is grappling with smoking, anger, or a porn addiction, the last people they want to find out are those at church! However, if we understand that the church is also a community of sinful people, we'll be more willing to admit our battles, because we know other believers are fighting theirs, too. When we see things this way, we won't judge others quite so harshly. Nor will we expect all the adults at church to have it all figured out. We will realize that all of us—teenagers and adults—are sinful people on a spiritual journey to know and love God more.

Jesus said, "I have not come to call the righteous, but sinners to repentance" (Luke 5:32). He was eager to help anyone who admitted they needed it. Strive to be compassionate to people, as Jesus was. And when you need help yourself, don't be afraid to turn to others at church for support and encouragement. That's what the church is for.

Live it out: Set an example at your church by being open and honest about your spiritual journey. When others see how real your spirituality is, it will free them to be honest too.

Pray about it: Start your journey of authenticity by being authentic with God. Tell Him all about the struggles and joys you experience as you follow Him.

DEC 2

Life's Ups and Downs

It is good to praise the Lord and make music to your name, O Most High.
Psalm 92:1.

Recently my mom sent me a box of my childhood drawings and schoolwork. In the stack of papers was a photocopied worksheet entitled "Life's Ups and Downs." The instructions read, "List three things you can do to make yourself feel better when you are unhappy." My list of answers included "pray," "sing"—and in the number one slot—"eat ice cream!"

Having spent the better part of adulthood trying to fall out of love with sweets, I realized as I looked at that worksheet just how long I have been using sugary treats as a pick-me-up. According to the crayon-scrawled date, I have been considering ice cream a top-ranking problem solver since the days of parachute pants, big hair, and the Reagan administration.

Now, of course, I'll be the first to admit that ice cream isn't the best solution for hard times. But I must say that praying and singing are pretty solid recommendations. I would still suggest them after all these years. In fact, the Bible has similar advice for dealing with a bad situation. The songwriter, or psalmist, David often used prayer and songs to turn his mind from his problem to God.

Paul and Silas were other God followers who relied on praying and singing instead of worrying and crying—even when they were in prison. Acts 16:25, 26 records, "About midnight Paul and Silas were *praying* and *singing* hymns to God, and the other prisoners were listening to them. Suddenly there was such a violent earthquake that the foundations of the prison were shaken. At once all the prison doors flew open, and everyone's chains came loose." If that doesn't make a person want to pray and sing, I don't know what will!

When you're facing tough times, I recommend you do what the Bible heroes did: pray and sing. Because now that I think about it, eating ice cream probably isn't the best way to fix problems. Even though I thought that was a really good idea when I was 6.

Live it out: When you are facing difficult times, try praying and singing. Pray specifically about your worries, and then listen to or sing along to some of your favorite praise songs.

Pray about it: Surrender your life to God in prayer, and remember that prayers can be spoken *or* sung. Many great hymns and praise songs are prayers set to music.

What's the Rush?

The Lord is good to those who wait for Him. Lamentations 3:25, NKJV.

If you're like most teenagers, you are counting down toward something. Maybe you're numbering the days until you get your driver's permit or driver's license. Or perhaps you're looking forward to the end of the school year or to your big family vacation.

Adults are no different. Just talk to any adult, and ask about their lives. Most likely they are rushing toward the next big thing in life too. The single adults are trying to get married. And the married adults are trying to have a baby. And the adults with babies are trying to get a bigger house, because now they need more room.

The Bible repeatedly tells us to slow down and wait on the Lord. He wants us to take time to enjoy *today*. As long as we are thinking only about things in the future, we miss the gifts that God is trying to give us right now.

The psalmist declares, "Let us rejoice *today* and be glad" (Psalm 118:24). Take time to slow down and enjoy what is happening right now, today. Don't miss an opportunity to laugh or learn or love. Above all, don't miss out on today because you're always focused on tomorrow. You may think you can't wait to move out of your parents' home or graduate from high school, but there are special things about these years that God wants you to treasure, not just endure.

Talk to God about your todays—and your tomorrows. As the psalmist says, put it all out there before God, and then wait and see what He does in your life: "In the morning, Lord, you hear my voice; in the morning I lay my requests before you and wait expectantly" (Psalm 5:3). Take life one day at a time with God, and you won't be disappointed.

Live it out: Enjoy today—whatever it brings! Pay attention to the little things that make today special, and take time to truly appreciate them. For example, if you are a part of a sports team that played a good game, enjoy it. Cheer on your teammates, and enjoy the activity. At the end of the day, think back and name three things you liked about it.

Pray about it: Thank God for today. Surrender your life to Him, and tell Him you trust Him with your present—and your future.

DEC 4

God Gets What You're Going Through

Surely he took up our pain and bore our suffering. Isaiah 53:4.

Ever felt as if God just doesn't understand what you're going through? After all, He isn't a teenager. He's never had to walk the halls of your school with all its bullies and mean kids. The Lord doesn't understand the temptations you face every day. I mean, He doesn't even live on this planet.

But here's the crazy thing about God: He does understand. He knows exactly what you're going through—better than anyone else. In fact, the Bible says that Jesus understands completely, because while He was earth, Satan threw every temptation at Him. As a result, He empathizes with—and identifies with—our weaknesses: "For we do not have a high priest who is unable to empathize with our weaknesses, but we have one who has been tempted in every way, just as we are—yet he did not sin. Let us then approach God's throne of grace with confidence, so that we may receive mercy and find grace to help us in our time of need" (Hebrews 4:15, 16).

Sure, the temptations would have looked a little a different for Him (it was 2,000 years ago, after all), but the *type* of temptations were the same. Jesus was a teenager. He was tempted to be disrespectful to adults. He was tempted to talk trash to a neighborhood kid, or to be mean to a classmate. He was tempted to lie to His parents. You name a temptation, and He faced some version of it. And, better than anyone, He knows how difficult it is to overcome temptations—because He resisted all of them.

Jesus feels love and compassion for you, because He knows exactly what you're going through. As the book of Hebrews says, you can go to Him confidently, and He will give you extravagant amounts of mercy and grace. He has a tender heart toward you, because He knows how hard it is to face temptation and win.

Live it out: When you feel overwhelmed by a temptation, what do you normally do? Next time you feel about to cave in to temptation, take a minute and pray. Tell God how hard it is to say no, and ask for His help.

Pray about it: Praise Jesus for coming to earth and facing the sinful world for us. Praise Him for understanding you. Praise Him for showering you with tons of mercy and grace.

Would You Like Fries With That?

I praise you because I am fearfully and wonderfully made; your works are wonderful, I know that full well. Psalm 139:14.

In the past 40 years Don Gorske has eaten more than 25,000 Big Macs. (You heard me right: 25,000 Big Mac attacks.) Don admits to eating two of the McDonald's burgers every day, along with a couple of parfaits every day and the occasional order of fries. He has skipped eating the burgers only eight days during those 40 years. (The day of his mother's death merited a skip, as did a few emergencies.)

Gorske even keeps a diary of how many burgers he has eaten, and he saves all the receipts of every burger purchase. (He explains that he was inspired to record his consumption by watching McDonald's track its number of hamburgers sold.)

Even though none of us have eaten 25,000 burgers, we're all tempted to throw back a little junk food now and then. When we make food choices, it's always good to remember what Paul recorded in 1 Corinthians 3:16: "Don't you know that you yourselves are God's temple and that God's Spirit dwells in your midst?" When we realize how wonderfully designed our bodies are, we're more likely to treat them with respect and to make healthy food choices. You don't have to eat 25,000 helpings of spinach or 25,000 brussels sprouts, but you might decide to have an extra veggie now and then. When you select what goes on your plate, keep in mind healthy principles. Choose wisely: you will feel better mentally, physically, and spiritually—and will honor God, the Creator of your body.

Live it out: What small change can you make to your diet to help you treat your body like the temple of God?

Pray about it: Thank God for the wide selection of food available to you. Ask for wisdom and willpower to choose foods that will help fuel the amazing body He gave you.

DEC 6

Write a Letter Day (Texts, Messages, and E-mails Don't Count)

You yourselves are our letter, written on our hearts, known and read by everyone.
2 Corinthians 3:2.

If someone wrote you a love letter, would you read it? I sure would. In fact, every time I've ever received a love letter, I read it so many times I practically had the whole thing memorized. (I know, that's a totally girly thing to do. But there is something very special about a letter filled with kind words.)

You've heard it said, I'm sure, that the Bible is a love letter from God. Considering that, you'd think we'd all be eager to read it! What's more, buried within that one huge Letter are lots of other fascinating letters. The New Testament is packed with actual letters sent to believers written by such men as Paul, James, Peter, and John. Even though composed long before computers or even ballpoint pens, the messages in those letters are still meaningful to us today.

This time of year there is a special but little-known holiday: Letter Writing Day. The day honors the old-fashioned joys of sending and receiving letters. And as you can tell by flipping through the New Testament, letters are very important in Christianity.

In one of Paul's letters to the Corinthians, he makes a very interesting comment about letters. He says believers themselves are a letter from Christ. When they live out loud what they have learned, it's as if they are a letter sending a message:

"Do we need, like some people, letters of recommendation to you or from you? You yourselves are our letter, written on our hearts, known and read by everyone. You show that you are a letter from Christ, the result of our ministry, written not with ink but with the Spirit of the living God, not on tables of stone but on tablets of human hearts (2 Corinthians 3:1-3).

What message is the letter of your life sending? Is it a love letter or hate mail?

Live it out: Send a handwritten note to someone today. Sure, an e-mail or text could do the job, but with a handwritten note, a piece of you will be in the same room with the person who receives it. They'll be able to hold something that you created just for them.

Pray about it: Thank God for the Bible, His love letter to you.

Live It Out!

You, Lord, give true peace to those who depend on you, because they trust you.
Isaiah 26:3, NCV.

An idea that stood out to me from this week's devotional readings:

_____

_____

_____

A verse from this week's devotions that was powerful to me:

_____

_____

_____

A "Live it out" challenge I tried this week:

_____

_____

_____

Something that happened this week that was a blessing:

_____

_____

_____

My prayer today (thanks, requests, praises):

_____

_____

_____

DEC 8

Getting Into the Christmas Spirit

For to us a child is born, to us a son is given, and the government will be on his shoulders. And he will be called Wonderful Counselor, Mighty God, Everlasting Father, Prince of Peace. Isaiah 9:6.

It's beginning to look a lot like Christmas! Actually, at the mall it was starting to look that way about three months ago. Nevertheless, the rest of us are just now catching up with the retailers who pulled out Christmas decorations while we were still buying back-to-school supplies.

No matter what the local mall would lead you to believe, the Christmas season isn't really about stuff. So think beyond the presents and create a little Christmas cheer all around you. Here are a few things you can do to get in the spirit:

- **Share a sweet treat.** Bake bread or cookies and deliver them to shut-ins or a nearby nursing home.

- **Make a merry message.** Ah, go ahead, put a friendly Merry Christmas greeting on your outgoing voicemail message on your phone.

- **Volunteer to be a part of your church's celebration.** Whether your church is doing an elaborate Christmas pageant or just a small church service, sign up to be a part of it. Volunteer to read a scripture, sing a song, or even put on one of those embarrassing Wise Men costumes. Whatever it is, do something to awaken the true meaning of Christmas.

- **Read the Christmas story.** Read Luke 2:1-20, and use your imagination to picture what that first Christmas must have been like. Bring the story to life in your mind. What do you think the shepherds were feeling? What might that night have been like for Mary? She was a teenager, after all, who was becoming the mother of the Savior!

Live it out: This week, do one of the things on this list, or come up with your own ideas for getting in the Christmas spirit.
Pray about it: Ask God to help you remember the true reason for the season this Christmas.

The Best "Thing" Ever

The Lord has sought out a man after his own heart and appointed him ruler of his people. I Samuel 13:14.

If you stop and think about it, everybody has a "thing." You know, the *thing* that other people use to describe you. Here's what I mean. If your friends were trying to portray you to someone else, how would they do it? Whatever descriptive words they use reveal your *thing*. For example, if they say, "She's the girl who is always so nice and happy," then your thing is being nice and happy. Or if someone comments, "He is the smart guy who always raises his hand in class," then that killer awesome brain of yours is your thing. Or if people say, "He's the guy who sits alone and never smiles at anyone," well, then it might be time for you to flash those pearly whites every now and then.

In truth, God designed everyone to be beautifully complex. None of us is actually so simple that one word or phrase could capture who we are. Nevertheless, all of us do have traits that stand out—the things that people notice first about us. When our dominant traits are good, it brings glory to God. So when we are loving and joyful, it's as if we are living out a testimony.

In the Bible the hero David had quite possibly the best description or *thing* of all time. Even though he messed up and didn't always get it right, he tried to rely on God and trust Him. He wanted to hear the Holy Spirit; and when God tried to teach him lessons, he would listen and accept correction. And that's why he got his thing: Samuel described David as a man after God's own heart (1 Samuel 13:14). Isn't that an awesome thing to say about a person? Sometimes TV and music and high school can make you start to think that the most important things are being cool, good-looking, rich, well dressed, skinny, or famous. But really, the highest compliment anyone can pay you is to say you have a heart like God's.

Live it out: Memorize 1 Samuel 16:7, and repeat it when you need a reminder of the most important things in life.

Pray about it: Read Ezekiel 36:26. Tell God you are ready for Him to change your heart day by day to be more like His.

Whom Would Jesus Invite to Dinner?

The Son of Man came eating and drinking, and you say, "Here is a glutton and a drunkard, a friend of tax collectors and sinners." Luke 7:34.

A few times in my life I've been in a conversation when someone asks the common icebreaker question "If you could have dinner with absolutely anyone, which five people would you pick?" Almost always people choose a few celebrities hot at the moment, maybe an important historical figure, and fairly often Jesus makes the short list.

Now ask yourself this: with whom do you think *Jesus* would want to have dinner?

The painter Paolo Veronese had a creative answer to that question—and it got him in deep trouble with the Roman Catholic Church.

It all began in the 1500s when Veronese received a commission to paint a depiction of Jesus' Last Supper. In his painting he included some traditional elements, such as Jesus seated with His disciples at a long table. However, the artist took some liberties and also included drunk people, a troublemaker with a bloody nose (who had obviously just been in a fight), little people, outcasts, and even a stray dog.

Veronese didn't do it to be heretical, but because he felt it was a way to represent Jesus' welcoming, kind spirit toward outcasts and the marginalized. The artist sought to portray the loving and inviting way of Jesus. The Roman Catholic Inquisition, however, didn't find that painting quite so charming. In fact, they regarded it as irreverent and offensive. They even refused to let the artist claim it was a Christian painting, and they forbade him from naming it *The Last Supper*.

Even though Veronese's painting was considered scandalous, it is a beautiful reminder that Jesus was indeed friendly and welcoming to people who didn't feel as if they belonged. Who wouldn't want to have dinner with someone so wonderfully accepting and compassionate? He would definitely be at the top of my list of five people with whom I would like to have to dinner.

Live it out: What can you do to show an accepting spirit toward people who often get left out or ignored? Think of someone in particular to whom you can extend kindness this week.

Pray about it: Thank God for being welcoming and compassionate to you.

Mirror, Mirror on the Wall

For the entire law is fulfilled in keeping this one command: "Love your neighbor as yourself." Galatians 5:14.

Have you ever met someone and immediately not liked them? Perhaps you can't even put your finger on it. So you say, "There's just something about that boy I don't like." Recently I heard a more clever—and appropriate—response. A friend was telling me about someone he couldn't stand, and he said, "There's just something about that boy I don't like about me."

That's deep. My friend went on to explain that we often detest the traits in others that we dislike in ourselves. For example, if you don't like a guy who is trying too hard to look cool, then maybe you hate it when you do that yourself. Or if you see a girl being flirty and trying to get attention, perhaps you're a little upset because you do that same thing—or wish you could. Or maybe you hate someone for always being negative even though you're known to have a negative attitude of your own. The bottom line is simply that we often notice the traits in other people that we ourselves have. We see the things we share. Other people can be a mirror, in a way, to show us what is in us.

Here's where things get sticky, though. We usually go a lot easier on ourselves than others. If we're trying too hard to be cool, we say, "Oh, I'm just popular." Or if we're negative, we say, "Oh, I'm just realistic." And if we're flirtatious, we might excuse it with "Oh, I'm just friendly." But when other people do those same things, we criticize them.

That's why God gave us this call to action: "Do not seek revenge or bear a grudge against anyone among your people, but love your neighbor as yourself" (Leviticus 19:18). When we make the same mistakes that others do, we don't seek revenge on *ourselves* or hold a grudge against *ourselves*. We give ourselves a break and just keep trying to work it all out. So why not offer the same compassion to other people? The next time someone annoys you, just show them a little love.

Live it out: Is God convicting you to be more loving to someone who has been annoying you? Show some extra kindness to them today.

Pray about it: Pray that God will help you "love your neighbor as yourself."

DEC 12

My Hero! My Deliverer!

You are my help and my deliverer; you are my God, do not delay. Psalm 40:17.

A little snow and ice wasn't going to stop me from visiting my family for Christmas. A blizzard had pounded Maryland, leaving thousands of travelers stranded in airports and on the roads, but I was still set to go. Despite days of delayed and canceled flights, mine to Oklahoma was still scheduled for takeoff.

Headed for the airport, my fearless husband slowly muscled our four-wheel-drive vehicle through the interstate's fast lane. Things were fine, just fine, until that thumping sound. We had a flat tire. Not one to be easily discouraged, my husband accepted the challenge as if it were a game. That is, until the tire wouldn't come off the axle. After trying every trick he knew (and searching online for any help), we called roadside assistance. They warned us there would be a delay because of the high volume of calls they were getting because of the weather.

One hour passed, and we weren't worried. I could still even make my flight if we got the tire changed quickly. Two hours passed, and we were still laughing. It would be a great story to tell. Three hours went by, and we were getting cold and hungry. Then four hours, and we kept checking back with roadside assistance—who continued to say they would get there when they could. After five hours, darkness had fallen and another snowstorm had blown in. The roads were icier than ever, and a warning had been issued that vehicles should be on the roads only in cases of emergency. By six hours we were running out of ideas. Just when we were losing hope, we heard honking behind us. A friend had spent the past few hours creeping his way over the icy roads to come to our aid. With coveralls, a sledgehammer, and a hearty laugh, he set to work on the tire. Joy and relief swept over us.

Throughout the Bible, when God showed up to help His followers, they too were overcome with joy and relief. We never truly appreciate deliverance unless we've been waiting and longing for it. If you're waiting for God to show up to help, keep praying and believing. He will come. And when He does, you will be overwhelmed with joy and relief.

Live it out: Write down the areas in your life in which you need God to be your deliverer.

Pray about it: Pray over the list you created, asking God to show up in those areas.

A Little Faith and a Lot of Power

But Jesus said, "Someone touched me; I know that power has gone out from me."
Luke 8:46.

She felt invisible. And hopeless. For 12 years doctors had said there was no cure for the disease she had. And now she was out of money, so she couldn't even afford to go to them anymore. Not that there was really any point in seeing them anyway, since they would just say she had no hope.

However, when she heard about Jesus, a tiny hope sparked inside of her once again. She would go to Him, and she would be healed. Her excitement increased, and she was filled with the kind of courage that comes only from desperation.

Just imagine the crowds on that day as countless people crammed in to see Jesus. They were loud and aggressive (and maybe even smelly from traveling and working on fishing boats and farms). Luke 8:42 says, "As Jesus was on his way, the crowds almost crushed him." When the sick woman walked down the path and saw this, her stomach—and her hope—must have dropped. How would she ever make it to Him? But she did not give up. She knew He was her only hope. Perhaps she whispered to herself, "It's now—or it's never!" And she pressed through the mob.

Finally she came up behind Jesus. As He walked along, she touched a tiny corner of His robe with a really massive amount of faith. And that was enough. She was instantly healed. Jesus immediately stopped what He was doing and asked who had touched Him. (I can just imagine one of His disciples muttering under his breath, "Ummm . . . it's a little hard to say, since, well, all the people in town are here!")

Jesus had sensed the touch of faith. "Someone touched me," He said. "I know that power has gone out from me" (verse 46). Even today Jesus never lets a touch of faith go unacknowledged. When anyone reaches out to Him in faith, He notices. And when He detects a person's touch of faith, He will send power out to help them.

Live it out: Reflect on the power of God. In what areas of your life have you reached out in faith to Him and seen His power?
Pray about it: Ask for God's power in your life. Reach out and ask Him to heal the broken places in your heart and mind.

DEC 14

Live It Out!

Give glory to God in heaven, and on earth let there be peace among the people who please God. Luke 2:14, NCV.

An idea that stood out to me from this week's devotional readings:

_____

_____

_____

A verse from this week's devotions that was powerful to me:

_____

_____

_____

A "Live it out" challenge I tried this week:

_____

_____

_____

Something that happened this week that was a blessing:

_____

_____

_____

My prayer today (thanks, requests, praises):

_____

_____

_____

Hey, Don't Forget About Me!

And if I go and prepare a place for you, I will come back and take you to be with me that you also may be where I am. John 14:3.

You might be from a small town if you think trips to Walmart are a grand adventure.

I grew up in a small town. Actually, I grew up *near*—not even *in*—a small town, on a ranch in Oklahoma. So when I was very young, trips to town (including stops at Walmart and Sonic drive-in) were pretty exciting stuff. (Before I sound completely like a hick or a senior citizen, I should clarify that I did not go to town in a covered wagon.)

On one Christmastime trip to Walmart, while excitedly picking out gifts for stocking stuffers, I wandered away from my mom and got lost. *She must be right here in the next aisle,* I thought frantically. No, she wasn't there. *Surely the next aisle.* Not there, either. With each mommyless aisle, my fears—and tears—increased. In my little mind the only thing I could think was *Did she go home without me?*

Fortunately, I did not have to grow up as an orphan in Walmart. My mother eventually found me crying as I wandered through the scented soap aisle.

Now that I have an adult's perspective on the situation, I can see how irrational it was to think my mom had gone home without me. Even during a frantic Christmas season at Walmart, she couldn't have forgotten her own child. She wanted me safe and sound at home with her.

Jesus understood a child's fear of being left behind. In fact, He recognized that adults have it sometimes too. While He was on earth He told His followers that He would be leaving them—but only for a while—to prepare a home for them. But He promised that when He went away, He would not forget them. He would come back for them Him (John 14:1-6).

If you ever feel abandoned and alone, remember that Jesus promised not to leave you behind. He is eager to return, to excitedly grab you up, and to take you home with Him. After all, God isn't the kind of Father who would leave you wandering the aisles of Walmart alone. He wants you safe and sound at home with Him.

Live it out: How does it change the way you live to know that Jesus will soon come back for you?

Pray about it: Thank God that Jesus will return to take you home to heaven.

357

DEC 16

An Unexpected
Encounter With God

The King will reply, "Truly I tell you, whatever you did for one of the least of these brothers and sisters of mine, you did for me." Matthew 25:40.

If you volunteer at your church (say, you help with a children's program or lead song service), then you probably feel you are doing something for God, right? Definitely! That's a great way to serve God. But He says there's also another *unexpected* way to help Him.

In Matthew 25 Jesus describes this surprising type of service. Speaking to a crowd, He explained that when the King returned to earth, He would thank His followers for their service. Here's how that Second Coming conversation between Jesus and His followers will go: "'Come, you who are blessed by my Father; take your inheritance, the kingdom prepared for you since the creation of the world. For I was hungry and you gave me something to eat, I was thirsty and you gave me something to drink, I was a stranger and you invited me in, I needed clothes and you clothed me, I was sick and you looked after me, I was in prison and you came to visit me.'

"Then the righteous will answer him, 'Lord, when did we see you hungry and feed you, or thirsty and give you something to drink? When did we see you a stranger and invite you in, or needing clothes and clothe you? When did we see you sick or in prison and go to visit you?'

"The King will reply, 'Truly I tell you, whatever you did for one of the least of these brothers and sisters of mine, you did for me'" (Matthew 25:34-40).

According to Jesus, whatever you do for the down-and-out underdog, you do for Him. When you help someone without a job, without a family, without a home, or without a hope—when you help them, you are helping God Himself. If you want an encounter with God, aid someone in need.

Live it out: This week, look for an opportunity to encounter God by helping someone in need.

Pray about it: Pray, "God, when I see someone in need, help me have the courage and willingness to meet their need."

If You're Happy and You Know It

Happy are those who keep my ways. Proverbs 8:32, BBE.

Everybody just wants to be happy. Jesus understood the desire, so He preached about happiness in His most famous sermon. In fact, He got the crowd's attention by starting the Sermon on the Mount with the Beatitudes, a list of things that He promises will make us happy. (The word "beatitude" comes from the Latin adjective *beatus*, which means "happy.") At first glance it looks as if there's a pretty good chance that list will make us *miserable*, not joyful. But take a closer look, and you'll see Jesus has amazing and unexpected ways of bringing happiness in our lives:

"Happy are the poor in spirit: for the kingdom of heaven is theirs.

Happy are those who are sad: for they will be comforted.

Happy are the gentle: for the earth will be their heritage.

Happy are those whose heart's desire is for righteousness: for they will have their desire.

Happy are those who have mercy: for they will be given mercy.

Happy are the clean in heart: for they will see God.

Happy are the peacemakers: for they will be named sons of God.

Happy are those who are attacked on account of righteousness: for the kingdom of heaven will be theirs" (Matthew 5:3-10, BBE).

Some of those happiness promises sound pretty wild, right? (Happy are the *sad*? That doesn't make any sense at all!) But Jesus knew what He was talking about. He was trying to explain that we will be happy during our times of sadness and weakness, because that is when we are closest to Him. We will be happy when we make peace instead of picking fights or honest and kind instead of deceitful and manipulative. He was so certain these things would make us happy that He tagged a promise on to every Beatitude. (Go back and look again at those promises—they are big guarantees!) Just think of it this as Jesus' Happiness Plan: happiness will be headed your way if you follow these unexpected principles.

Live it out: Which of the Beatitudes do you relate to most? Put it to the test this week. Follow Jesus' plan, and see if it brings you a sense of deep happiness and peace.

Pray about it: Thank God for bringing happiness out of bad experiences.

Awesome Holiday Memories

I thank my God every time I remember you. Philippians 1:3.

Everybody loves having good memories. But not everyone takes the time to *make* them. Here's the thing: you can't create special memories sitting on the sofa watching TV. You have to get up and do something special to make a special memory. This holiday season, jump up off the sofa and create some memories that you and your friends will treasure for years to come! Here are just a few ideas:

- Make a Nativity scene in the snow—or in the sand if you live in a warm climate.
- Find some of the tackiest Christmas decorations in the mall and take goofy pictures in front of them.
- Write notes to your schoolteachers and church youth leader. Tell them they are a special gift from God to you!
- Rally your church youth group to do a special project. For example, host a babysitting night at the church so that parents can go to holiday events or run errands. Or collect extra Christmas decorations from your parents and decorate the homes of shut-ins or others who could use a little Christmas cheer. (Be sure to go back after Christmas and take them down, so those stockings aren't still hung by the fireplace in April.)
- Drive around town with your family and friends looking at Christmas lights. Rank each house on a scale of 1-10, with 10 being Blow-the-Circuits Beautiful and 1 being Bah-Humbug Boring.

When the apostle Paul wrote to his friends in Philippi, he told them, "I thank my God every time I remember you" (Philippians 1:3). When we share special memories with people, it builds a bond with them. Make memories with your friends this Christmas, and, just like Paul, you'll thank God every time you remember them.

Live it out: Make memories! Invite a few friends to join you in one of the activities listed above.

Pray about it: As Paul did, thank God for the special people in your life.

A New Kind of Christmas List

Every good and perfect gift is from above, coming down from the Father of the heavenly lights. James 1:17.

Christmas involves a lot of lists. In folktales, Santa makes a list of all the good—and all the bad—little boys and girls. And in real life, moms compile lists of all the things they need to buy, bake, wrap, and mail. Meanwhile, children prepare lists of all the toys they want.

This Christmas, why not make a list of your own? Pull out a pen and paper and prepare a new kind of Christmas list. Using the guidelines below, write as many things as you can on your list:

- **Spiritual gifts God has given you.** List all of the spiritual gifts, talents, and strengths God has endowed you with. Maybe you are sociable and make friends easily. Perhaps you write great stories or poems. Or it could be that you are athletic and coordinated. List anything you feel blessed to have as a part of your identity. After you list the strengths, write beside each of them a way you can use that gift to honor God.
- **Gifts God has brought into your life.** List all the things and people for which you are thankful: your comfy bed, your pet dog, your best friend, your youth pastor. All of these are gifts from God to you.

Live it out: Make your list, and check it twice. After you finish your list, hold on to it so that you can refer to it again. Add things to it when new gifts come to mind. On days you feel discouraged, go back and read the list. It will be a good pick-me-up.

Pray about it: Thank God for the many gifts He has brought into your life. Especially thank Him for His ultimate gift: "The gift of God is eternal life in Christ Jesus our Lord" (Romans 6:23).

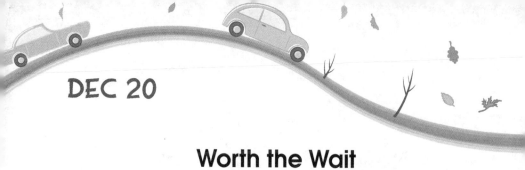

DEC 20

Worth the Wait

But when the set time had fully come, God sent his Son, born of a woman, born under the law, to redeem those under the law, that we might receive adoption to sonship. Galatians 4:4, 5.

If you want time to slow down, then start waiting for something. Whether it is a special event or the end of a school day, time just seems to creep by. Imagine, then, what it must have been like for the people watching for the Savior to come. They had been waiting for *years—thousands of years!*

After Adam and Eve left the perfect Garden of Eden, they immediately began hoping the Savior would be born. Every time Eve had a son, she and Adam dreamed that the child would be the promised one to save them. But no, none of them were. Eventually they probably started putting their hopes in the grandchildren—maybe one of *them* would be the Savior. But again they were disappointed and left waiting.

For thousands of years God's followers watched for the Savior. Although God knew the people were anxious for the Messiah to arrive, He did not rush. He had a perfect time in mind. Scripture says, "But when the set time had fully come, God sent his Son" (Galatians 4:4). God waited for that perfect, set time.

And it was worth the wait! Born in an unlikely town to an unlikely teen mom, Jesus arrived according to God's plan. The baby everyone looked for had finally come to "save his people from their sins" (Matthew 1:21).

Live it out: In what areas of your life do you feel as if you are waiting for God? While you are waiting, don't complain. Instead, use the time to get to know God more.

Pray about it: Thank God for the arrival of the Messiah—the perfect Savior at the perfect time!

Live It Out!

"The virgin will conceive and give birth to a son, and they will call him Immanuel" (which means "God with us"). Matthew 1:23.

An idea that stood out to me from this week's devotional readings:

_____

_____

_____

A verse from this week's devotions that was powerful to me:

_____

_____

_____

A "Live it out" challenge I tried this week:

_____

_____

_____

Something that happened this week that was a blessing:

_____

_____

_____

My prayer today (thanks, requests, praises):

_____

_____

_____

DEC 22

Going With God's Plan

"I am the Lord's servant," Mary answered. "May your word to me be fulfilled."
Luke 1:38.

If God chooses you to do something big, just go with it. That's what Mary did. She didn't refuse or make excuses. Although it didn't seem to make any sense that God chose her to be Jesus' mother, she didn't protest. She was a teenager from Nazareth, a little village with a bad reputation. Of all the women in all the places in all the times in history, God selected her. And she went with it.

God sent an angel to tell Mary that she would become pregnant with the Savior of the world. It was arguably some of the most important news ever delivered on earth, so it must have been pretty intimidating to her. Luke records the story:

"But the angel said to her, 'Do not be afraid, Mary; you have found favor with God. You will conceive and give birth to a son, and you are to call him Jesus. He will be great and will be called the Son of the Most High. The Lord God will give him the throne of his father David, and he will reign over Jacob's descendants forever; his kingdom will never end'" (Luke 1:30-33).

The angel went on to explain to her how it would happen: "The Holy Spirit will come on you, and the power of the Most High will overshadow you. So the holy one to be born will be called the Son of God" (verse 35).

Then the angel looked at this scared but willing teen girl and summed up the entire plan: "For nothing will be impossible with God" (verse 37, ESV).

Mary believed that God was going to do the impossible through her. She agreed to be a part of the plan and told the angel, "I am the Lord's servant. May your words to me be fulfilled" (verse 38).

If God asks you to do something great, follow Mary's example. You'll never regret it.

Live it out: Make a commitment to be the Lord's servant. Like Mary, tell God that you are willing to do whatever He wants—even if it's something that seems impossible.

Pray about it: Thank God for using a teen girl from a small town to do incredible things. Ask Him to use you in whatever way He wants.

The Wise Men

After Jesus was born in Bethlehem in Judea, during the time of King Herod, Magi from the east came to Jerusalem and asked, "Where is the one who has been born king of the Jews? We saw his star when it rose and have come to worship him." Matthew 2:1, 2.

Almost every Nativity set has the same crew of characters: Baby Jesus, Mary, Joseph, three Wise Men, a few shepherds, a cow, a donkey, and a sheep. Notice, there are always three Wise Men. So there were three of them, right? And they arrived at the stable to see Jesus in the manger, just like the shepherds?

Not exactly. Here's what we know—and don't know—about those Wise Guys, otherwise called Magi. We don't actually have any idea how many of them there really were. They did bring three gifts—gold, frankincense, and myrrh. But that doesn't mean it was one gift per person. Maybe they all brought some of each of the gifts; or maybe there were two bringing gold, two bringing frankincense, and two bringing myrrh.

One other snag in the story? If you picture the Wise Men showing up the night of Jesus' birth, right alongside the shepherds, you don't have the story straight. By the time the Wise Men arrived, the little family had already settled into a home.

No matter how many Wise Men there were or when they got there, they are an amazing example of God followers. They studied the prophecies so carefully that they knew when to look for a star that would indicate the birth of the divine king. They literally followed a star in the sky for miles and miles looking for a baby! How cool is that?

This Christmas, be like the Wise Men: search for God, and don't stop until you find Him!

Live it out: You can read the exact prophecies the Wise Men read that led them to follow the star to Jesus. Use a Bible commentary or an Internet search to look for "messianic prophecies." Does it build your faith in the Bible and in God to know that the prophecies came true exactly as predicted?

Pray about it: Bow down and worship God, as the Wise Men did.

The Gift of Giving

Remembering the words the Lord Jesus himself said: "It is more blessed to give than to receive." Acts 20:35.

If you could have absolutely any gift this Christmas, what would it be? Imagine how you would feel if you actually received that dream present. You would feel elated, right? Now, consider what the Bible says about giving and receiving. It tells us that it is even more exciting and wonderful to give than to receive. In Acts 20:35 Paul says, "We should remember the words the Lord Jesus himself said, 'Giving gifts is more satisfying than receiving them'" (GW).

It feels really great to receive a gift, so it is a really big claim to say that presenting gifts is more satisfying than receiving them. The Word of God doesn't lie or exaggerate, though, so you can be sure it's true. If you're still in doubt, put this claim to the test this Christmas. Give something (a gift or an act of service) to someone who really needs it, and experience the thrill that comes from it. Here are some ideas to get you thinking about what you can give:

- Buy a special present for a classmate who doesn't have much.
- Write your parents a note thanking them for all they do for you.
- Donate to charity some of your clothes or items you no longer use.
- Give a single parent in your community a "coupon" for a free babysitting session.
- With the aid of a pastor, teacher, or parent, find a soup kitchen or homeless shelter that needs help serving a holiday meal. Invite friends to join you, and it will be even more enjoyable.
- Invite an elderly neighbor over for Christmas dinner, and ask them questions about their life—the jobs they've had, the places they've been, the people they love.
- Send a care package to a soldier.

Live it out: Make this Christmas all about giving. Choose ideas from this list, or come up with some of your own. Give, and then enjoy the pleasure of bringing joy to others.

Pray about it: Thank God for all the gifts He has given you. Ask Him to open your eyes to opportunities to give yourself this holiday season.

A Message for the Ordinaries

And there were shepherds living out in the fields nearby, keeping watch over their flocks at night. Luke 2:8.

During Bible times shepherds were the ordinary guys. In modern times they might be mechanics, or farmers, or guys who work at Home Depot. They earned an honest living, but there was nothing flashy or fancy about them. That's what makes it so cool that a skyful of angels came and told shepherds about the birth of Jesus. God could have sent those angels to announce the birth to wealthy, powerful world leaders. Instead, He dispatched the angels to a field full of ordinaries:

"And there were shepherds living out in the fields nearby, keeping watch over their flocks at night. An angel of the Lord appeared to them, and the glory of the Lord shone around them, and they were terrified. But the angel said to them, 'Do not be afraid. I bring you good news that will cause great joy for all the people. Today in the town of David a Savior has been born to you; he is the Messiah, the Lord. This will be a sign to you: You will find a baby wrapped in cloths and lying in a manger.'

"Suddenly a great company of the heavenly host appeared with the angel, praising God and saying, 'Glory to God in the highest heaven, and on earth peace to those on whom his favor rests'" (Luke 2:8-14).

God knew what He was doing when He chose to tell this group of ordinaries about the baby Jesus. It was the biggest news they had ever heard, so they excitedly told everyone who would listen: "When they had seen him, they spread the word concerning what had been told them about this child, and all who heard it were amazed at what the shepherds said to them" (verses 17, 18).

If you feel like an ordinary, don't be discouraged. With God, extraordinary things happen to ordinaries. Even Jesus Himself was born an ordinary. And there's nothing ordinary about that.

Live it out: Be like the shepherds: tell someone about the birth of Jesus!
Pray about it: Thank God for sending Baby Jesus to be born for all of us ordinaries.

DEC 26

When Jesus Stands Up for You

But Stephen, full of the Holy Spirit, looked up to heaven and saw the glory of God, and Jesus standing at the right hand of God. Acts 7:55.

Stephen was sold out for Jesus. The Bible says, "Now Stephen, a man full of God's grace and power, performed great wonders and signs among the people" (Acts 6:8).

He sounds like a really likable guy. You'd think everyone would appreciate him. Not so.

The religious leaders couldn't stomach him. They wanted him silenced, so they seized him and brought him before the Sanhedrin.

As Stephen stood before these angry men, he remained filled with God's grace and power. In fact, as his enemies looked at him, they couldn't help noticing that his face "was like the face of an angel" (verse 15). (Again, how can you not like a guy like that?)

Stephen went on to give a passionate speech about Jesus. (This guy really loved the Lord!) Yet it did not move his hard-hearted listeners. In fact, his speech just made them angrier: "When the members of the Sanhedrin heard this, they were furious and gnashed their teeth at him" (Acts 7:54).

As he faced his raging opponents, Stephen did not back down. He would stand up for Jesus—no matter what. And when he did, a beautiful thing happened: Jesus stood up for Him. *Literally.* "But Stephen, full of the Holy Spirit, looked up to heaven and saw the glory of God, and Jesus standing at the right hand of God. 'Look,' he said, 'I see heaven open and the Son of Man standing at the right hand of God'" (verses 55, 56).

The angry mob rushed at the angel-faced Stephen, dragged him out of the city, and stoned him. Through it all, he continued in prayer, even asking forgiveness for his torturers. And in his final moments he certainly must have taken comfort in that glimpse of heaven in which he saw Jesus rise from His throne and stand up for him.

Whenever you stand up for Jesus, you won't be standing alone. He'll be standing up for you, too.

Live it out: Don't shy away from opportunities to stand up for Jesus. He'll stand with you!

Pray about it: Thank God for always protecting and standing up for you.

Defeating Your Enemies

In your unfailing love, silence my enemies; destroy all my foes, for I am your servant. Psalm 143:12.

Seventy-two psalms—almost half the book of Psalms—speak about enemies. That's interesting and adds some drama to the psalms, but what if you don't feel as if you have any enemies? No one is out to get you, so what do those verses mean to you?

Enemies aren't just people with a weapon and a grudge. An enemy can be anyone or anything that can overcome you. That means lust, the desire for popularity, money, or addictions can all be your enemies. With that in mind, all those psalms about enemies take on an entirely new meaning, don't they?

Think about some of your "enemies" as you read these verses from Psalms:

- "In you, Lord my God, I put my trust. I trust in you; do not let me be put to shame, nor let my enemies triumph over me" (Psalm 25:1, 2).
- "Then my enemies will turn back when I call for help. By this I will know that God is for me" (Psalm 56:9).
- "I will exalt you, Lord, for you lifted me out of the depths and did not let my enemies gloat over me" (Psalm 30:1).
- "With God we will gain the victory, and he will trample down our enemies" (Psalm 108:13).
- "You give us victory over our enemies, you put our adversaries to shame. In God we make our boast all day long, and we will praise your name forever" (Psalm 44:7, 8).
- "The Lord is with me; he is my helper. I look in triumph on my enemies" (Psalm 118:7).

Live it out: Make a list of your "enemies"—all the things that have the potential to overcome and destroy you if left uncontrolled. Now choose a verse about overcoming your enemies to memorize. Repeat it as a prayer every time you sense your enemies trying to defeat you.

Pray about it: Thank God for guaranteeing you victory over your enemies!

DEC 28

Live It Out!

One thing I do: Forgetting what is behind and straining toward what is ahead, I press on toward the goal to win the prize for which God has called me heavenward in Christ Jesus. Philippians 3:13, 14.

An idea that stood out to me from this week's devotional readings:

_____

_____

_____

A verse from this week's devotions that was powerful to me:

_____

_____

_____

A "Live it out" challenge I tried this week:

_____

_____

_____

Something that happened this week that was a blessing:

_____

_____

_____

My prayer today (thanks, requests, praises):

_____

_____

_____

When Goodness and Love Follow You

Surely your goodness and love will follow me all the days of my life. Psalm 23:6.

David knew the importance of a shepherd's protection and guidance. After all, he had been a shepherd himself. His most famous psalm, Psalm 23, describes God as the ultimate shepherd offering guidance and protection, goodness and love:

"The Lord is my shepherd, I lack nothing.
He makes me lie down in green pastures,
he leads me beside quiet waters,
he refreshes my soul.
He guides me along the right paths
for his name's sake.
Even though I walk
through the darkest valley,
I will fear no evil,
for you are with me;
your rod and your staff,
they comfort me.
You prepare a table before me
in the presence of my enemies.
You anoint my head with oil;
my cup overflows.
Surely your goodness and love will follow me
all the days of my life,
and I will dwell in the house of the Lord
forever."

Live it out: Look back over Psalm 23 and think of specific times in your life in which the Lord has been like a shepherd to you. When has He protected you? When have you felt His goodness and love?

Pray about it: Turn Psalm 23 into your prayer today.

Like Trying to Eat an Elephant

Who dares despise the day of small things? Zechariah 4:10.

Question: *How do you eat an elephant?* Answer: *One bite at a time.*
OK, so you're never going to eat an elephant. Good choice. All the same, the old joke makes a pretty good point. When you are facing a big task, it can feel as if you're trying to eat an elephant. You look at the massive thing and wonder where even to begin.

For me, writing this devotional book was a little like eating an elephant. When I started, I thought, *Sure, I can write 365 things about God and life. It's a big project, but no problem.* But before I'd even made it through the July writings, the ideas were running low. And I still had a lot left to do. It was like standing in front of an elephant with a plastic fork, wondering how I was going to consume the massive thing.

The answer, just as in the corny joke, is to take it one bite at a time. In this case, one day at a time. I prayed and asked God for one more day's writings, and He would give it. One day at a time (literally) I chipped away at this thing. After 365 bites I had eaten the elephant.

Most important things in life don't happen overnight. Forming great friendships, making good grades, breaking a bad habit, understanding the Bible, learning a new hobby or sport—all of them take time. If you look at it as a whole, it can feel as if you're staring into the eyes of an elephant while holding chopsticks. Don't get discouraged. Instead, just start eating . . . one bite at a time. Each small bite you take will help you accomplish the larger goal.

For example, if you want more friends, start with small gestures. Strike up a conversation with someone over lunch, or invite a classmate to join you for flag football after school. You won't be best friends overnight, but you definitely will be one step closer to being friends.

The Bible says we should never resent that big things start as small ones: "Who dares despise the day of small things?" (Zechariah 4:10). All great things start small, so pull out your plastic fork and start eating that elephant.

Live it out: Think of a big goal you have, such as learning a new language or making more friends. Do one thing today to take a bite out of that goal. Just keep taking one bite at a time until you reach your goal.

Pray about it: Ask God to help you have the patience and endurance to reach your goal.

The Magnificent Future

He who testifies to these things says, "Yes, I am coming soon." Amen. Come, Lord Jesus. Revelation 22:20.

One of the best things about being a Christian is knowing there are better days ahead. We realize that there's more to life than what we see right now. Even if things seem terrible today, God has promised us perfect days to come.

Here's a reminder of how amazing life will someday be when God makes everything new and perfect:

"Then I saw 'a new heaven and a new earth,' for the first heaven and the first earth had passed away, and there was no longer any sea. I saw the Holy City, the new Jerusalem, coming down out of heaven from God, prepared as a bride beautifully dressed for her husband. And I heard a loud voice from the throne saying, 'Look! God's dwelling place is now among the people, and he will dwell with them. They will be his people, and God himself will be with them and be their God. "He will wipe every tear from their eyes. There will be no more death" or mourning or crying or pain, for the old order of things has passed away.' He who was seated on the throne said, 'I am making everything new!'" (Revelation 21:1-5).

"Then the angel showed me the river of the water of life, as clear as crystal, flowing from the throne of God and of the Lamb down the middle of the great street of the city. On each side of the river stood the tree of life, bearing twelve crops of fruit, yielding its fruit every month. And the leaves of the tree are for the healing of the nations. No longer will there be any curse. The throne of God and of the Lamb will be in the city, and his servants will serve him. They will see his face, and his name will be on their foreheads. There will be no more night. They will not need the light of a lamp or the light of the sun, for the Lord God will give them light. And they will reign for ever and ever" (Revelation 22:1-5).

Live it out: Read Revelation 21 and 22 and try to imagine what the new heaven and new earth will be like.

Pray about it: Thank God for the promise of a magnificent future.

MORE MOMENTUM!

CHECK OUT THESE ENCOURAGING WORDS AND ACTIVITIES THAT WILL HELP KEEP YOU MOVING IN THE RIGHT DIRECTION:

= PROMISES FOR LIFE DETOURS

Sometimes the road of life has some unexpected twists and turns, roadblocks and detours. For those wild times, here are some words to cheer you up and cheer you on:

= WHEN YOU ARE AFRAID

"For God has not given us a spirit of fear, but of power and of love and of a sound mind" (2 Timothy 1:7, NKJV).

"So we can be sure when we say, 'I will not be afraid, because the Lord is my helper. People can't do anything to me'"(Hebrews 13:6, NCV).

"So do not fear, for I am with you; do not be dismayed, for I am your God. I will strengthen you and help you; I will uphold you with my righteous right hand" (Isaiah 41:10).

= WHEN YOU NEED STRENGTH

"He gives strength to the weary and increases the power of the weak" (Isaiah 40:29).

"The Lord gives strength to his people; the Lord blesses his people with peace" (Psalm 29:11).

"But he said to me, 'My grace is sufficient for you, for my power is made perfect in weakness.' Therefore I will boast all the more gladly about my weaknesses, so that Christ's power may rest on me" (2 Corinthians 12:9).

"My flesh and my heart may fail, but God is the strength of my heart and my portion forever" (Psalm 73:26).

= WHEN YOU ARE ANGRY

"My dear brothers and sisters, take note of this: Everyone should be quick to listen, slow to speak and slow to become angry, because human anger does not produce the righteousness that God desires" (James 1:19, 20).

"A gentle answer turns away wrath, but a harsh word stirs up anger" (Proverbs 15:1).

= WHEN YOU ARE TEMPTED

"On reaching the place, he said to them, 'Pray that you will not fall into temptation'" (Luke 22:40).

"Watch and pray so that you will not fall into temptation. The spirit is willing, but the flesh is weak" (Matthew 26:41).

= WHEN YOU NEED WISDOM

"If any of you lacks wisdom, you should ask God, who gives generously to all without finding fault, and it will be given to you" (James 1:5).

"I will instruct you and teach you in the way you should go; I will counsel you with my loving eye on you" (Psalm 32:8).

"How much better to get wisdom than gold, to get insight rather than silver!" (Proverbs 16:16).

= WHEN YOU DOUBT GOD'S LOVE

"See what great love the Father has lavished on us, that we should be called children of God!" (1 John 3:1).

"For I am convinced that neither death nor life, neither angels nor demons, neither the present nor the future, nor any powers, neither height nor depth, nor anything else in all creation, will be able to separate us from the love of God that is in Christ Jesus our Lord" (Romans 8:38, 39).

"But God demonstrates his own love for us in this: While we were still sinners, Christ died for us" (Romans 5:8).

= WHEN YOU ARE WORRIED OR OVERWHELMED

"I can do all things through Christ who strengthens me" (Philippians 4:13, NKJV).

"Cast all your anxiety on him because he cares for you" (1 Peter 5:7).

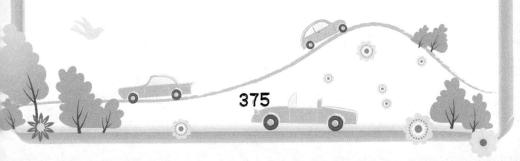

"And my God will meet all your needs according to the riches of his glory in Christ Jesus" (Philippians 4:19).

= WHEN YOU ARE DEPRESSED

"He heals the brokenhearted and binds up their wounds" (Psalm 147:3).

"When you pass through the waters, I will be with you; and when you pass through the rivers, they will not sweep over you. When you walk through the fire, you will not be burned; the flames will not set you ablaze" (Isaiah 43:2).

"A cheerful heart is good medicine, but a crushed spirit dries up the bones" (Proverbs 17:22).

"'He will wipe every tear from their eyes. There will be no more death' or mourning or crying or pain, for the old order of things has passed away" (Revelation 21:4).

= WHEN YOU ARE MAD AT SOMEONE

"For if you forgive other people when they sin against you, your heavenly Father will also forgive you. But if you do not forgive others their sins, your Father will not forgive your sins" (Matthew 6:14, 15).

"Be kind and compassionate to one another, forgiving each other, just as in Christ God forgave you" (Ephesians 4:32).

= WHEN YOU NEED PEACE

"And the peace of God, which transcends all understanding, will guard your hearts and your minds in Christ Jesus" (Philippians 4:7).

"The Lord gives strength to his people; the Lord blesses his people with peace" (Psalm 29:11).

"You will keep in perfect peace those whose minds are steadfast, because they trust in you" (Isaiah 26:3).

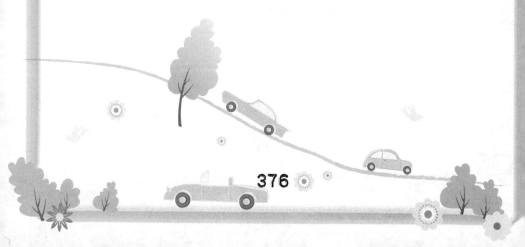

FINDING GOD AROUND EVERY TURN

KEEP TRACK OF SOME OF THE AMAZING THINGS YOU SEE
GOD DOING ALL AROUND YOU.

DATE   I SAW GOD AT WORK WHEN THIS HAPPENED:

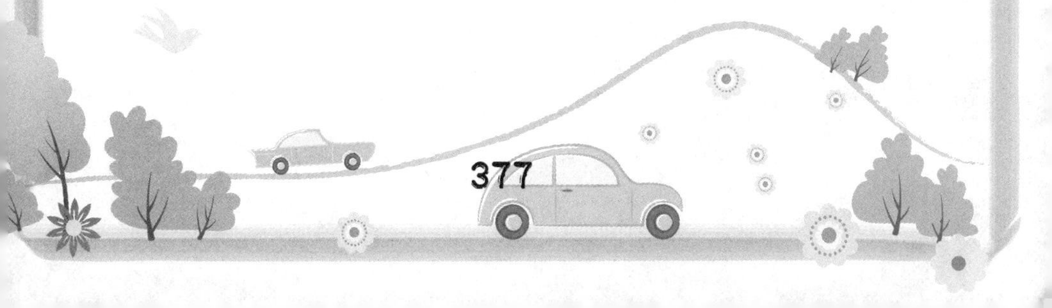

_____   _____

               _____

_____   _____

               _____

_____   _____

               _____

_____   _____

               _____

DATE	I SAW GOD AT WORK WHEN THIS HAPPENED:
_____	_____
	_____
_____	_____
	_____
_____	_____
	_____
_____	_____
	_____
_____	_____
	_____
_____	_____
	_____

DATE	I SAW GOD AT WORK WHEN THIS HAPPENED:
_____	_____
	_____
_____	_____
	_____
_____	_____
	_____
_____	_____
	_____
_____	_____
	_____
_____	_____
	_____

PRAYING ABOUT WHAT'S AROUND THE BEND

NOT SURE WHAT GOD IS UP TO? NEED TO TALK TO HIM ABOUT A FEW THINGS? RECORD YOUR PRAYER REQUESTS HERE.

I AM PRAYING ABOUT THIS:

= FRIENDS AND ACQUAINTANCES

_____

_____

_____

_____

_____

_____

_____

_____

_____

_____

_____

= FAMILY

_____

_____

_____

_____

_____

_____

_____

_____

_____

= PERSONAL GROWTH

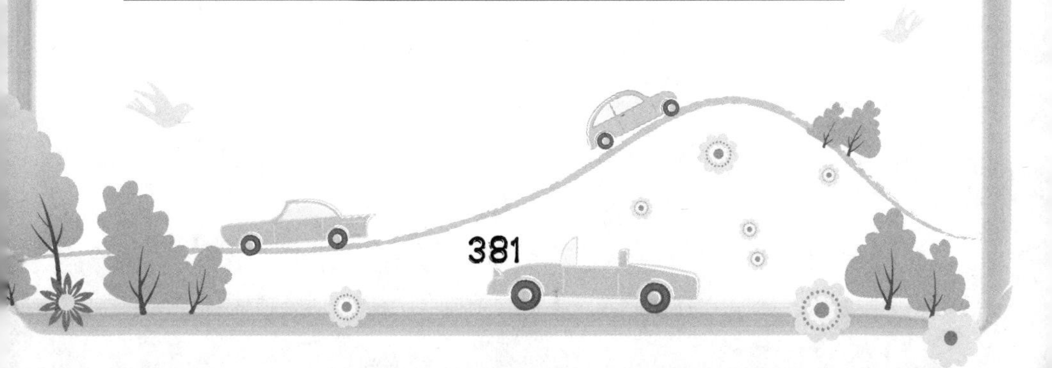

_____

_____

_____

_____

_____

= DECISIONS AND DILEMMAS

= SCHOOL/WORK

_____

_____

_____

_____

_____

_____

_____

_____

= THE CHURCH

_____

_____

_____

_____

_____

_____

= NATIONS/WORLD